THE GROTTO

By

ARMANDO VISELLI

Order this book online at www.trafford.com
or email orders@trafford.com

Most Trafford titles are also available at major online book retailers.

Printed in the United States of America.

ISBN: 978-1-4269-5890-8 (sc)
ISBN: 978-1-4269-5889-2 (e)

Trafford rev. 03/08/2011

 www.trafford.com

North America & international
toll-free: 1 888 232 4444 (USA & Canada)
phone: 250 383 6864 ♦ fax: 812 355 4082

Chapter 1

I have always claimed that the best years of our lives are when we go to school, but we never realize it until it is too late.w I wanted a job so badly that I quit school even before I graduated, and yet, when I got one, I couldn't hang on to it

I was only sixteen and in a matter of not even a year, I had already changed three jobs, but instead of climbing the ladder I was going down deeper and deeper.

When I lost my first job as a bell boy at the Hotel Torino, one of the best in Rome, right away my father decided to employ me at a clothing and fabric store owned by Signor Spizzichino (Mister Cheap) an old Jewish merchant of Piazza Vittorio, which he knew from way back. That day on the way to the store he kept repeating to me don't forget my son that working for somebody will never get you anywhere, but as far as I can remember, I have never seen a business man starve to death. Look at the Jews, those people sure know how to make money, so stick with this guy, learn his trade and maybe someday, who knows, maybe you can start your own business.

I knew the man and the place so well because I had been there so many times with my father to buy mostly some remnant pieces of fabric. Usually the best cloth to be found in the market but that was either out of style or there was not enough material for a whole suit, therefore could be bought very reasonably. Naturally as far as I remember, not once was a deal was closed before a big long story and lots of genuine crying from both patron and store owner was involved. The buying was especially planned by my father only bright and early on Monday morning. We waited at the corner for Signor Spizzichino to open the store door and as soon as he had disappeared inside we would walk right in behind him .A trick that my father played on him every time and he didn't like it at all. I don't know how much truth there was in it, but being very superstitious, Signor Spizzichino hated to lose his first customer. It brought him bad luck on all the oncoming week.

That scene is so vivid in my mind that I can still see the two of them going at it, arguing back and forth. First my father would look around and choose what he liked, than ask for the price. Once he knew it he dropped the material and immediately turned to something else, making him take down sample after sample, each time asking for the price but always showing a dissatisfied look in his face, until he put his hand on top of the original choice saying:

"Signor Spizzichino, this is the one I want. Without any doubt it is the best, it's all wool, but on the price we are a mile apart. I will give you"... and pulling out the wallet and counting the money. Here this is all I got. , waving the bills in front of his face.

At the sight of money, the dead eyes of Signor Spizzichino, a light built little man with a big nose and a guttural voice, would give a sparkling sign of life but that was all and raising his hand over his head with a crying voice he would say. "Please, please Mr. Viselli. I am here to do business, not to be ruined by you."

"Come on Signor Spizzichino, as you well know, I would never think of doing that, thank you just the same and friends as before. All right, you keep your merchandise and I keep my money. Vabene? Come on Armando. Let's go someplace else." And pulling me by the hand he would start for the door.

"Un momento, un momento, Mr. Viselli", would then holler Signor Spizzichino running after us. "Please give me another ten lire and the cloth is yours."

My dad would stop, turn around and very seriously say: "Signor Spizzichino. Have you ever seen blood come out of a turnip? I don't have another penny. Let's go Armando, we are wasting our time."

"Wait Mr. Viselli, let's split the difference. Give me another five lire."

Pulling two lire from his pants pocket and putting them on top of the others, very unhappily he would say: "Signor Spizzichino, take them, but don't forget this boy is going to be hungry all day. Those two lire were for his breakfast."

Right at that moment he could care less if I starved or not, all he could see in front of his eyes was the two extra lire and reaching for the money he would put the big bill right up in the air against the light and once sure that they were not false, he would place them in a thick oily wallet hanging from a gold chain, swiftly put it back in his coat pocket and crying he would add: "Another deal like this and I will go broke."

I think they were both good actors and enjoyed teasing each other.

No doubt he was a very shrewd business man, but a poorly minded person, always afraid that somebody would steal from him, he was very different and trusted no one.

Not too long after I started working for him, one afternoon his old crabby wife came to the store with a good size parcel. I was repairing a step ladder in the back of the store when she appeared thru the door calling my name.

"Coming, coming," I hollered back, and when I got there Signor Spizzichino had the parcel on the counter and was writing something on it.

"Do you know where the Concentration Camp of the English prisoners of war is?" He asked as he kept writing.

"No, I never heard of it."

"Well it is not very hard to find, it is past Cinecitta' on Via Tuscolana and the Tranve dei Castelli goes right by it. You can't miss it. I want you to deliver this parcel to the son of an old friend of mine. I am sure he will appreciate what I send him, food, cigarettes, brandy and a wool sweater. His name is Samuel Pascovich, it is written all over the parcel, you can't make a mistake. Try but I doubt very much if they let you see him at this hour, if you cannot deliver it personally, leave it at the guard house, here is two lire you got more than enough for the street car, now go and hurry back."

Once I got there, it was not as easy as he had described it. The easiest part was to pass the guard at the gate, after that it was all like a dream to me.

I was introduced in front of the fascist lieutenant who started to ask me all kinds of questions. Who are you? What are you doing here? Who are the people that gave you this parcel? Why didn't they deliver it personally? Are you related to the prisoner? Are they related to the prisoner? What is in this parcel? Do you collaborate with the enemy? Do you know that I could have you arrested for this? He kept going on and on, he wrote down every little bit of information, and when he finally released me, I cursed all the fascists and all the Jews on earth.

I was not home when three days after my unforgettable experience at the camp; two carabinieri came to the house and asked my father all kinds of questions about myself, the prisoner and Signor Spizzichino.

After what happened that afternoon, I couldn't say exactly what it was, but it was not the same thing anymore, I was very uncomfortable with the whole set up, Signor Spizzichino, his wife, the store and everything that had anything to do with them, never the less I tried my best to please him, and worked my little butt as hard as I could, but it was one thing to be his customer and a completely different thing to work for him, he never seemed to be satisfied. Because of my father I endured quite a lot, but at the end of the month, when he handed me a lousy thirty lire, one miserable lira per day, I almost had a fit. Cheap, cheap bastard, as bell boy, sometimes I made that much in tips in one single week. No wonder he had a hard time to keep his help.

That night when I got home and told my father he really surprised me when he said: "I knew it. What did you expect millions? Don't forget you are learning." Maybe he was right, but that was the last of our association, because even against my father's will, I never went to work there again, instead I let Viano my best friend, talk me into going to get a job with him as labor at the Railway Depot of Scalo Sar. Lorenzo, where the pay was decent, the work although dirty and greasy was very interesting and the hours, lots of overtime.

Tile foreman of the labor pool Mr. Panto was the one that assigned us to our day after day jobs, almost the same routine, in fact unless something very unusual happened, we always worked inside the round house, either with the boiler maker to repair the boilers, or around the steam engines to put out the fire and clean the oven on the oncoming locomotives, or get them ready with coal and water, lubrication and a new fire. The other assignment was with the mechanics, with them, besides the fact that I was learning something new every day, there was no limit on the amount of working hours. The department was going steady twenty four hours a day and still that wasn't enough. After every trip the big locomotives 685 used for the long haul with the 735 called the Americana, were always brought in for repairs. Ninety percent of the time scarcities of good oil and grease, plus cheap metal were the main cause of all their troubles. Because of poor lubrication the big bearings on the wheels main axle, became so hot that actually melted away.

We were in bad shape, but there was a war going on, that was all that was available and no matter how, limping, puffing, sweating, pushing or pulling, those locomotives had to be on the road on time.

One day a terrified fireman brought in a 735 full of machine gun holes, the engineer, a big friendly guy, which we all knew and joked around with, was laying dead near the oven door with his head completely blown off. Man, what a gruesome sight he was. We had heard so much about what was going on down south, especially in Sicily and around Naples, but this was the first time we really witnessed the death of a victim of the war. Rome had been declared "Open City" from the first day of the hostilities, therefore beside a few little variation in our daily routine nothing had changed drastically. In fact if it wasn't for my brother Peppe being away in the Navy, we would have never noticed any big difference in our house. Food was rationed but papa' was always buying flour in the black market, therefore when we finished our rations, mamma would switch to homemade bread and noodles. Every time nonna Teresa visited us or we went to her farm, she kept us well stocked on dry beans, lentils, chick peas, homemade sausages, lard and oil. As for cheese we could have supplied an entire army ourselves.

Without exaggerating, our parents' bedroom was like a storage place. Behind a huge dresser that covered all one wall, papa' had driven long spikes into the wall, from which were hanging at least a dozen gigantic provoloni.

One night we were all sound asleep, when suddenly we were awakened by a thundering crash, as though if the wall and the pavement of the whole house had collapsed. In a matter of seconds the whole family was up and under the reflected rays of a bluish painted light bulb, with terror in our eyes, all you could hear was: What was that. What happened? We looked all over, we even climbed on the roof, thinking that maybe a bomb or some kind of mysterious object had fallen on top of us, but we couldn't find anything. We went back to bed and we forgot all about it. At that time, papa' had been recalled in the army and was stationed in the grenadiers barrack, near the Parioli, but almost every night he came home to sleep. All his fellow soldiers were more or less the same age, around forty, veterans of the first world war, aggregated to an auxiliary division, which seemingly nobody knew exactly what to do with, but lately they were seriously talking of shipping them out, Russia, Creta, Greece, nobody knew, in the meantime they were on the alert twenty four hours a day and all leaves were cancelled. Finally one day we got a phone call front papa'; "tomorrow we are leaving. Bring six pair of heavy socks, four knitted wool vest and four heavy long underpants. While you are at it, bring me a nice dish of homemade noodles, which it could very well be my last one for a long time to come. And don't forget, tell your mother not too much sauce, also wrap up a big slice of provolone cheese, maybe a couple kilos. You got everything? Hurry up; we might be leaving anytime now. Ciao."

When I got there, calm and poised he was waiting at the gate laughing and joking with the sentry. After one of the guards let me in, we joined a group of his Roman bon vivant friends and their respective wives, sitting on the grass under a giant walnut tree and having a real picnic. After the banquet was over, we waited until ten o'clock in the evening, but the order to leave never came. Papa' shoved the cheese in the haversack, and told me to take the clothes back home. He was afraid that somebody might steal them. He accompanied me to the gate and with the big bundle of clothes under my arm, in the dark I walked over a mile to get to the street car. This went on for a whole month. They were leaving, they were not leaving, and every time if it wasn't me, it was my brother Carmine, or mamma that had to go. By then, everybody was getting on everybody's nerve. The barracks were in the middle of nowhere and to walk for a good fifteen minutes in the open under the scorching sun was not very pleasant. Everyone was fed up, a day didn't go by without someone complaining, especially the wife of one of my father's fellow soldier. One day while he was enjoying his favorite dish, she was pacing up and down the little path that we had made, she was steaming. She waited until he was finished, she put everything away, then as calmly and as respectfully she could possibly be, she said:

"Now listen to me Teodoro. What you just finished eating was the last of the spaghetti that there was in the house. I have no more money, no more of any food and most of all no more patience. This nonsense has gone far enough, if you are leaving tomorrow or ever, don't call me anymore, because for all I care, you can go to hell. Understand? Good bye." She angrily picked up her bag, turned on her heels and before he had a chance to say anything, she had passed the gate and disappeared behind the high walls surrounding the barrack.

Teodoro's wife never showed up again, but we kept going and one day papa' reminded me to bring him another piece of cheese. When I got home, I asked mamma to prepare it for the next day, and since there was only a small piece left in the pantry, we had to remove the big dresser in the master bedroom to get to the provoloni hanging high on the wall. And what did we find? One huge provolone weighing at least seventy five pound resting on the cement tile floor, the big straw rope from which it was hanging severed. Thus we were finally able to solve the mystery of the big bang that scared the hell out of us a while back during the night.

Among all the gossip going around the camp, one day we heard that Mussolini was coming to give his farewell to the departing troops. Nobody believed it, it was only the usual fib, the same old bull, but when the order was given to raise a platform for him, every doubt dissipated from everybody's mind.

I had never seen him before, and that day I took advantage of the situation to satisfy my curiosity. The security measures were very tight but the orderly officer knew me well and at the last moment he let me pass.

The huge quadrangle was crowded with soldiers standing at attention, when a flourish of trumpets announced his arrival. He was wearing his fascist uniform and ordinary army helmet. Quickly he scrambled up the ladder and once he reached the podium platform, holding himself to the parapet in front of him, made of rough two by fours, he immediately began:

"Camerati. Soldati."

Since their coming to power in the twenties, there had always been bad blood between the fascist and the military. There was lots of rust and the ill feeling had opened a deep wound in the heart of the old king's guard, beginning from the generals to the last professional soldier. While the fascist militias, a minority group, were enjoying all kinds of favoritism, those same privileges were denied to the others, who actually were the real backbone of the Italian army, navy and air force. For instance, just to mention a few, while the militia men were making ten lire a day, the ordinary soldier was paid a miserable lira per day, where the militia man had free rides on buses and street cars, the regular army, sailor and air force man had to pay. The same thing had to be said for the theaters and cinemas. There was an endless list of injustices inflicted on the regulars, therefore it can only be imagined what went through the soldiers mind when they got wind of his coming. Lots of them hated Mussolini's guts and immediately began to think how they could give him a hard time or better yet scare the hell out of him without making it look so obvious.

To make sure that he had plenty of vision all around him, the soldiers built the podium sky high but very narrow at the base, making it quite unstable and shaky at the top. Naturally everybody knew about it and the general opinion was that as soon as he started to rock the boat, he would get panicky and come down in a hurry. But I doubt very much if height ever bothered Mussolini at all, because clinging nonchalantly with both hands to the two by fours, vigorously he began his speech. The more he talked, the more he got excited, the more excited he got the more he kept swinging the podium, until all the soldiers standing in front of him, began to wonder if the son of a gun would ever land on top of them. Man, what a switch that was. He sure gave lots of them a hell of a scare, and I would have staked my life on it that many of them must have felt quite relieved when he finally decided to come down.

Finally the troops were shipped out to Greece, but thank God, two days after Mussolini's visit, my father was sent home forever and went back to his old job as a street car conductor. He had been exonerated for having a numerous family, because of my brother Peppe the oldest son that was already in the service.

Chapter 2

That morning the birds woke me up. Rubbing my eyes I went to the window, I opened it and looked outside. Wow! What a beautiful day! The sun already high, the sky clear, not a single cloud and the air so fresh and good. It was exactly what I had prayed for.

"Carmine get up," I called out to my older brother who shared the room with me. "I bet the other guys are already waiting for us."

"So ... Let them. Who cares." He replied sleepily. Shoving his head deeper under the cover.

"Come on." I insisted. Pulling the blankets away from him. "It is the most gorgeous day I have ever seen and it is a crime to waste it in bed."

While he sat on the edge of the bed yawning and scratching his head, quickly I rushed to the bathroom, washed myself and, dripping, with a towel still in my hands, broke into the kitchen, where mamma was busy preparing breakfast.

"Boungiorno mamma, is the picnic bag ready?"

"It certainly is. It has been ready since six o'clock. I prepared it right after your father went to work."

"Thanks mamma. You are an angel." Getting closer I tried to kiss her, but she wouldn't let me.

"Go away silly, there are many more interesting things to do besides wasting time with you." She said pushing me aside. "Come upstairs, your shirts are ready I pressed them all yesterday."

Dancing, I followed her like a happy little dog.

"Here, this is your, and give this one to your brother." She added thoughtfully.

"Thanks mamma." This time I did steal a little kiss and quickly going down the stairs I bumped into Mario, my younger brother, who was wandering around the house barefooted, holding his shorts up and asking questions;

"Are you going to the beach? Can you take me to?"

"I am afraid not. You know we can't, papa' wouldn't like it. You know what he always says."

"Ya ya I know. If you can't take care of yourself, how do you expect to take care of me. Same old story. In the meantime I have to stay home."

Feeling sorry for him I tossed half lira in the air saying: "Here, catch it. Buy yourself some candies and don't forget Maria, give her some too."

"Are you going to talk forever or are you going to bring me that shirt," yelled Carmine impatiently. "Come on, Viano is at the door."

We were almost out on the street, when mamma called back "Be careful when you go swimming, that lake is very treacherous, and for a change comeback early tonight will you? Don't make me spend all night worrying and waiting."

At the usual corner, we met the rest of the gang and all together, laughing and joking we walked to the street car stop on Via Prenestina. After the short ride we got off on Viale Manzoni where boarding the Tranve dei Castelli we had to scramble for the seats and got separated from each other.

From Rome, the street car follows the Appia Highway all the way to the many little towns and villages. Among them and about fifteen minutes ride away from the main line, there is Castel Gandolfo, which is altogether not more than twenty kilometers and a little more than one hour's ride.

Most of the passengers were Air Force soldiers, going to Ciampino Airport and as we got there they descended leaving the tramway almost empty. I got up with the intention of joining my brother, but seeing that he was already busy talking to a beautiful brunette sitting opposite him, I quickly changed my mind.

Sitting back and enjoying the scenery was very relaxing. First it was a farm house here and there, then fields of golden wheat, as far as the eye could see, then hundreds of fruit trees and finally as we began climbing, vineyards after vineyards.

Past Frattocchie, the street car slowed down and leaning my head out of the window I tried to get a glimpse ahead to see what the holdup was. Wow! We were going uphill, straight up and brother........what a hill.

Here begins the land of the famous Colli Albani, once the original sight of the ancient Rome, and now the largest and best source of supply of white wine for all the roman bonvivants.

At a snail's pace we arrived at Ercolano, where the tramway stopped to let us off. We were saving ourselves a full hour by taking the short cut to the lake, but boy o boy, climbing that desolate hilly lane full of rocks and cracks on the uneven floor, was real hard work. In fact nobody seemed

empty. How did we do it no one could explain it, but they were empty.

"Let's fill them up again." Suggested Viano laughing loudly.

"Damn good idea Viano" I agreed heartily, and that done we headed back.

My face was getting hotter by the minute, but, "it must be the sun," I said to myself, "it can't be the wine" that is for sure, it can't be the wine. I felt as if my feet were hardly touching the ground, everything seemed so rosy and quite, quite beautiful. My friends seemed to be having the same experiences, so singing yelling and laughing our heads off, swinging the fiaschi up in the air and sipping slowly from time to time to clear our throats, we finally got back to camp. From then on, until we got home at three o'clock in the morning, is something that I recall very vaguely. As in a dream I remember walking back to castel gandolfo and on the way my brother hurled curses at me for getting into this miserable condition. Indistinctly I recall that we didn't take the short cut this time, and thank God for that, because in the dark I would have never made it, instead we waited for the street car for Albano and from there the one to Rome, the struggle to get on it, my friends and the guy with the mouth organ encouraging me to sing which I did and before long I had all the passengers harmonizing with me, including the conductor, who if am not mistaken, was just as drunk as I was. I remember the two carabinieri that stopped us at Porta Maggiore because we were disturbing the peace, and finally papa' in his night shirt waiting for us at the gate saying "Look at you. You are disgracing the whole family. Go, go to bed now, we will take this up again tomorrow when your head is free of butterflies."

Chapter 3

In this world, there are many things that are not right. For instance, just to cite one. In a week we have more working days than rest days, and definitely this is very wrong. To be fair, I believe we should have at least an extra day off, say Monday for instance. I bet everybody would appreciate it, especially if someone had the same type of weekend I had. If this were the case, it would be like cheese on the macaroni, I could have stayed in bed as long as I liked and when I decided to get up, maybe my head might have felt a lot better.

It would be nice, wouldn't it? Cut it out you dreamer, it is time to go to work and make it fast, before papa' comes down. If he finds out you are still in bed, then there will be real trouble and nobody is going to save you from a good beating. Carmine has left long ago, so you won't have any excuse for being here.

Mentally I lashed myself into painful action and with great effort I made it to the shop. Sneaking under the boss's window so he wouldn't see me, I was just set to punch the time card, when a lovely voice reached my ears.

"Well. Look who is here! Poor Armando, late again eh?" Whined Mr. Panto as gracefully as a rhinoceros could be. "What's the excuse this morning? Oh don't say it, I know. The street car was too crowded and you had to walk all the way. What a shame. I bet you must be tired already. Well, well," he went on sarcastically. "I hate to see you overdoing it, if you ever get sick on account of this, my conscience would bother me for the rest of my life. No, no, I am sorry but I can't have any part of it. You better go home this morning, have a nice rest and when you do come back tomorrow morning, and do I a favor will you? For a change, make damn sure to be on time."

"Damn you, you old goof." I grumbled between my teeth. He sure crossed me up. I had already planned to spend all morning sleeping in the oven of a 735, instead I had to start replanning and in present conditions I was in, just to think, it took a tremendous effort.

On every other occasion when I had been late, I had begged and promised him I would never be late again, until my obvious sincerity touched his tender heart and he would relent and give me permission to go to work, but right now I couldn't care less, and putting the time card back in place, I turned on my heels and walked out, leaving him standing in the doorway with a very satisfied smile in his face. I had just gone a little way when he called out:

"Armando?"

"Yes Mr. Panto," I said turning and looking him straight into the eyes. Thinking that he had changed his mind like he had done so many times, instead:

"Don't forget now, we start at seven o'clock." He said adding sarcasm to his sweet voice. "Remember?" Have your fun today. Somehow, someday I will get even with you, you pompous ass. I murmured again between my teeth.

I was too tired even to talk, my head felt hollow, sounds were magnified a hundred times and echoed around as if I was in an empty hall, my intestines were ready to come through my mouth at any second, my whole body was aching all over and my legs were not too steady either, so without uttering another word, slowly climbed the endless stairway and quit the premises. But I didn't go far, along the narrow avenue leading to the main gate, under the shade of a wild chestnut tree, I saw a bench, I stopped, dropped on it and closed my eyes.

I don't know for how long I stayed, but when I got up, and started walking, the fresh air revived me. My physical condition was not at its best, but at least the headache was gone and my mind was a little clearer, only the eyes still burned in the bright light of the sun, but that too in time would go away, I hoped.

So, I thought, this is how one feels the morning after the night before. Well … It is a lesson learned the tough way, but never again, never. This is the first and the last time, as one drunk said to another.

Finally reaching home, I was kind of glad to be there, but as I went through the gate, seeing papa' down in the hole digging, sent my spirits down to a new low. Poor papa'. I knew he meant well and maybe he was right but Carmine and I couldn't see it, to us it was a waste of time, material and energy. Yet he swore on it. He was convinced that our present war was fought in the trenches, the same way as it had been fought in 1914-18. So by building a shelter as the one that he had in mind, a big hole in the ground covered with heavy planks and dirt on top, it would be safe enough for us in case of an aerial attack.

Fortunately it was never finished and never tested, otherwise I wouldn't be writing this story.

But why did he have to start working again on that darn shelter today of all the days? I groaned under my breath, and sleep will have to wait for the time being.

When he saw me, he leaned heavily on the shovel and with contempt in his eyes said:

"Well what are you doing home at this hour? Did you get fired?

"No, I didn't. There has been a change in the schedule and I will have to work next Sunday." I was lying and he knew it but he didn't say anything.

"Very well, then go change your clothes and come back here to help me. Maybe we can make some progress with the shelter today."

From the look on his face I could see that he was not in a good mood, so I hurried into the house as I was eager to please him. Mamma was combing my little sister Maria's long wavy hair, going by I gave her a quick hug but got no response and continued to my room. When I came out I run into Mario.

"What is the matter with mamma?" I asked.

"She is mad at you and Carmine, because last night you came home so late."

"You see? Aren't you glad you didn't come?"

Oh Lord! The first shovel full of earth seemed to weigh a ton. Before long I started perspiring, the sweat came down my forehead, over my eyes, behind my ears, my cheeks and my neck, streaming down my chest in little rivers and soaking into the band of my shorts.

While papa' broke up the hard packed soil with his pick, I rested and wiped my forehead. When he got tired I took over. I spit upon my hands so I could get a better grip and lubricated the blisters that were beginning to form, then I dug in and shovel after shovel the brown earth was tossed out.

We were more than five feet deep and thank God, papa'
thought it would be enough, he threw the pick on one corner
and said: This will do the trick, and turning to Mario who
was sitting on the ground watching us:

"Ask your mother to give you some money, go to the
hardware store to buy half kilo of spikes and hurry back."

After we had driven a wooden post into each corner, we
assembled all the two by six planks near the edge and all we
needed were the nails, but Mario was not back yet. So we
waited and waited but Mario was nowhere in sight.

"I wonder why that kid is taking so long. The store is
not that far and he left almost an hour ago. Do you think
he is making them?" He asked me laughing.

Looks like things are brightening up I thought. His
humor was getting better and the tension that had been
between us up to then, eased off, but not for long.

"Go find your brother," he ordered me. "And don't take
all day either, otherwise if I have to go after you too, you
will both get it. Hai capito?"

I walked to the end of the street, through Via del Pigneto
and at last there he was, coming down from Via Alberto da
Giussano. "Where in the devil have you been?" I asked.
"Papa' is furious. Didn't you get any nails?"

"No. They didn't have any. I went to two stores. The
one in Via del Pigneto sent me to their other store in Via
Brenestina, hoping that they might have some left, but they
didn't have any either," he explained.

"Well ... Let's go then. Papa will have some ideas."

We were just entering Via del Pigmeto again when the
alarm went, sounding the alert to take shelter. Here we go
again, I thought. It was one of the usual false alarms that we
had heard so many times, but we had never seen any enemy
planes over the city as yet. They had not and they would
never dare to bomb Rome. It was long ago declared an

"Open City" so, as if nothing had happened, we proceeded slowly toward home.

Boom! Boom! Boom! A couple anti-aircraft guns were shooting now, the shells leaving white snowflakes in the sky as they exploded. Ahead of us, a woman holding heavy shopping bag with her two hands, stopped and resting it on her prominent big belly, looked up and yelled:

"What are those crazy fools shooting at? I don't see any airplanes. The way they shoot, only God knows where the shells will fall next. Believe me we better take cover someplace, because it is not safe here in the open."

She had hardly finished speaking when we heard a steady humming noise coming from high above, but looking up in the sky we could see nothing. More sirens were going at full blast now with a terrifying high pitched scream, but still feeling that we were not in any immediate danger, leisurely we started moving, talking and joking about the men on our defense guns. Meanwhile the humming got louder and louder, and only then, we began to realize that something was not quite normal.

Inquisitively I looked at the lady next to me and saw terror in her eyes.

"Come on Mario, let's hurry, papa' will be working and" ......but I had no time to finish the sentence. Suddenly our world was shattered by an ear splitting roar, the earth trembled under our feet, as bewildered and confused I looked behind me. It seemed impossible, but there it was, the front of the building where Sergio lived, disintegrated right before my very eyes.

I don't know how or why I did it, but faced with the reality of a raid, without consciously thinking, I stuck my leg out and tripped the poor pregnant woman who well flat on her face, then "Down Mario down" I shouted, at the same time dragging them down on the pavement with me.

A split second later and we didn't know if we would survive this or not, as a shower of rocks, branches, pieces of wood, steel, bricks, with an immense cloud of earth and dust rained down on us. Bombs were falling and exploding everywhere around us, making a thundering and frightening noise.

There must have been hundreds of bombs, thousands of them, who knows. It lasted ten seconds, thirty seconds, one minute half hour, it seemed it would never end. Then all at once ...... silence.

I waited for a few seconds, then cautiously raised my head and looked around. I pushed myself up on my feet and shook off the debris, like a big dog when he comes out of the water. My first impulse was to look at my brother, help him to get up and inquire if he was in pain somewhere in his body, but other than a look of fear and panic on his dirty face, there was nothing wrong. By the time I turned to help the lady, she was already moving up the street screaming hysterically, leaving behind her the shopping bag full of groceries; after that, hand in hand, and as fast as our feet could go, we ran the short distance home, to mamma and papa' who met us halfway on the street crying.

"Here they come again! Here they come again!"

Was the cry that went up from all sides, as everybody rushed back into their homes.

"This time let's all go down the hole," said papa'. "Come on, come on." He urged hurrying us through the gate.

The drone of the planes could be heard once more, louder and louder as they came closer and closer and the same nightmare started all over again.

At last our curiosity was appeased and we saw them very clearly this time. They were the famous American four engine planes, called the " Flying Fortresses " They came in wave after wave, formation after formation, while hundreds of thousands of people must have been watching them, wondering where the bombs would fall next.

"Look, look papa' they are flying right toward the Scalo San Lorenzo." As if they had heard me, they started their infernal music. The earth started trembling once again, the windows in the house were rattling as though someone was hitting drums with a wooden stick on the glasses, the doors swung open by themselves, and the air was filled with smoke, gas smell and a reddish cloud of dust. We could see the dropping of the bombs so clearly, they looked like wood matches falling from their box hurrying down to accomplish their deadly mission.

As one formation moved away, another one moved in to take its place. Some of them passing over the same area, some others quite close to us, others farther away, but all doing the same thing, dropping bombs continuously.

Again, how long this devastating bombardment lasted, would be hard to say, maybe ten minutes, maybe half an hour, but to us it seemed like an eternity. It seemed hard to believe, but at last they stopped. We searched the sky looking for them, but there were no more in sight. Immediately a sense of relief came over us, the tenseness disappeared from our bodies, but the fear was still showing on our tired faces.

Mamma put down Maria who had been in her arms all during the raid, shook the dust off her little dress and looking at papa' with anxiety in her voice she asked:

"Where will Carmine be at this moment?"

"Only God knows, but if he had time to take cover he should be safe, the shelter they have is one of the safest in this neighborhood."

We were all so thirsty that I jumped out of the hole and went into the house to get some water, but …"mamma mia" What a mess.

In the kitchen a part of the ceiling had come down, with several holes in the roof from which rays of sun where coming through. The soup all over part of the floor and on top of the plaster, scattered pots and pans, broken dishes and pieces of window glasses everywhere. I fished out a bottle from under the sink, placed it below the tap and opened it. Crrrr. Crrrr. Only a funny noise came out of it, but no water. I shut off and tried it again, but not even a little drop.

The two tubs outside where mamma washed were still full, with a fine layer of dust on the surface, but apart from that the water seemed to be good. With my hand I pushed the dirt to one end, and immersing the bottle into the clear water I filled it up. I drank half of it, refilled and walked back to the hole. Handing the bottle to papa' I said "This is from the tub, the water is not running from the tap anymore." But I don't think he understood what I said or just didn't care, because after helping himself, he passed it around.

The planes were approaching again, the sound of their motors was so familiar to us now that it was impossible to mistake them for anything else. At that moment I wished it was only a trick of my imagination, a bad dream in the middle of the afternoon. Soon it would disappear from my mind and everything would be normal again, but unfortunately it was not so. The silver silhouettes shining under the strong sun, almost blinded me, as I tried to count them, flying in a triangular formation of nine, making an impressive display of might power, carrying their deadly loads of destruction in their broad bellies.

"Oh Lord no, it can't be," yelled papa' with fear in his voice, looking up toward the new comers. In fact their course was not entirely the same as the one taken by their predecessors, they were pointing straight in our direction. As they came closer and closer, an air of expectancy built up, and up, and up, they were just about a few hundred feet from us when the unbelievable happened. Their bomb-bay doors opened wide open and their contents belched forth under our terrified eyes. Protecting our ears with our hands, we cringed, getting closer to each other, forming a single body, and with our hearts in our mouths we waited for the impact.

Unless someone has been under a bombardment and knows exactly what I am talking about, it is quite impossible to describe the feeling, the cold sweating, the praying, the terrible scare. Also, I can't describe the strength of that infernal blast; the vacuum of air was so strong, that we were tossed from one corner to the other corner of the hole, like a ship on an angry infuriated sea. We were completely helpless. No human creature can stand the blow of such unnatural phenomena. This was it. It looked like the end was near for all of us and everything around us, yet, although it could have been our last hour, we didn't lose faith in the great power of the Almighty God.

Time after time, we invoked Him desperately. Please God save us. Please don't let us die. He must have taken pity on us, our crying and our prayers must have touched Him, because He did, yes, He did spare our lives after all.

At ten minutes to two, the danger was over. The whole world around us, started to live again so did we. The hole were we had spent all the last three hours, even though was just a plain hole, had been our salvation, because in spite of the fact that we were all covered with dust, we were safe and sound, but if we had stayed inside the house it is doubtful if we would be alive. The whole roof of the back of the house, had vanished into the air, what was once our parents' bedroom with all our precious provolone cheese, was nothing but a pile of rubble, stucco, pieces of wood, shingles, stones and bricks, the front door was completely torn off the hinges, all the mirrors and glasses were now in thousands of little pieces, but this was not our main preoccupation. We had been so busy thinking of ourselves that we had forgotten entirely about nonno."

"Mario!" Shouted papa'. "Go outside and ask anybody if they have seen your grandfather, and you," he said to me "go to the Officine Centrali and inquire about Carmine, and hurry back; I have to be at the depot for three o'clock."

I rushed toward Via del Pigneto while my brother went in the opposite direction. Our street was full of debris and holes, and if this could have been any consolation to us, many of our neighbor's houses had vanished entirely, they had been replaced by great big craters in the earth. The crying of despair, the moaning and groaning of the wounded, was so depressing that it was sending cold chills right down my spine. You could smell death all around us. All the neighbors were outside and if they were not helping somebody else, they were inquiring about someone dear to them, and the only words I could hear, were "Have you seen my son? Have you seen my mother, my father, my brother, my daughter?" The lucky ones have a reassuring answer, stopped running and inquiring, while the rest of them kept wondering and asking over and over the same painful question.

I was one of the luckiest. Carmine was coming down the street like a thunderbolt, shirtless, with his pants ripped on one side from the waist down. We ran toward each other. Never till now had I realized how much love I had for my brother.

"Armando!" He called, a sob in his voice.

"Carmine!" I replied. The lump in my throat made my voice sound like a croak, as we embraced warmly. I kissed his dirty face, he kissed me and then he tried to speak, but nothing came out, I knew exactly what he wanted to say and beat him to it.

"They are all safe and sound, only nonno Edoardo was not with us and we don't know where he is, but Mario is already searching for him."

"Oh Lord, thank You" he said, then as an afterthought "And you, what are you doing here. Were you not supposed to be at work?"

"No, I didn't, but it is a long story, I will tell you all about it later, now let's go home."

No need to describe the joy of my parents on seeing Carmine well and unhurt. My brother was really broken hearted when he saw the terrible shape our house was in, but since we were only one of many in the same predicament, we felt very grateful just to be alive, and out we went again to look for our grandfather.

We searched for him in every likely place where he might have been, we asked hundreds of people if they had seen him, but there was no sign of nonno.

Via Pausania the next street parallel to ours, had been really demolished by the bombs, with four apartment buildings completely destroyed. There it was nothing but a mass of desolation. The people were busy with picks and shovels digging through the ruins, taking out dead bodies and some that were not dead, but badly wounded, while agonizing cries could be heard from their relatives and from those who were still trapped under the cellar beams.

We looked at the dead lined up on the ground, covered with canvas, blankets, sheets, potato bags, anything that could be found. One by one, we went over them all, and each time a different face, some badly mutilated and almost unrecognizable, some were of old friends, some just ordinary neighbors. The corpse of a woman was my first experience with death; it was as if someone had hit me over the head with a sledge hammer. It was revolting, ugly, and hard to believe that this was once a lovely woman. Now, nothing but a big piece of meat passed through the cement mixer. Her once beautiful long hair, was the only part of her body that could be identified as belonging to a woman. Oh God, what a horrible sight.

The second body, the third, the fourth one and after that I didn't feel anything, it didn't bother me anymore. When we finished one group, we moved to the next one, we went through the same motion time after time, and the only thing we were able to articulate was thank God he is not here.

On the next block where the houses of the railway people began, called Villini dei Ferrovieri, there was less commotion, the reason for it, was that the houses themselves, had been built on very large lots, therefore, being the buildings well apart one from the other, the casualties were at the minimum, even though, the damages were very heavy. In fact, nine villini out of ten, had been hit very hard by the bombs. The same thing was on the next block. A cluster of bombs had fallen right on the middle of the street, creating a crater that went from one sidewalk to the other, and a U.M.P.A militia man, wearing a steel helmet, sent us away from the dangerous area. It seemed that quite a few bombs were down in the hole still unexploded. As we entered Via del Pigneto on the way back, Carmine said: "Wow. Look at what they've done to Sergio's place."

"I know. I saw it blowing up at the very beginning of the raid. You should have seen the way it went up in the air, it looked like a house made of paper." The grocery store and all the front part of the apartment were a pile of rubble, two crews of firemen were fighting through the ruins with pick and shovel to free three firemen, who had become trapped themselves while they in turn, were trying to rescue a group of women and children who had sought shelter in their cellar.

We proceeded slowly and the sight that our eyes met on all sides was always the same, bodies mangled and sprawled all around. Asking and looking as we went along for our beloved nonno, but our hopes of finding him in one piece were dwindling. We had just passed our street, when a woman called to us "If you are looking for your grandfather, you will find him at the pub of Sor Richetoo."

We rushed to the place and even before we had set foot in the premises, the pub owner came out to meet us saying: "If you are here to get your nonno, don't worry it is all right. He has been here since eleven o'clock. When I heard the alarm, I called him in and together we went down to my wine cellar to take cover, but now, I'll be damned he doesn't want to come out."

"Why?" We both asked a bit worried. "He is not hurt is he?"

"No, no, no. the crazy fool has been digging into my best barrel of wine." Replied Sor Richetto. At which we couldn't help it to burst out laughing. . Thank God, at last among so much grief, horror and destruction, someone was having a little bit of fun.

"No bad feelings Sor Richetto. Tomorrow I will pay every cent for what he drank. For the time being, thanks a lot for taking care of him." Said Carmine, then turning to me with a smile in his eyes "Come on, let's fish him out."

We rushed toward the cellar door and down the four steps. There he was , slumped in a chair with his feet propped on a barrel, holding a fiasco almost empty in his hands. Dear old grandpa was obviously saturated, and at first, he didn't seem to be disturbed by our appearance, but when he recognized us he tried to get up, yet if his memory was still good, his legs weren't and he fell heavily over the barrel.

We picked him up, we pushed him up the stairs, and after thanking Sor Richetto once more, out we went. Luckily everybody on the street was busy taking care of their own problems, and nobody paid too much attention to us as we were going by. In fact, in an effort to steer Nonno home, we had to waltz from one side of the street to the other, and when we finally got there, we left him in the shade of the apple tree, hoping the fresh outside air would help to sleep it off. Even if he wanted to, we couldn't have taken him anywhere else, because there wasn't any other place to take him anymore.

Papa' had gone to report for duty and we were undecided as to what to do, when my friend Viano's father dropped in to see us, mumbling in a dazed way to himself. "Armando have you seen my son?" He asked very preoccupied.

"No. I went to work but I was late and the boss sent me home. Why?"

"I just came from the Railway Depot and a sub foreman told me that this morning he was assigned to the mechanics department to replace you. I inquired around but no one seems to have seen him, so I thought that he must have come home, but he wasn't and I don't know where to look or what to do." Tears were streaming down his wrinkled cheeks, as he stood there motionless.

My heart filled with compassion for the poor old man, but I didn't know how to console him or help him, finally: "Don't despair Sor Oberdan." I was able to say. "He must be around somewhere, and sooner or later he will show up."

"I hope so, but it is already four o'clock and by now if nothing has happened to him, he should definitely be here. Do you understand?"

From his attitude I could see that he was desperate, what he wanted was action not words. After all Viano was my best friend and it was my duty to go and look for him, therefore without any more hesitation I offered to go personally to the depot and inquire about him. "Sor Oberdan would you like to come along?"

"No, you go ahead. My wife is so worried and I am afraid to leave her again."

"How about you Carmine? Would you like to come?"

"No, no. I better stick around, mamma might need me, beside I am very tired and to be honest I have seen enough slaughter for today. Take Mario with you."

So I did....... No matter where we walked, the rage and resentment of the people was at the highest, and the unanimous public opinion was that if Rome was an "Open City" it should have never been bombed. "Open City, means unprotected, means "Off limits" to everyone, the Americans were well aware of it, still they went ahead with their diabolic plan. The world would soon know of the ignoble act committed by them against the Eternal City and condemn them accordingly.

As we passed by a group of people standing in front of a store still undamaged, we stopped to listen. "You should have seen what they did to the Quarter of San Lorenzo?" A little guy was saying. "I have just come from there. Believe me, very few houses have been spared from the massacre, and from reliable sources it seems that over ten thousand people have been killed, maybe more. Campo Del Verano looks like a battle ground, the cemetery was upturned from end to end, and hundreds of graves were desecrated."

"Poor souls! Not even after death can they rest in peace." Remarked a woman. "Besides, what quarrel can they have with the dead?"

At this point, a loud murmur could be heard among the group as they vented their indignation against the sacrilegious, after they had just heard that not even the centuries old Cathedral of San Lorenzo had been spared.

When we got to our usual street car stop I couldn't recognized it.

It seemed hard to believe that only yesterday morning, with nothing but pleasure in our minds, our happy an carefree group, waited on this very corner for the street car to go to Castel Gandolfo. Look at it now. The traffic on Via Prenestina was paralyzed with big craters all over. Two tramways with respective trailers were sideways abandoned right in the middle of the road. There wasn't any sign of automobile or truck, only an endless procession of thousands of families on foot, evacuating the city with any kind of conveyance they could find, bicycles, wheel barrels, hand carts, loaded to the maximum and carrying the indispensable. They were moving as fast as they could, with no particular destination, but one, to get away. At Prenestina Square, another tramway was laying on its side, near a huge crater of about fifty feet in diameter filled with water, which resembled a small artificial lake. We learned that this was where the water main had been hit and explained why our fountains were dry. Ambulance, militia men and firemen crews were busy fishing out dead bodies from the areas flooded basements. Poor people. They had managed to survive the direct bombing but could not escape their fate, as tons of water from the broken main rushed into their cellars so fast they had no time to get out.

The officine Centrali where Carmine worked, offered a very sad sight too. The once huge hangers with their shiny tin roof, were now a gigantic pile of twisted and contorted steel, now good only for scrap. The beautiful one million lire tramway with all its modern splendor of design and performance that had just arrived from the Milano factory, stood charred and burned where it had been parked. Here too, crews of firefighters were trying to hold the blaze that was reaching out its hungry arms, trying to engulf a shed where the paints were stored.

Three hundred feet away, at the gates of the Railway Depot, a policeman stopped us, but after he recognized me he let us pass. The gravel road that I had walked over twice a day, for the past six months, was pitted with large holes and blocked with fallen trees, was no longer a familiar place. Even the friendly bench where I had slept on it only nine hours ago was not there anymore. At the end of the road, there were steps, about hundred and fifty of them, they were gone. We managed to get down hanging on to the broken up pieces of steel and cement. The orderly pattern of tracks, buildings, round houses, turntable, the tall water tank tower and the bustling activities of steam engines, shunting back and forth with the smoke streaming from their stacks, engineers, firemen, mechanics, labors, and further back as far as the eye could see, things that we see every day in normal times, were now scenes of the past, and unbelievably as recent as eleven o'clock this morning.

A big 685 steam engine was standing straight up in the air, its front sticking up through the roof of what was left of the round house. Where once there were four tracks, now there were big holes, rails contorted, twisted like big snakes, with the ties still fastened to them. Where just a few hours ago there had been sidewalks and people walking on it, now there was but wreckage pieces of tracks, pieces of broken machinery unrecognizable was once useful equipment. A part of the coal chute that had been erected a couple of hundred feet to one side of the administrative building, was now part of it. The water tower was upside down, with water everywhere. Two engines were up in the air facing each other, resembling to black monster resting after a long exhausting battle. Skeletons of hundreds of freight cars, coal bunkers, passenger coaches, were scattered and burned. This gigantic mess, this mammoth desolation, was all that remained of what was once the pride of the Scalo San Lorenzo and the Italian Railway.

When our tired eyes refused to look any longer at this dreadful and unforgettable sight, we walked toward the office. My boss Mr. Panto was the only person around. He was wondering about as though in a daze, and his appearance scared me. His hair standing straight up on his head like needles, face as black as coal, his once white shirt wide open showing his hairy chest, shouting incomprehensible words and waving his arms around, resembling more a devil than a human being. I was going to talk to him, but I hadn't gone more than couple of feet, when an older man unnoticed to me before, stopped me.

"Don't go near him." He said. "He doesn't know what he is doing."

"Why? What happened?"

"Somebody brought him news that his wife and two sons have been killed in San Lorenzo." He explained. "They just found their bodies in the ruins of the Cathedral. They must have gone there to take cover, thinking that the old church would have been the safest place to be, instead they lost their lives."

"Poor Mr. Panto!" I said touched by this tragic news. "Where you here when the planes came?" I asked the man.

"Was I here? My son, I can't understand why, but as you can see I am still kicking around. When I was younger I went through the earthquake of Messina, but that was peanuts compared to this. And ...." I listened for a while and finally we had to interrupt him, otherwise he would still be talking.

"I have never seen you around here. Where do you work?"

"I am mechanic and I work in the electric engine department."

"Are you?" My interest in him aroused.

"Yes, yes. I have been sick for a long time, and today of all days I had to come back to work. I was down in the pit changing a pair of brake shoes on an engine, when all hell broke loose and..... "

Hurriedly I cut in "Do you by any chance know Minera Viano?"

"Who? That nice looking kid with dark curly hair?"

"Yes, that's the one. Do you remember seeing him after the bombardment?"

"Well .... Just a moment, let me think ..... He was sweeping the floor near the pit, and that was the last time I saw him."

"What about after that?" I asked again impatiently. "Do you remember seeing him again anywhere else?"

"No, no. I don't recall seeing him." He said calmly, scratching his head and forcing his mind to work. "You see" He continued "A search was made for the casualties, and the dead were brought to the bunkhouse and laid on the floor, while the wounded were carried to the hospitals. Go have a look, they haven't been taken away yet. In fact the way things are moving, they will be there forever."

Thanking the old man for his assistance, I told Mario to stay put, then with robotic maneuvers, avoiding falling into several huge craters full of water that dotted the path leading to the bunkhouse, unexpectedly I found myself face to face with a red flag saying: Danger Unexploded bomb. I almost blacked out. Petrified with fear, a cold sweat began to run down my spine as I looked down the hole, then recovering quickly I slowly worked my way around a safe distance from us, and advancing more cautiously than ever, I reached the bunkhouse and pushed the door wide open.

As the stench of charred human flesh stung my nostrils, I approached with a certain repugnance the lines of covered bodies, and one by one, I began to look at them. When I recognized some friends behind those black masks, people that I knew, that I had worked and joked with only the day before, I felt my nerves lightening up. After I had passed what seemed to be about fifty, I could not see Viano among them; hope surged back into my heart, but burr. There was not a living soul in there, and suddenly realizing I was surrounded by corpses, fear gripped my heart with its icy clutch and quickly making the sign the cross, I forced my shaky legs to move, and somehow they carried me out into the open once more, where hurriedly I gulped fresh air into my starved lungs.

"Well, any news?" Mario inquired, getting up from the cement steps where he had been sitting all this time.

"No" I said. He is not there.

"Let's go home then, I am getting hungry." He said, yawning and stretching, obviously bored by something he did not fully understand. "Don't forget I had only a bowl of bread and coffee since this morning." He continued plaintively in his boyish way.

"Lucky old you," and at that, I realized that I had not touched food since the night before. Strangely enough only then I realized that my stomach and headache were completely gone. Only fear and excitement like the one we had, could have performed such a miracle in such a short time.

The day before only twenty four hours ago. Yet it seemed so much had happened. The whole world had been turned upside down. Why? I asked myself. Why? Not finding an answer, I turned to my baby brother and putting my arm across his shoulder in a protective way I murmured: "All right, let's go, I am hungry too." The closer I got to the house the worse I felt, as a sense of emptiness gradually took hold of me. What it was I could not explain. Maybe I was getting tired, or it could have been the hunger. No ..... That was not it. I had been hungry before. This was different, something I couldn't describe, something inside me, deep, deep down. Finally I knew what it was. I had to face Sor Oberdan and I was scared. How should I tell him that we were unable to find his son? He was so worried. Maybe I should have continued searching, but where? Rome is a big city, and there are a million places where he could be. Well ... There was no reason why my conscience should bother me, after all I tried my best.

Oh stop worrying. I told myself. It has been a long exciting and exhausting day and your mind is completely confused. Think positively for a change.

Perhaps Viano has already had his supper, and by now he is laughing and telling jokes with the gang under the street light pole, our usual gathering place. How nice it would be if that was true.

At the corner of Via del Pigneto and ours, Sor Oberdan was waiting for us, with hope and anxiety showing on his face. "Did you find out anything?" He asked with a tremor in his voice.

"No." I answered without raising my head, avoiding to look directly at him. "But I went through all the victims and his body was not here."

That was the moment I dreaded. I wished I could have disappeared, vanished into thin air, for watching and listening to him talk, was something too hard to bear.

"I knew it. I knew it." He kept repeating, breaking down completely. "Good-bye to my generation. The Minera name is finished. The only son I had is dead." My heart was bleeding for him, but I couldn't let him go on torturing himself like that, and swallowing the big lump in my throat that had been choking me, I tried to calm him down saying: "Don't give up hope so easy Sor Oberdan, tomorrow I will tour all the hospitals, I am sure one way or another we will find him."

"Poor son of mine, poor son of mine," he went on. "You were the only thing that I lived for. Oh Lord! If it is true that you can do miracles that everybody talks about, please make one now. Please give me back my son."

After that, he covered up his face with both hands and walked away dragging his red feet, leaving us with a feeling of helplessness and futility.

As we followed him, his appeal to God was so fresh in my mind that it made me think and wonder. I know it is a sin to take His name in vain and worse yet to question Him, and I hope that my doubting will be forgiven, but if He is as powerful as they claim, if He is everywhere and sees everything, why did He allow so many horrible things to happen? Maybe, this was one of His many ways to show His disappointment for our behavior, but tell me, what could have Viano done, to deserve to die? He was so young, why should he pay for the mistakes of somebody else? It is claimed that He is just and fair why then doesn't He punish the real responsible ones, the ones that transgress His laws and commandments? Why did thousands of innocent have to be killed today instead of a few ambitious greedy bastards? Tell me why? I am afraid the answer will never come.

Papa' was back home now, he didn't have to work. Everybody was sent to their respective families because of the great chaos that was reigning all over the city.

Between him and Carmine they had made only a little dent in the mass of debris, as Mario and I pitched in to remove the worst and make a pathway into the kitchen and to our food pantry. To our great surprise, the little room was intact and what came out was the crock of homestead sausages, a big plate of boiled potatoes that had been cooked the night before and all the bread that we could find.

Mamma had improvised an outside fire and in no time supper was ready. I slapped the sausage between two thick slices of bread and like the rest, once in awhile, I reached for a forkful of fried potatoes in the frying pan. I was enjoying with gusto every mouthful, when I heard papa's voice:

"Armando. See if nonno is feeling better now, ask him if he wants something to eat."

Biting hungrily into the sandwich, I walked toward the apple tree where he was lying, his mouth wide open snoring loudly. "Nonno is still asleep." I shouted "Va bene, va bene, don't bother to wake him up then. He doesn't need any food anyway, his belly is still full of wine."

I had just regained my seat, when holding in her tiny hands a tin cup, my little sister cried: "Mamma can I have some water, I am thirsty."

"It won't be long now." Mamma replied. The water is not cold enough yet. And dipping a ladle into the big pot, she filled up the cup and set it on the improvised table made of two planks resting on two equal piles of bricks.

"But mamma, the tubs of the fountain are full of water, why can't I drink it?" Asked Maria.

"Because the air must be infected with bacteria after what happened today. This is why I am boiling it, to sterilize it and make it safe to drink."

"What does that mean mamma?" She asked again.

"It means that by boiling the water we will kill all the invisible little animals so we don't catch any disease."

"But mamma", went on Maria not yet satisfied, "I don't see anything. Come see," walking toward the fountain, "it is nice and clear."

"That's enough," snapped mamma losing her patience. "Sit down and wait for the water to cool off."

Poor little doll, she is so innocent and naïve.

After the last crumbs of food were devoured, we remained seated around the table. Darkness had descended upon us, all was calm, not a sound could be heard. Our friends and neighbors, who always liked to sit on their front steps, enjoying the fresh air of the cool evening, were not there, neither were the kids, who under the benevolent eyes of their parents, usually played hide and seek, exploding with the shrill of delight when the seeker found the hider. The hilarious voices of my friends gathered on the corner beneath the street light, were missing too, as was the dim blue light that used to brighten our front yard. In the sky with its thousands of stars, the moon circled unperturbed high up, keeping watch as we talked low, so as not to disturb the silence that reigned around, while we discussed the day's events and its many highlights over and over again.

This was one of the days that would remain impressed in our minds for the rest of our lives. Monday, July 19, 1943, would never be forgotten. From here on, this day would be remembered as "Black Monday" Black is right, because from this day, the thousands of those who survived would wear a wide black band on their left coat sleeve in mourning for the loved ones that were lost to them forever.

It was past midnight when at last we decided to go to sleep, but before we get tired, papa' had a last word to say:

"Let's all kneel down and thank our Lord for sparing us, and say a prayer for those whom we will never see again."

Sor Richetto the pub owner wasn't wrong when he complained about nonno drinking all his wine. As we lifted him up like a bag of potatoes and carried him to his room, he heard nothing and felt nothing. That done, we placed a couple of blankets on the floor right next to his bed and we started to get comfortable, when mamma came into the room with another bunch of blankets.

"Here, keep them folded and use them for pillows." She was almost outside the room, when something made her change her mind, and turning back toward us her shadow reflecting on the wall she said: "Good night and God bless you all."

Chapter 4

I was very tired when we went to bed, yet I couldn't sleep, as many, many thoughts traveled through my unstable mind. I was really shocked when it suddenly dawned on me how fragile we are, how easy it is to pass from life to death. I also realized that in such moments of great peril and distress, the whole family seemed to gel together, to get closer to one another, to be more compact, as we loved, and feared, we shared and worked together more than ever before. I had the impression that we had become humble again, that we appreciated little things that in normal time we would take for granted.

Also I couldn't believe how in such moments, how easily we all accepted and accommodated accordingly, without arguing or complaining. In fact, while papa', mamma and Maria, had taken over our bedroom, we had to move in with nonno, and everybody was more than happy to do so. If such circumstances would have occurred in normal times, I am positive, we would be still screaming, crying and maybe even fighting over it. Therefore, the sole fact that we had made the best of what was left without uttering a single word of dissatisfaction, proved to me that I was right, my conjecture were correct, which made me arrive at a very simple conclusion: It wouldn't hurt to be more humble, more human and less greedy. Next morning-at sunrise we were up without the help of the alarm clock or the usual call from mamma. I had bad nightmares all night, and my mouth felt like it was full of sand. A good cup of coffee would have certainly done the trick, but what coffee? We had forgotten what it tasted like a long time ago. I must have been dreaming again. It was a cold glass of water that I got instead, like everybody else, and I had to consider myself fortunate at that.

We were all set to report to work, when papa' had something to say on the subject:

"Armando! Forget the railway job for the present time. When those cheap bastards provide a decent shelter for their employees, like the one there is at the Officine Centrali, then we will see. Beside there is enough to keep you busy around here if you really feel like working. Also, another good reason for wanting you to stay home is because your mother may need you. Is that clear?" And turning to Carmine in the same commanding tune "Come on you. It is getting late and even if we won't be able to work, the least we can do is to report on time."

Experience had taught me never to argue with papa's orders, so I accompanied them as far as the gate where I followed them with my eyes until they turned on Via del Pigneto, then immediately after, with mamma and Mario, we started the slow operation of removing the debris. Not more than a few minutes had gone by, when the noise we were making woke up nonno.

"Bunch of wild animals," he shouted, cursing and swearing. This house is getting impossible to live in. "They won't let a guy sleep in peace any more. I am beginning to wonder where the decency and respect has gone." He said appearing in the doorway, holding his pants up and shouting with all the strength of his 79 year old frame. Oh grandpa, at his age he was still a powerful man that is when he was sober.

I doubted very much if he was still drunk, but of one thing I was sure. He had no idea at all of what had happened the day before, because very convinced he said: "What in hell goes on here? What are you trying to do wreck the house down?" But suddenly, as if somebody had cut his tongue off, he stopped talking, and the towel he was holding in his left hand slipped to the ground. Then slowly moving toward us, raised his hand to his mouth and biting his forefinger in horror he exclaimed "Mamma mia." Che e' successo? Did we have an earthquake?"

"No nonno" I explained, taking his arm and helping him to sit on a pile of bricks. "Yesterday the Americans bombed Rome, and now we are cleaning up the mess."

"Bombed?" He murmured, keeping his eyes down and muttering to himself. "This damn war, in my days we fought on the front line, soldier against soldier, now they bring the war right on your front step. Bunch of riff raff." Then suddenly, looking around with his inquisitive eyes, as he began remembering, with a voice quavering with emotion cried out: "Where is Sebastiano and Carmine?"

"They are all right papa', no one was hurt, not any of us. They went to check in, but I guess they will be back shortly." Said mamma taking hold of his hands.

"Well..." A sad smile showing on his lips now "As long as we are alive, the hell with the house and whoever built it." He said, forgetting that it was he himself that ten years ago built it with papa' "Our skin is what counts first. In no time we will have it cleared and maybe with God's help, we will be able to repair it. As a matter of fact, this time we will build an addition to it, so when this stupid war is over, and Peppe comes home, (My oldest brother was his favorite) he can have a room all to himself. And you know what?" He went on jokingly "He won't have to complain anymore about my snoring."

Then laughing like a child, stood up, picked up the towel from my hands, tied it around his neck and with the agility of a fifteen year old kid, walked to the fountain and before mamma could stop him, splashed some water on his face and without bothering to dry up, he joined us at our unpleasant task.

We kept working at it all morning until eleven o'clock, when the sirens alerted us for another air raid, but luckily nothing happened, it was a false alarm. The quiet was resumed, everything returned to normal and shortly after, all exited papa' and Carmine came rushing home. They had learned that on the Tavoletti's farm there was lots of fresh water available, so gathering all the damigianes, pails and pots, with four trips we accumulated enough water for at least a couple days.

To keep my promise made to Sor Oberdan the day before, around two o'clock, in the height of the heat, Carmine and I took off for the nearest hospital to search for my dear friend Viano. On the way out, we looked everywhere hoping to see some of our neighbors and friends, but without too much luck. Most of them must have deserted their homes the day before. A supreme quiet reigned all around us and at that moment Via Marmocchi, like many others was a lifeless street.

We chose San Giovanni Hospital as our first stop because it was the closest to the bombed area and most likely the one where Viano could have been brought. Any time I had occasion to visit this place, I was always impressed with its intensity, as a matter of fact, and I became lost as in a maze with its wide endless corridors going off in each and every direction. As we ran up the several steps of the entrance and into the spacious lobby, I expected to see the same familiar scene as then with quiet and silence reigning everywhere, instead we stopped aghast at the chaos that existed inside.

White clad figures of nurses and doctors, the good sisters, with large aprons over their habits, bent over hundreds of people laying on the floor, benches, chairs and cots. All casualties of the bombing. We didn't know what to do, where to turn, everybody seemed so busy we hated to disturb them. Finally regaining our composure, we walked over to the information desk and to the girl at the switchboard, but she too was so busy that Carmine could only get a few word in as she excused herself and turned back to the light that kept constantly illuminating the large board in front of her. Discouraged we left her and tried to find someone else who could answer our questions, but seeing no one paying any attention to us, we slowly started moving into a long corridor, where a nun was talking to an orderly.

There we hoped was our chance, we stopped right in front of them and without too much regard for what they were saying, I asked "Excuse me sister" Looking at me as though annoyed for the rude interruption, exasperatedly she eyed both of us from top to toe saying: "What Is that you want?"

"We are so sorry to have so rudely interrupted your conversation sister," butted in Carmine noticing the spark of fire in my eyes. "We would like to know where we can get some information concerning a friend of ours. He disappeared yesterday and no one knows if he is dead or alive."

"My dear young man" She answered coldly "They brought hundreds of wounded people and many of them have not been identified as yet. What is the name of the person you are looking for?" She then asked kindly.

"The name is Viano Minera. He is sixteen years old."

"Come with me to the office." Quickly we followed her. On a desk she picked up a bunch of papers and handing them over to us, she added "Here, you may look over them, see if your friend's name is on it." Avidly we went through the several lists of names, but no trace of the one we wanted, and shaking our heads, in chorus we murmured "No sister, it's not here."

"Well... I am sorry boys. This is all I can do for you." Then, as an afterthought, "by the way, how old did you say your friend was?"

"Sixteen. Dark curly hair, five foot five, about my size," I answered promptly.

"Maybe, maybe," as if talking to herself, "I remember an army truck bringing in a group of wounded yesterday just before the second wave started. Among them there was a young man that had been found unconscious near the railway tracks of the Scalo San Lorenzo. He had no clothes on at all and his body was all covered with wounds and burns."

"That's him, that's him." We both answered excitedly. "Where is he now sorella?"

"Follow me. You wouldn't find him in a million years." She said with a gentle smile on her face and leading the way. How right she was. Corridor after corridor, all crowded and with the same confusion as was in the lobby, through a pavillion, past the maternity ward and finally into a small dark room. "There he is," she said in a hushed voice pointing at the third bed on the left. And make it very short, because he must be in terrible pain. Then without giving us a chance to thank her, she nodded, smiled and left.

We tip toed cautiously toward the bed and stood there looking at him. He must have sensed our approach because he wiggled his fingers, the only part of his body except his eyes and mouth that were not bandaged. Oh God what a spectacle. He looked more like an Egyptian mummy that a living creature.

"Ciao Viano, come stai?" I asked.

"Not too good," he answered feebly. "Every time I move it hurts everywhere. The nun told me that as soon as the burns on my back have healed, the doctor will try to remove the little pieces of shrapnel from my body." He stopped talking, then taking a deep breath he added, "have you seen my parents? How are they?"

"Don't worry about them, they are all right, in fact they should be here any minute now." Carmine added lying. Then remembering what the sister had told us, we cut it short " We have to go now, so take it easy, and do exactly what the nurse orders you to do, I bet in a week's time you will be back home."

"You dreamer" He grinned. "Who do you think you are kidding?"

"Be patient and you will see it won't be long" I said, quickly wiping back the sneaky tears with the palm of my hand. "If I have time I will come to see you tomorrow. All right? For now good bye Viano."

"Ciao, ciao." He answered with a feeble voice.

At the door we turned back to wave at him, but he had already closed his eyes.

"You had a lot of nerve in telling him that his parents are coming," I said reproachfully to Carmine. "They don't even know if their son is dead or alive yet, besides, his mother has been in bed since yesterday afternoon, and I doubt very much if Sor Oberdan will take a chance on leaving her by herself."

"Well.... What did you wanted me to say? I had to take a chance." Carmine answered. "And don't be a pessimistic mother in law all the time," he added. "I bet anything with you that when we bring them the good news, sick or not sick, they will rush to the hospital at a hundred miles an hour. You will see?"

The sounds of the sirens caught us in the middle of Porta Maggiore square, and as a safety precaution we stopped under the very thick arches of the old roman walls, but nothing developed and soon after we proceeded toward home.

Sor Oberdan met us on the stair landing where he had been waiting since we had left, and it is almost impossible to describe the commotion we caused. The joy and happiness of knowing that his son was alive again, brought him back to life instantly, because as soon as he had enough information as where to find him, he turned on his heels and climbing the steps four by four, without even holding to the railing, he began screaming and yelling to his wife: "Elena, Elena, our Viano e' vivo! Our son is alive"

By the time we reached our gate, we saw the old couple come out hand in hand, walking like two young kids in love going to get married.

"Look at them! Didn't I tell you," Carmine said.

I tried to say something, but the words were hard to come, my heart was full, filled with gratitude toward God that had made it possible, because thanks to Him once again, those two poor souls were happy, once again they had something to live for. The love of their son.

Chapter 5

The night before we had a family conference, and after a long discussion, mamma and papa' decided to send my sister Maria, my brother Mario and myself away to Ceprano, a town hundred kilometers south of Rome, to stay on the farm of my mother's parents, our nonni Agostino and Teresa, and depending on the frequency of the air raids, they would join us in the near future. Due to the unusual circumstances, we had to go to the Casilina station, only a secondary place, on the outskirts of the city and not too far from where we lived, to catch the mixed train of coaches and boxcars that was already formed and ready to leave when we got there.

People were running up and down, not knowing exactly which way to go. They were disoriented and confused. Kids were crying and hanging to their mothers skirts with a frightened look in their eyes, men and women, young and old alike, carrying suitcases, bundles, boxes, baskets and bags of all shapes and color, loaded with personal belongings, as many as they could carry, all valuable things that they could not bear to leave behind. In many cases, this represented all of what they had been able to salvage from their destroyed homes.

The inside of the coaches and boxcars were jammed tight, and although everybody was making an extra effort to push further inside to make room for the newcomers trying to climb aboard, many of them had to be left behind, hoping that soon, another train would take them away too.

The saddest heart breaking moment came when the convoy started moving and a general cry of voices, saluting each other exploded into the air, from the people on the train and the ones remaining on the platform. We did the same, and as papa' disappeared from our sight, warm tears came rushing down our cheeks.

Although we were packed like sardines, for the first few kilometers nobody complained much, but after a while everything seemed to get under everyone's skin and big sighs were heard among the passengers. Handkerchiefs were brought steadily to the foreheads indicating the discomfort shared by everyone, because first of the suffocating heat, secondly of the poor air circulation, without mentioning that there was not a drop of water available anywhere.

When the train was moving it didn't seem too bad, but the villages or towns were not very far apart, and it seemed that when we stood still, which was quite often, we could hardly breathe.

Maria was complaining all the time that she was being squashed, so to make sure that she wouldn't get hurt, I kept her in my arms most of the time.

We had left Rome around two o clock, and to cover the hundred kilometer trip, we should have been able to make it in a little more than three hours, but at last when we got to Ceprano's station, we were so tired that we forgot to count them, we were happy to be there and that's all.

Jumping off the boxcar, the fresh air revived me, and I felt good to be able to move around freely again. First with the kids, then someone helped with the baggage, and with my little sister on one side and my younger brother on the other, we walked to the exit and out into the big square where we were supposed to board the bus to take us into town. I looked for it, to the left, then to the right, but it was not there. I turned about hoping to see somebody, but there was not a soul in sight, no houses, no sign of life anywhere, only deserted fields and a solitary gravel road winding away in the distance. I turned my eyes to the little station behind us, hoping with all my heart to see somebody, but there too, nothing. At this point I became a little worried. There must be people working inside, so I put the suitcase down, sat Maria on it, ordered Mario to take care of her and a little panicky now, I broke into the waiting room, but nobody, into the wash room, the baggage room, still nobody. It was incredible.

A cold chill began to creep up and down my spine and a cold sweat all over my body. "This is it. We have arrived, but how are we going to get to the farm?" I was talking to myself now. I wished papa' was here, he would know what to do. Now that I think back, I don't recall seeing anyone get off the train. Frightened thoughts began racing through my mind. Could it have been that we got off at the wrong station? No, no. The dispatcher was there calling loudly: Ceprano. Ceprano. I am certain of it and he must be somewhere, damn it! Where in the hell is he hiding? I was just about ready to scream, when I noticed him sprawled on a chair with his feet on the desk, holding the newspaper over his face.

Oh thank God. When he heard me approach, he moved the newspaper to one side, looked over his steel rimmed spectacles and nonchalantly he inquired: "What is it young man?"

"I arrived a few minutes ago and expected to find the bus outside. Do you know the reason why it is not there?"

"Certainly, there won't be any bus, because the train you got off was not a regular one, therefore it was not on their schedule. I am afraid you will have to walk your way into town." Getting up and looking through the window he asked:

"Are those two kids with you?"

"Yes they are."

"Well... You better get moving then. That is the road you have to follow." Pointing at it with his finger. "And make it fast, otherwise the night will catch up with you."

After thanking him for the information, I got back to my little family, and hand in hand, we began the long march into the open, under the setting and yet very hot sun.

Maria and Mario were running freely now, always ahead of me, picking flowers, throwing stones and laughing and shouting for many insignificant things. It took so very little to make them happy, and I was very pleased to see them enjoying themselves. After all there was no danger of any sort around here, no cars, no trucks or bicycles, so I let them be until we entered the town.

Every time I came here, I felt the same way. The narrow streets, the smell of freshly baked bread, the women still wearing the old fashion dresses reaching down to their ankles, the old people sitting along the edge of the fountain, cows and horses, resting near the drinking trough, the calm and unhurried manner of the natives, fascinated me.

At a bar we stopped for a brief rest, treated ourselves to an orangeade and a sandwich each that mamma had prepared before we left, and once again, feeling like new, we proceeded toward the Casilina Highway. When we passed it, it was almost dark and we left its paved smoothness for a lumpy gravel road, with fences and high trees all along it.

The suitcase I had been carrying was getting heavier and heavier, my two little vagabonds were not scampering anymore, and now and then I had to stop and wait for them, beg them, tease them, coax them, but it was just like talking to the wind. Now they had only one speed: slow. Actually it was a long walk because I was kind of getting tired myself, and for children of seven and eleven, they were well behaved and I was very proud of them. All this was good and well, I admit, but it did not solve my problems, we still had a long way to go, and in spite of my feelings, I kept pushing and urging. The further we went, the darker it grew and when the moon shone to light our way, we sure appreciated the full value of its coming. Now and then we passed a very poorly Illuminated farm house, and without weakening each time we passed by, the barking of the dogs scared the wits out of my sister and brother, who naturally ran closer to me looking for protection and reassurance.

In doing so, they reminded me anew that they were my responsibility which in a way made me feel like a grown up man, but only for a second, because it was a good thing that they couldn't read my mind, otherwise they would have known, that I was just as scared as they were, and maybe more.

Finally we came to a fork in the road, I looked for the little shrine that was to indicate which way we had to follow, and there it was on our right. Realizing that we didn't have much further to go, I couldn't help giving a big sigh of relief.

"Well.... It won't be long now." I said trying to encourage my little ones, but to no avail. Maria's cup had been filled, it was overflowing, large tears were pouring down her doll like face, as she complained that she couldn't stand it any longer. At first I coaxed her, I promised her the sky, the sun, the moon and the stars, but she wouldn't budge, I got mad and this made things worse.

There was only one thing left to do:

"Come on Maria" I said heaving her up on my shoulder and putting a leg on each side of my head. "Are you comfortable now?

She answered by grabbing a handful of hair in each hand, and digging her tired heels into my chest, she hung on for dear life when I bent down to reach for the suitcase.

The road had become a path now, its uneven terrain with deep ruts and holes made by the spring rains, made walking very difficult, but the idea of getting home soon gave me a new strength. Slowly but steadily we climbed the path of the steep hill until we were almost half way there, then gasping for breath I had to stop. I put the suitcase and my sister down, sat on the still warm earth to rest and with the handkerchief, began wiping the perspiration dripping down profusely from my neck and chest, while Mario who had been quite a little man till now, took his shoes off and shook out the minute stones that had been bothering him.

After a while, I got up, brushed my pants and bending down to get closer to her face I asked: "Do you think you could make it to the top all by yourself?" But there was no answer. Her eyes half shut kept staring at me as if they would say "Come on, don't be such a slave driver, can't you see I had enough? What is the matter with you, don't you want to carry me anymore?"

"Va bene. Va bene. Come on, hop on, this ride won't last too long." But by the time we reached the top of the hill and the side of the house, it was all I could take, I felt as though the whole world was resting on my poor shoulders, and as if my arms had been stretched to the ground. As I unloaded my heavy burdens in a hurry, in consolation I said to myself:

"It's all over now, your problems are over, but as the proverb says: Never count your chickens until they are hatched."

A huge white long haired dog, disturbed from his sleep, came bounding from nowhere, barking and snarling at us. "Mamma mia! What is it a lion? Nonna, nonno! Open up. Open up," I shouted banging my hand on the door, while I reached for the suitcase and put it between us and the dog. Thank God, that kept us at a safe distance, but the dog kept on barking louder and louder.

"Who is it?" My grandfather inquired loudly.

"It is us nonno, your grandchildren from Rome."

"Oh per la Madonna!" I heard him exclaim. "Teresa, Teresa, get up. They are our daughter Archangel's sons."

They must have been in bed, because when nonno Agostino came to the door, he was in his night shirt. "Look who is here!" He shouted excitedly, kissing and hugging the three of us. "Come on inside." He said leading us into the bedroom where nonna was struggling with the kerosene lamp that wouldn't light.

"Here, sit her here." Nonno went on lifting up some clothes from the wooden chairs, then, irritated for stumbling against the leg of the bed in his bare feet, he rushed through the door and to the dog who was still barking furiously, he bellowed: "Shut up Baronet. Shut up you damn fool. Another sound out of you and by San Rocco, I will cut your tongue out."

The noise had awakened my aunt, my uncle, all my cousins and all the neighbors who in no time at all were around us asking questions, and showing nothing but surprise and shock at hearing the bad news.

Are they kidding me, or where is this, another part of the world? Imagine only today for the first time they heard rumors that Rome, the capital city of Italy had been bombed, and yet, with me here telling them, they still find it impossible to believe.

After I had described as best as I could the whole story, they began to be convinced, and only then the specter of war was brought home to them in all its stark reality, which was evident even to me, by the expressions of horror on their simple faces, as they kept asking questions and relaying the bad news to the neighboring farmers that kept pouring into the house like flies, much to my dismay, in fact at one point I couldn't helped asking nonno:

"Where are all these people coming from? We did not see a single solitary soul since we left the Casilina Highway."

"I know. We go to bed with the chickens around here. He explained. But when they heard Barone barking and the lights in the house going on, they knew something was wrong and they came to find out."

Even before they were all gone, I saw that my tired out little blonde angel was put to sleep in her bed by nonna, then with that load off my mind, I joined the rest in the kitchen, where aunt Giovannina had put out some food on the table.

Believe me, it was about time, and it was good. Mario and I dug into the salad bowl, where fresh cucumbers, lettuce and tomatoes were swimming in olive oil and vinegar. Our aunt was having a hard time to keep up with us, as the thick slices of mixed white flour and corn bread, disappeared from the table as fast as she put them down, while everyone around us, with big wide eyes, looked in surprise.

They may have been thinking that we had not eaten for a week, and who knows, maybe they were right. I bet if our parents were there, they would have wondered what had happened to our good manners at the table, but luckily they weren't, and so we went on enjoying our food. We would take care of the good manners some other time. In the meantime, nonno Agostino, with a clay decanter in his hand, watched my glass like a hawk. Every time he refilled it with the most beautiful scarlet wine, he poured some into his own, and lifting up his elbow, nonchalantly kept repeating : "Salute! Eat and drink my sons, there is nothing better than a good meal after a long hard day."

As I emptied my glass for the fourth time, I began to feel a warm glow all over me, I would not have minded having a couple more, but remembering the promise I had made to myself just a few days before, I stopped drinking right then.

This was a big disappointment to my grandfather, because he had to stop too, before nonna Teresa got mad. It seemed that she had been keeping a close watch on him since he came back from the hospital, where the doctor told him to moderate the use of wine, in order to keep his blood pressure down.

To push the chair away from the table and get up after consuming a decent meal, sometimes it is not as easy as it seems, and this was one of those times. Because my belly ached from eating too much. After I undid my belt to relieve the pressure which it helped momentarily, but the unpleasant feeling still remained, nonna Teresa lead Mario and myself to our temporary new room, were we had to make the last effort of the day by taking our clothes off, then we flopped into the bed that had been piled high with nice clean corn husks of last year's crop, that had been left in storage only for this purpose.

Oh boy. After those last couple of days, this was heaven, we couldn't ask for anything better. We relaxed till we were as limp as two strands of overcooked spaghetti, then, falling asleep side by side, we slept the sleep of the innocent.

Chapter 6

The following morning I awoke slowly. It was bright outside, so very still, so very quiet. I looked up and.... What is this slanted roof over me? Where am I?

For a moment I was disoriented, lost. Letting my eyes wander down I was in bed. I began to feel about, and touched someone. Then raising myself on my elbow, and seeing the familiar face of my brother, it all came back to me. The horror of the past days seemed like a bad dream from which I had just awakened.

Getting out of bed, I went to the window and looked down into the valley

How beautiful it was, green everywhere, the grass glistened with the early morning dew, and how peaceful and quiet everything was.

Sighing sleepy, I turned away from the window, and seeing my clothes on the chair, got dressed, and on my way out shook Mario.

"What is now?" He asked irritably, sitting up and rubbing his eyes. It was hard to resist his little boy sleepiness.

"If you intend to go with me, you'd better get up, I will wait for you outside."

Suddenly he was wide awake, and scrambling out of bed in a flash, excitedly called: "Wait, wait for me. It won't take me long to get ready."

Climbing the four steps into the kitchen and seeing nobody, I wondered if they were up yet, so without calling or making any noise, I walked out.

Oh, what a lovely morning. Breathing the clean fresh air deeply into my lungs, I made the round of the house. And in the barn I found nonna squatted on the stool, her old fashioned skirt spread about her, busily milking the white cow, the long streams of milk splashing down into the pail which was already half full, while Barone, lying on the straw with his nose resting on his paws, did not move from his position. I was sure my steps made no sound, so I was startled when without turning toward me, nonna said:

"Buongiorno Armando"

"Good morning nonna"

"Did you sleep well?" She asked, then dipping a tin cup into the foamy milk ; she handed it over to me : "Here drink it, it is still warm.

Avidly I brought the cup to my lips, but the odor and the oily look of it, almost made me vomit, and emptying it back into the pail: "Sorry nonna, I don't think I like it," and leaving her laughing heartily, I called out the dog:

"Come on Barone. Would you like to go with me?"

For a moment he looked at me as though thinking it over, then leisurely got up and with Mario now beside me, we went down the hill among the vineyards and fruit trees. My o my! What an abundance and what a choice. Green plums, red plums, pears, peaches, figs black and white; really, we didn't know which fruit to start on, and finally the figs happened to be our favorite.

At first we picked them from the low branches and popped them into our mouths, skin and all, then we began peeling the skin off, but we were getting full and fussy, so we started to examine them more carefully and those we liked the look of, we ate, those we didn't, we tossed to the dog, who caught them in mid air and swallowed them in one gulp.

Soon we got tired of this game and moved to other trees and other fruits, but our appetites were sated, so we walked down to the well and drank some of its icy water, an operation which we should have never done.

Have any of you dear readers ever eaten a lot of fresh figs early in the morning and then, right after drank water? If you ever do, make sure to have a secluded ditch nearby, and lots of paper, it might come in very handy.

Barone had accepted us as a part of the family already, and we loved it. We had always dreamed of having a dog of our own, but our wish could not be realized on account of the severe restrictions of city life, so only those people fortunate enough to own a dog, can understand how we felt to have already won the affection of this beautiful beast, even if only temporarily.

Our friend was a real champion of the canine race, with his thick pelt all long white hair, bright intelligent and gentle brown eyes, and a huge and powerful head erect on a colossal body, always on the move, leading or following us wherever we went, dashing after a bird, leaving patches of hair here and there all along the wire that held the vines, which were already loaded with rich green clusters of beautiful grapes.

We spent the first couple of days getting acquainted with our young cousins and boys of the neighbors, running up and down the surrounding hills, with always something new to see, visiting people we really didn't know, but who welcomed us very warmly just the same. They loved to talk and we enjoyed every minute of it.

Saturday morning came with a small flurry of excitement, because that was the day reserved for one purpose only, washing. In this area the wells created somewhat of a problem for all the residents, during the summer months they were very unpredictable, in fact in most of then the water level went way down and some went completely dry. On nonno Agostino's farm there were two wells, the one closer to the house about five hundred feet downhill, was the one they kept covered all the time, and was the main supply of drinking water for the household, the second one was further down, and was used for doing the laundry and for watering the animals.

Every time I saw my grandmother coming up with a water jug on her head, I watched fascinated, fully expecting to see the water cascading over her any minute, but so far that had never happened, and she kept climbing the steep hill with a poise and grace, that had been acquired over the years in performing just such tasks.

The donkey, borrowed for the occasion from uncle Domenico, my grandfather's youngest brother, was being loaded bright and early that morning, with baskets and baskets, bundles of all size and shape full of soiled laundry belonging to us and our close neighbors, and by the time the caravan started moving, the poor beast's head and tail, were the only visible part of his body.

As we followed the well beaten path which went through different farms, we were met with greetings by the friendly folks, who had lived in this incomparable way of beauty, scenery and history, yet very tired and poor land, all their lives as their ancestors had done and as their sons would do in years to come.

Everybody seemed to know everybody else, and after the usual polite inquiry about us, nonna or my aunt Giovannina had to explain our presence in the group. Being strangers among them, we were the center of great attraction, and in one of these encounters, I happened to meet my "Commare" Nina, (Godmother) for the first time. Of course she didn't recognize me, but after nonna introduced us, suddenly I found myself crushed to her buxom and powerless in her strong arms, with her crying one minute and laughing the next.

"How old are you? You look so big and have grown so much," she said relenting her grip and stepping back to have a better look at me. "Oh my God how the years have flown. The more I look at you the older you make me feel. It seems like yesterday when I stood in church, holding you in my arms, you had on a long white lace dress, and kept crying all the time, while the priest was reading the baptismal rites. My oh my, you don't know how good it is to see you. Now that you know where I live, don't forget to come to visit me again. By the way, how is the Commare and the Compare? I haven't seen them for ages." She meant my mother and father. After I had explained to her noticing that my grandmother was beginning to get restless, she said: "Don't go away yet, wait a moment," rushing into the house and coming out almost immediately, "here, take this with you" handing me a red handkerchief tied at the ends, loaded with homemade sausage and fresh eggs: "I might not be home when you come back this evening, but don't forget now, I will be expecting you. Good bye."

Very much touched by her outburst of affection, I kissed her good bye for the moment, and leaving her standing at the door, I rejoined the rest of the group with Barone trotting in front of me and leading the way.

As we went along, in one field, two aged men and three women stood side by side, each with a spade turning the hard soil, singing as they worked, making it seem so easy, although their bodies were wet with perspiration, as they worked under the hot morning sun. As we passed they stopped, and while saluting us, they wiped their foreheads. One of them reached for the jug of wine kept cool in the shade of a tree, and after helping himself, he passed it around to his companions who, like him drank avidly.

It had not rained for over a month, the earth was dry, everything was suffering, everything was drying on the vines, lima beans, chick peas, beans, green peppers, tomatoes, lettuce, all needed water very badly, and everyone was complaining about it. If they had some rain it would be a blessing for the crops.

The hot sun really hit us when we crossed the open fields, and we appreciated the little shade we got, when we entered the short strips of green field where the corn had grown as high as my shoulder and swayed in the gentle breeze. Here and there, people wearing big straw hats, were picking up freshly cut wheat and tying it into shooks, then standing them on end to dry. Here too, were the same familiar friendly scenes, the same friendly and warm greetings over and over again, till at last we entered the white provincial road. We followed it for a while and finally we arrived at the tumbling narrow river called "Liri" that at that point was no more than a couple of hundred feet wide, and at the most, from one to four feet deep.

The little donkey that up to now had been going at a steady pace, appeared to appreciate the fact that everybody was helping to unload the burden from off his back, because as soon as the last basket of clothes was down, he broke out braying loudly as if he would have liked to say: "Well, that is done my dear friends, now I am going to enjoy a well earned rest." Then moving to the rive edge, he drank and drank until having satisfied his thirst, he started wandering around chewing at the grass that seemed to be thicker and greener here.

Right away everyone got busy, nonna Teresa and aunt Giovannina began looking for a good spot, and once they found it, they moved their clothes to it, a great big rectangular flat stone, about a foot over the water level.

Standing barefooted, with their dresses pinned above their knees so they wouldn't get wet, without wasting time they got to work. Soaping, pounding, slashing, rinsing, squeezing and washing over and over again till the pieces were clean, as hard work can make them, while my cousin Angelina and my sister Maria, both the same age, were busily engaged in a child's game, using a stone for soap and a piece of rag, trying to copy the older women. As for myself, I wouldn't have minded playing with the other boys, but they were far too young for me, so to pass the time, I tried to help by carrying the washed clothes away from the river, piece by piece and spreading them out on the shrubs, bushes and grassy ledges, to bleach out in the warm sunshine, at the same time keeping an eye on my brother Mario and warning him now and then, not to cross to the other side of the river, where the current appeared to be quite strong.

After a while though, tired of doing woman's work, I called him and with Barone, who had chosen me as his new master, we went for a walk along the sandy river bank.

The temptation was too great when we noticed a field of watermelons.

"This is God's paradise" I exclaimed all excited. "Shall we steal one?" I whispered to Mario, as though afraid someone might hear me.

"Sure, why not. Let's go." He said without thinking twice, and faster than the blink of an eye, we ran into the soft sandy field looking for the biggest watermelon, moving from one plant to another, lifting up the wide green leaves.

"Look at this one, look at that one," we both shouted in turn, as we had the time of our lives making up our minds, with so many to choose from. Barone must have thought we were playing some kind of a game, because he ran with us wagging his tall vigorously, putting his head between the leaves as though helping us to search. We kept doing that for quite a while, then: "Here Mario! This is it," I yelled at my brother, pushing the leaves aside to bring out to light a huge watermelon, when suddenly I felt something slimy moving through my fingers and then, right in front of me, two coiled green hideous looking snakes raised their ugly flat heads, their beady little eyes seeming to stare straight at me. With a jerk I withdrew my hand, then feeling a cold chill going down my spine, for a second being unable to move as if hypnotized, I gasped: "Mamma mia".

"What is it?" Mario asked, realizing that something had happened and rushing toward me, but there was no time for me to explain. Barone who had seen the snakes at the same instant as I did, with a leap of his ninety pounds of canine fury, pounced on them, but they slithered away, and he was after them in a flash.

I never realized how fast snakes could move until that moment. Rushing and reaching for their hole, they almost got away, in fact the first one disappeared into the earth, but the second one was not so lucky, he never had a chance. Barone stopped him with his paw, then with his fangs showing, grabbed the snake by the back and lifting him up and snapping him down several times, in not more than thirty seconds put an end to the very short fight, then, leaving the lifeless body of the reptile laying on the ground, he turned his massive head toward us, and with his gentle big eyes seeking approval for what he had just accomplished, he came closer to me to get the caress that he had justly earned.

In the excitement of the moment, the desire for watermelon had completely vanished from our minds, and we walked back with Barone between us, the hero of the hour we wished we had a mountain of bones to reward him with, but we had to content ourselves to share with him the slice of bread and cheese we had for lunch, and a little, I mean a little piece of homemade sausage that my commare had given me that morning. The reason being, homemade sausage especially in the summer time is a rare delicacy and very hard to come by. The watermelon would have made a real nice dessert on top or our dry meal for the whole gang, but the incident of the snakes discouraged all further pilfering, which was just as well anyway.

Around three o'clock, a good part of the clothes were almost dry and the women were beginning to fold them and place them into the wicker baskets and other containers.

The donkey was brought back into the scene and slowly loaded once more, but not as heavily as this morning. This time, some younger women were going to carry their bundles of clean laundry on their heads. When I noticed this change, deep inside me I felt very happy. The way they had loaded him coming down here, seemed to me a bit exaggerated for such a tiny beast.

When the last piece of the clothes had been put away, and all the children were near their mothers, the caravan started moving for the return trek home, and then the singing began. Their songs were completely folkloristic, sweet, gentle and above all melodic. It was the eternal love between man and woman that was glorified a thousand times. Their songs were absolutely enchanting, at times expressing their happiness, other times expressing their sadness, they revealed the purity and simplicity of their souls, they voiced the general feelings, the closeness to their every day way of life, which made them include everything around them, that surrounded them, the trees, the grass, the fields, the wheat, the water, the earth, the sky, the balmy air, the animals, the birds. When they sang, they sang freely, and wholeheartedly, lifting up their argentine voices to God, praying and praising Him for the daily bread they received.

Those hymns refreshed my soul and filled my heart, reminding me that even if I was not raised here, I was born here, and that ciociaro blood still ran through my veins, making me proud to belong to this honest, sincere and valiant race, that in the past contributed so much to the glory of the Roman Empire. The singing went on all the way, through the valleys and hills, so their men would know that they were coming back.

The sun was setting as we approached my grandparent's house on top of the hill, and the serenity of the surroundings was soothing after the long eventful day, the cow lifted her head lazily as she heard our voices, and turned back to the sweet clover that she had been contentedly chewing on, some of the chickens were hopping into their coops, preparing to roost for the night, leaving the tardy ones in the fenced yard still scratching and pecking at the earth.

A cool breeze had come up, replacing the waves of heat rising from the parched earth, the leaves on the trees were moving now, the air was so mite, inviting us to relax, but here, it seemed that there was always something to do, and rest and relax would have to wait until after supper. We all helped to unload the bundles and brought them into the respective bedrooms, we said goodbye to the other groups that were not very far from their destination, and only then nonna began getting ready for supper.

Nonno Agostino chopped up some wood and I carried it into the smoky kitchen, then somebody asked for water and

I chivalrously offered to go get some, which I should have never done, because by the time I climbed the steep narrow path back up to the house, the water jug was weighing a ton, and my legs and back were sore and stiff. Poor nonna, she had done it all her life and never complained.

Maybe life out here was not so comfortable, maybe it didn't vary very much from one day to the next, with no electricity, no telephone, no radio, nothing to read, in fact even if you had a magazine or a book, you couldn't waste too much time reading it during the day. As anyone knows, farm life is not for people who like leisure, and it would have been a sacrilege to keep the oil lamp lit at night just for reading, especially at that time, when kerosene was a very expensive item and almost impossible to get. Still in spite of the discomfort and hard work, I loved this primitive type of living, (once again some farmer blood showed up on me) and truly I would not have minded it a bit if I could have remained here forever.

Everybody here was very poor and money was scarce, children and adults alike, wore their clothes full of patches, and were very poorly educated, especially the old people, because they never had a chance to go to school, as a matter of fact that was a privilege enjoyed mostly by the wealthier class in the old days. The younger ones, were and still are, sent to study at the closest country school, about four or five miles distant. Rain or shine, their only means of transportation, their own good will and strong legs, on roads that have been packed by the rushing raid and the treading of the "Cioce" (type of sandals worn originally by the old Romans and still used by these people). For the majority, school lasts only until they are old enough to hold a rope and lead the cows or the water buffalo to pasture for the few rich land owners. This is as good a way as any to earn their first piece of bread, and as they grow older, the spade and the hoe, are their best friends for the rest of their lives, unless they get smart and venture out to the city, where the women work either as servants or foster mother for the wealthy families, and the men in any kind of construction jobs they can get, because they never had an opportunity to learn a trade.

From what I was able to gather, thousands of them were lucky enough to migrate to the New World around the beginning of the century until after the end of the First World War. Working hard and saving money, then sending it to their families they slowly alleviated and gradually started to change the standard of living in this part of the country, but that didn't last. Mussolini claimed that it was degrading and humiliating for the Italian people to go to work abroad, he enforced a heavy restriction on migration, and in doing so, all hopes for improving their lives were lost forever, and the situation dropped back almost to the former conditions, which have remained so for many years to come.

Although poverty was the order of the day, they didn't seem to mind it. Maybe they didn't know any other way, and maybe they knew, but preferred to let things ride as they were, after all there was not much they could do about it, and this could explain why they were so happy and cheerful, simple and hones, always willing to lend a helping hand. If the conversation happened to turn to war matters, to them, it was nothing but a momentary bad inconvenience that deprived them of the love of their sons, husbands and brothers, and the sooner it would be over, the better it would be for all.

As I have already mentioned it, I was born here just a couple of months over sixteen years ago, in one of these beautiful hills, in an old frame house, where from the inside, you could see the daylight between the cracks of the boards.

From here, after five winters that my father worked and commuted from Rome every two weeks, he decided to move his entire family, then of three children, to the small brick house in the city, built little by little by him and his father at night after working hours.

For the first time since we had arrived in the country, the thought of the house took me back to my parents, my brothers, nonno Edoardo, my friend Viano, and the hundreds of pleasant and unpleasant memories as well. How were they making out? What were they doing right now? Would my parents and brother come as they promised?

At that moment, my mind wandered from one thing to another aimlessly. Homesick and worried, I feared for them. Before we left, the raids were more frequent than ever. Had they been bombed again? They should have left everything and should have come with us. The more I thought, the more I worried, but at the end, I always came back to the same point. Nobody knew but themselves what had actually happened.

With a growing splitting headache, I forced myself to forget everything and everybody, but when success failed me, I turned to God with hope and humility and with all my heart I began to pray:

"Please Lord, wherever they are, take good care of them all," and crossing myself, I left the matter in His mighty hands.

Chapter 7

Religion is very strong among the population of this country town. Following the traditions of their ancestors, they respect and venerate their Saint Protector on July 28, the Festa of Sant'Arduino.

At the house, everybody had been talking and waiting for this day, and busily preparing the best dresses to wear for the occasion.

That morning, nonno and nonna were the first to leave for Ceprano. It was quite customary for them to get there as early as possible, attend the Prima Messa at six o'clock and thereafter do their shopping. From then on, nonna was free to converse with her friends and relatives and in their company watch the procession, then as soon as it was over, she picked up her groceries and parcels left in custody of her merchant friends and without any delay, went back home and got dinner ready.

While we were sleeping, very late the night before, papa', mamma and my brother Carmine had arrived from Rome. Our family was reunited now, with the exception of nonno Edoardo, who preferred to remain to look after the house, and to welcome my older brother Peppe in case he came. The letter they received last Friday, gave them the understanding that his ship, was anchored in the harbor of Naples for minor repairs. He was trying to get a leave of absence, but not to count too much on it, because the navy is unpredictable. Today here, tomorrow there.

That morning, seeing before us the graceful figures of our little mother and our tall, broad shouldered father, descending the hill side by side, with Maria and Mario behind them, and Carmine and I bringing up the rear, filled my heart with joy.

My prayers had been answered, and I couldn't think of words to thank our Lord, because my heart was filled with gratitude. With them here, it was a different matter all together, it felt good to be relieved of all responsibilities, of taking care of my young brother and sister, which since our arrival here actually had been little or no problems at all.

On the way to town, was a continuous renewal of old acquaintances for mamma and papa', who knew just about everybody from way back. Gradually, as we met them, the women separated from the men, the groups enlarged as we went along, while the children mingled. They were always quick to make friends with us, proudly showing their new clothes, discussing how they would spend their few cents in the afternoon when we would go back to the fiesta.

After we crossed the Casilina Highway, the families grouped together again, and entering the main street of Ceprano, everybody went their own way, as we had to slow down and watch ourselves because of the heavy traffic of carts, wagons and the sporadic truck and automobile, that forced us off the center of the road.

The reason why we didn't walk on the sidewalks is because there weren't any, beside were they should have been, it was lined with livestock of all kinds on both sides of the road. Horses, cows, calves, donkeys, mules, pigs, goats and sheep that had been brought in the night before and early this morning from the local farms and surrounding towns and villages.

This religious holiday, was also very good for businesses, because thousands of people came from everywhere to buy or to sell their merchandise.

For Mario, Maria and myself, this was all new. We were fascinated in seeing so many animals, their owner hurrying around, some of them busily brushing and slicking them up. Carmine was more familiar with this scene, and did his best to explain things to me.

"Wait and see how those guys become eager beavers when they spot a prospective buyer. You will enjoy seeing them at work" he said.

The opportunity presented itself, when papa' and mamma encountered some old friends of theirs, and moved to one side to stop and chat.

"Come on Armando," my brother called, pushing through the crowd and coming to a sudden halt near a wagon, were several horses were tied to it. "Look at that tall skinny guy, I have seen him at work before. He is terrific. Watch him."

Studying the look of passersby, with the hope of distinguishing a prospective customer, he smoked nervously and spit at every puff. A stocky farmer was admiring a beautiful black mare, and it didn't take long for the skinny guy to notice him.

Approaching the farmer with a disinterested attitude, we heard him say:

"You sure know what you want, don't you? Look at it. Isn't that a beauty?" Carmine nudged me with his elbow whispering there he goes, watch him now.

Moving with the agility of a panther, he went from one animal to the other, opening a horse's mouth to show his teeth, lifting the foot of another one, displaying his merchandise with consummate skill, giving very little chance to the farmer to get a word in, until he brought him back to the black mare.

"This is the pick of the crop my friend, and this is what you want. I know it. Look at her broad chest, look at those limbs. This horse is all heart, and you can be sure she is not spavined. Here," handing the rope to the farmer, "take her out for a trial, I am sure she won't disappoint you."

The latter, lead the black beauty by the halter, circled around a few times, then with a small grin on his face, gave the rope back to the merchant.

"Well? What do you think of it?" Asked skinny nonchalantly.

"Looks all right," replied the stocky fanner quietly, standing with his calloused hands on his hips, then fidgeting and unable to wait any longer he asked:

"How much do you want for it?"

At this point the haggling began. Heads shook, arms and hands gestured in the air, they were shouting as if they were ready to jump at each other's throat any minute. "You can say whatever you want, but a horse like this one, for two hundred lire is a present to you." Said skinny, turning his back to the farmer.

"Ha ha," replied the farmer not quite convinced. "Why should you make me a present? Do you like my face so much? If I was a lovely young lady, it would be understandable, but unfortunately I am a man, married and with five kids" the farmer went on, mocking the merchant and looking and winking at the few spectators that had gathered to watch the proceedings, causing a ripple of amusement among them.

Skinny's face turned red as a hot pepper, but not discouraged, took the sarcasm good naturedly and kept patting the horse's neck. When the laughing was over, he broke the silence:

"One hundred and ninety five lire is my last word my friend. Not a cent less. Take it or leave it, it makes no difference to me."

There went the sale into a cloud of smoke, I thought, as the farmer walked away, then turning to my brother Carmine: "Let's go. It is all over."

"Ha ha." My brother burst out laughing. "All is not lost yet. Give to Caesar what is Caesar's is an old saying. The merchant is an old pro, he will persist on his line and I am sure he will get what he wants. You don't think for a single minute that he would give up at the first sign of refusal, do you? Just watch and wait."

Knowing that sooner or later he would meet his own terms, the experienced merchant followed the farmer around like a wolf, crying out loudly, "don't go away, you will be sorry. There is nothing to compare to this horse in the market, I know my line, and when you come back for her, she won't be here, I guarantee you that."

The stocky farmer stopped, turned around, walked back to the beautiful mare, looked at her, then pulled out a red handkerchief as big as a towel, wiped his sweaty face and neck, then slowly fished out his fat greasy wallet, and concentrating his attention on it, carefully dug for some lire bills.

"This is all I have" handing it over to the eager merchant. " Count it. It is one hundred and ninety lire."

At the sight of the money, the merchant's greedy little piggish eyes gleamed, as he could not conceal his avarice, immediately reminding me of Signor Spizzichino, the Jewish store owner. Hurriedly the merchant's trained eyes counted the money quickly, then shaking his head, as if he was reluctant to accept the smaller amount, put them in his coat pocket, and looked at his customer saying:

"Very well my friend, it is a deal." And after shaking hands to seal the transaction he had to say a last word. "A deal is a deal, and you got the best of the bargain. I have the mate for this horse that will make a fine team, if you are interested, come back to see me, I will give you a good deal." Then freeing his hand from the tight grip, with an air of resignation, walked to the wagon and untied the horse.

The stocky farmer, stood there for a moment, rubbing his perspiring palms on his Sunday trousers, then reaching out one hand, with pride showing on his hard sun beaten face, began patting the horse's sleek nose and with the other took the halter rope held by the merchant. With the usual clucking sound, gently urged the superb beast off the circle and away they both went through a double line of admirers.

Once again my brother's prophecy was right.

"What did I tell you Armando?" Laughing and with a gleam in his eyes he continued: "Long Pole" as he called the merchant "Is the best of all the brokers that come to this market. I believe he is from Udine, a long way from here, and his colleague are a little jealous of him. As you just witnessed, he doesn't need the help of a shill, for he always handles the best merchandise. Come on, by now they must be looking for us, and you know papa'. When we wait for him it is all right, but if he has to wait for us that is a horse of a different color."

Worming our way to the place where we left them, we found they had already gone, so we kept going and soon we saw them standing near the church of Sant'Arduino.

"For God's sake, where have you been?" Papa' demanded impatiently. "Come on, hurry up, the mass has already started," herding us to the door and taking off his light straw hat.

Just inside to the right, he dipped my fingers into the marble font of holy water, touched my mother's hand and while both knelt down to the floor, at the same time they crossed themselves. We followed closely but only for a few steps, because of the dense crowd we couldn't advance any further, and remained standing there for the remaining part of the ceremony.

At eleven o'clock, the bells started ringing, gaily announcing the end of the mass and the beginning of the procession. Being close to the main door, we were the first ones to get out, and to make sure that we wouldn't miss anything, remained close to them, but it was like fighting a surging tide, and in a very short time we were pushed way, way back by the growing multitude of people coming out of the church. Realizing that it would have been foolish to remain there, papa' decided to change strategy. Holding each other by hand, so we wouldn't become separated, and forming a long line, we headed for a more advantageous spot.

It was a good thing that my parents were born here, otherwise we would have been still looking and circling around, because even if they had been away for a long time and the place had changed, they found their way around quite well. Along the river road, behind the main square and through narrow alleys, we finally made it to one of the main intersection, where four streets met, and this was where we stopped.

There was a lot of people already lined up, but still there was room for newcomers and trying to make ourselves comfortable, we began the long wait.

Every house of this busy corner and all along the cobblestone streets, were richly decorated with hundreds of beautiful and different colored flags, banners, pennants and ribbons. Every window was like a gallery, where a good view of the procession could be had. Kids sat precariously on window ledges, suspended from door knobs, light poles and every conceivable place imaginable.

Suddenly three consecutive loud bangs roared into the air, followed immediately by a simultaneous shout from the exited crowd of "Viva Sant Arduino, Viva Sant Arduino."

The music and the religious chant, reached us before we could see anything, and now people were coming from everywhere, packing in front of us, behind us, around us, and with the hot midday sun beating down on us, the jostling, the pushing and elbow jabbing, the tramping on our feet, became a little too much to take.

People were fanning themselves with anything available, and wiping at their red faces that were dripping wet. The men's white shirts and women light summer dresses were limp and clinging to their backs.

Papa' was almost ready to give up and move out, when, in all his glory and magnificence, Sant'Arduino, appeared in the form of a large statue. Standing on platform carried by eight men, four each side, with their shoulders supporting the long handles. They were all dressed like him, with a white loose cassock tied at the waist with a rope, a purple cape falling loose from their broad shoulders, and a heavy brown felt hat, hanging down their backs.

Just behind them, the relief bearers, four of them, each one carrying a staff of wood, and looking somewhat like a fork. This was to rest the platform on, when the eight men got tired and switched their positions around.

As he passed, we all genuflexed and shouting at the top of our lungs, we called his name. Beseechingly, a couple of women shouted their humble prayers and begged favors from him, raising their voices high above the general clamor.

The moment was so touching, that tears were streaming down the faces of men and women alike unashamedly, while his path, was strewn with flower petals and confetti, thrown from those on the windows above.

At a little distance came the Bishop in his white and red robe, holding with both hands the sacred chalice, preceded and followed by six altar boys, them too, all in white robes, each one carrying a lighted candle. Then came a priest with the holy water, blessing the crowd on both sides, while his two young helpers, waved the silver incense burners and filled the air with its sweetness. The crowd was hushed, and as they went by they made the sign of the cross.

Then appeared the sisters of the convent, all in black with white starch collars and bibs, leading the beautiful girls in their immaculate white long dresses, with their silvery voices singing the hymns: "Ave Ave Ave Maria. Ave Ave Ave Maria."

As they went by, everybody joined in their chant, and looking at them, I could not conceal my emotion, because this scene reminded me of my childhood and the beautiful and unforgettable years spent in the convent with the Sisters of the Sacred Heart of Jesus in Grottaferrata, a little town up in the Colli Albani, and the many hours spent together with the rest of the students, to get ready for the big procession on the eight of September in honor of Our Lady.

After the last sister had passed, the monks moved up next. Fingering their huge wooden rosary, padding along silently on their leather sandals, they led the large group of orphans wearing the same brown cassock. For a while they stopped right in front of us, as the bearers of the statue paused to change position and rest.

My heart swelled up with pity to see the young orphan boys wearing such a heavy woolen garment on such a blistering hot day, but they did not seem to show any sign of great discomfort.

When the procession started rolling again, the daughters of Maria, all dressed in the traditional pale blue, a long banner held by the first row, with the insignia of the order written in blue and gold just below the sacred image of Our Virgin Mary. This was the largest group, and extended way back, so by the time the tail end of them left us behind, the procession came again to a halt.

Something went wrong with the leaders, it seemed that they had to decide whether to enter the city hall square now or later, where, waiting were the mayor and all the big shots, including the captain of the Carabinieri, the doctor, the notary the lawyer, the rich merchant and the band of musicians that had arrived from Naples that very morning. After arguing back and forth, finally they came to an understanding and chose to pass by the hospital first. While this went on, the bearers were holding the statue, and by the time a decision was reached, they were pooped, so when the order was given to proceed, instead of moving forward, they called for the relief bearers with the four forks, adding more confusion and discontent.

Finally after a good rest, they got going again, but not for long. The street that they were turning into was quite narrow and as usual packed with spectators, so at the corner, the platform holding the statue being too long didn't go through, the confusion got greater and greater. Nobody knew exactly what to do, until the four Carabinieri following the procession, took the matter into their own hands creating more discontent among the people who were being pushed away from the area. Only then, with the street cleared, was it possible to make the turn.

Maneuvering the long platform slowly back and forth, they succeeded in going around the corner, and at that moment, I bet even Sant'Arduino must have been laughing.

After that little incident, they sped it up, and when the local band strolled along, everything was forgotten. Trying their best to keep time with the music, and paying too much attention to their instruments, the musicians forgot to march in unison, they were badly out of step, but no one seemed to mind it.

As a matter of fact, the spectators hoorayed and clapped their hands, proud of their own town band. The last of them had gone by, when mamma called out eagerly a note of pride in her voice: "There is papa' Agostino coming. Do you see him?" Lifting myself on the tips of my toes and craning my neck I saw him. Poor nonno, dressed in a warm looking black cassock and a green cape, looked exhausted. I could see him clearly, bent to one side and dragging a great big crucifix, moving very slowly between two men of his own age, wearing the same outfit and leading all the brothers of San Rocco, which were not a large group, then just behind them came the brothers of Sant'Arduino and the brothers of the Holy Trinity. They too, were dressed in the ceremonial cassock and cape but of a different color.

As they approached, the crucifix seemed to get heavier and heavier on nonno's shoulder, pressing him down. He was not walking any more, just dragging his feet, a few more steps and he would have been right in front of us.

"Nonno! Nonno!" Maria and Mario called loudly trying to attract his attention, but without success. He seemed to be having problems of his own, and he had a peculiar look on his face, as he dazedly kept staring ahead.

At last the procession stopped, and so did he. He raised his white head, looked around once more and with a final effort, walked toward us followed by his mates holding the ropes hanging from each side of the crucifix. Leaning the cross on the wall and making sure that it would not fall, very slowly, wiped his dripping forehead, on the sleeves of his cotton cassock, exhaled noisily as with a deep sigh of exhaustion then under the eyes of everyone present, untied the cape and the rope around his waist, unbuttoned his cassock, took it off, rolled the whole thing together, making a neat package, tied with the rope and tucked it under his arm, then very ceremoniously turned toward his mates and in a determined voice said: "Well. I don't know about you fellows, but I had enough of this for today." Then pointing his finger to the wall: "There is the Crucifix, whoever wants it, is welcomed to it. I am going for a glass of wine, before my parched throat cracks."

And leaving everybody standing there astonished and with shocked disapproval clearly mirrored on their sanctimonious faces, he headed for the pub on the corner and disappeared through the door and out of sight.

That was the end of the procession for us. Mamma embarrassed and ashamed of what her father had done, crying and sobbing, her breath coming out in deep gulps rushed us away from the scene as though it were our fault. On the other hand, papa' found the situation highly amusing and was laughing his head off, tears streaming down his fat cheeks, as he tried to regain his composure and console mamma.

"After all it is a very hot day, and you should not blame your father for what he has just done." He murmured placently. "If you want to know how I feel about it, at his age he has done his best, and in his place, I would have done exactly the same thing."

This brought a fresh outburst of tears, so he added righteously, "I understand that it was not nice to abandon the crucifix right in the middle of the road, and I don't say either that we should be proud of him, but you have to admit that he had lots of guts. Anyway, it is not for us to judge." Then taking mamma's arm under his, with a very soft voice he murmured: "Come on, forget what has happened and let's go home, we have a long way to go, and when we get there, try to be calm, otherwise you will upset mamma Teresa."

As though papa' knew exactly what was going to happen, receiving the bad news, nonna broke into a furious rage: "Just a bum like him could have done what he did. Oh Sant'Arduino! Please have mercy on us. Where is he now? In the tavern I suppose, bragging about how brave he was today with his dear old pals."

As she talked, she paced the kitchen floor, holding her long rolling pin in her hands. She sure made a terrifying picture and we dared not interrupt her. We knew she had to get it out of her system, and the sooner the better. When finally her rage was over, she called on everybody "Come on all of you, sit down, and let's have something to eat now. There is no use waiting for the old drunkard, he will come home when he is good and ready. This morning after the mass I had a feeling that I should have never left him alone. When the cat is away the mice will play." And walking toward the small table near the fireplace, she picked up the large white salad bowl full of nice, wide homemade noodles, and placed it in front of us, then with the ability of an experienced chef, filled up the plates one by one, as mamma held them out and distributed them around.

This, a dish well known all over Italy with the name of " Fettuccine all'uovo" is a meal all by itself. The "Fettuccine" mixed in the succulent rich meat sauce covered with lots of Romano cheese, were delicious and we all went for the second helping, but the rabbit and sliced potatoes, sprinkled with wine and rosemary, baked in the oven, with a rich green salad and lots of wine to top it off, was something out of this world........ My o my what a meal and an abundance of everything

Even the dog, laying at my feet under the table was having his share. When no one was looking at us, Mario and I managed to toss him some choice bits. This went on for a while, until nonna Teresa noticed our furtive movements and quickly put an end to it, by administering a solid kick to poor Barone, who yelped in surprise, and was unceremoniously thrown out.

Lucky nonno was not home yet. I bet he would have been on the receiving end of that one. But he would surely get his when he did come home.

With the heavy dinner over, a sense of peace and well being overtook everyone, and leaving the women to the dishes, we all went to our beds for the afternoon siesta.

How long we slept was hard to say, after all, here on the farm, time was of no importance. When we got up, it was just a bit cooler, the sun was setting in a fiery glow on the western horizon, and once more we prepared to return to town and the festivities planned for the evening.

Chapter 8

The main square was the center of attraction. A good section of it was taken by the band stand and several rows of benches. Hundreds of people were sitting on each other's laps, listening enchanted, to the beautiful tune of an aria of the opera "Madam Butterfly" played so well by the professional musicians.

Another big slice of space was occupied by tables and chairs, borrowed from different places and brought here to accommodate a small percentage of the large crowd that came here from miles and miles around to enjoy themselves.

The fat bar owner and his just as fat five daughters, were sweating it out. Outdoing themselves in keeping up with the demanding customers, carrying from the store behind them, pails of ice cream, trays and trays loaded with orangeade, lemonade and beer. They sold everything that evening, as long as it was wet and cold. Meanwhile, his wife called "La Balena" (the whale) hardly moving away from the counter, helped by two trusted younger employees, tried to satisfy the mob of children, who were anxious to spend their few pennies, hungry for candies. Candy coated almonds, caramels, chocolate bars, ice cream cones, soft drinks, and any other sweet thing available.

Wherever we looked, there were little stands selling carnival hats, trumpets, balloons, noise makers, celluloid wind mills, firecrackers, sliced watermelon on ice and hard donuts with caraway seeds, called "Ciambelle."

Besides all that, and what was left of the square, was jammed tight with people, and to get around was almost impossible.

This was the ideal working ground of the wise guys and smart alecks that moved from place to place, picking mostly on groups of young women, now and then, setting off harmless firecrackers, scaring the wits out of the poor girls, who yelled and screamed in pretended fright. Actually they loved it.

It was a good opportunity as any to be noticed and spotted by male admirers among the crowd, and from there on, the chase began. In groups of twos or threes, the girls walked away from the square laughing and giggling, sending sly glances backwards to make sure the boys were still following them.

Luckily we happened to be close to the wide street with no outlet that ran from the square onto the river bank and we stopped as the greasy pole climbing race was getting ready to start. Planted on the ground, was a very tall telephone pole about fifty feet high, maybe more, covered from top to bottom with grease, the blackest and smelliest kind of grease that could be found. "This is going to be funny" announced papa'. "Let's get closer, so we will have a real good view of what is going on."

If the reader does not know this game, I will explain it. The object is to climb the pole, and whoever succeeds in reaching the crossbar nailed to the top, collects everything, the reward in money and all the prizes attached to it.

Seven young men were waiting impatiently for the signal to start, to test their skill and their luck. At the word "GO" a tall fellow barefooted, wearing trousers tied at his ankles, thick shirt with long sleeves, a red toque on his head and a sack hanging below his hips, full of sand, looking much like a scarecrow, walked to the base of the pole, and with a jump began the climb.

Right away it looked like the guy knew his business, and immediately, ringing through the air, from somewhere, a voice began shouting encouraging words. Reaching frequently into his sand bag, and rubbing it on the greasy pole, he was able to make it up to the twelve foot mark, but to our disappointment, he stopped there. He couldn't advance any higher, his sand supply ran out on him and slowly he slid back to the ground.

The second contestant, immediately started climbing, giving the impression that he would go higher, much higher, but as he reached the twenty seven foot mark, lost his grip and came down a lot faster than the way he went up. Poor guy, he was doing so well. By the way he walked, we gathered that he must have hurt himself, and that automatically threw him out of the race for good.

Moans and jeers came from the dissatisfied crowd, as the third and fourth contestant made a very poor show of themselves, failing to reach even the twenty foot mark. Mocking remarks and dirty jokes came from all sides as the fifth contestant took his turn. He was a short boy of slight build, with bowed legs and extra long arms. And began climbing with the apparent ease of a monkey, causing a lot of excitement among the spectators, as someone began shouting: "Forza pecoraro, come on shepherd"

"Come on, come on, get going. For a guy that rides water buffalo all day long, to you, this should feel like riding a saddled horse." Some friend shouted teasing. At the eighteen foot mark, he showed no sign of tiredness, and slowly but steadily reached the thirty two foot mark. Appreciating his tremendous effort, the encouraging words and sympathetic yells from the crowd, became louder and louder: "He is good, he is very good. Forza pecoraro, you are doing fine. Come on, don't let us down now. Keep going, keep going, don't stop now." Thirty five, thirty six. Wow. He was terrific. Working his way inch by inch, as the grease seemed to get thicker and thicker, his climbing slowed down, but he still kept moving. Thirty seven, thirty eight, thirty nine, forty, forty one. The mob was getting hysterical, as they called aloud the foot marks. Suddenly the inevitable happened. Reaching for the bag to get some sand, he lost his grip and slowly slid back down a couple of feet. "Ohhhhhhhh. Ohhhhhhhh." Cried the mob in unison. He is not going to make it. There is too much grease on the pole. He has no more sand left in his bag. He can't make it and might as well give up, before he hurts himself.

Everybody was giving his two cents worth of advice, and I thought that instead of helping him they were hurting him. They kept on until a very distinct gentleman lifting his cane up in the air, shouted: "Shut up you hecklers. You don't know yourselves if you are dead or alive. Leave the boy alone. He has got the stuff, and by Sant'Arduino, he is going up right to the top. I guarantee you that." Then turning to his idol up there, with an impassioned voice and making himself heard by everyone, he yelled: "Come on. Forza Aldo. Don't let me down now. Show these town boys what a shepherd is able to do. Come on now, get going. Double salary and rest for a full week if you succeed."

With a renewed courage, valiantly the little shepherd clawed his way up again. Forty one, forty two, forty three, and there he stopped. Looking down and turning his bag inside out, from his lofty perch, he shouted: "I have no more sand!" Then hating to give up so easy, he called to the rest of the competitors: "Whoever brings me some sand, I will split the prizes with him. But when nobody answered his call: "Come on," he went on. "What is the matter with you guys down there. Can't you hear me? I will split half and half. Come on help me."

The crowd was getting belligerent and nasty words were hurled back and forth, finally the distinguished gentleman lost his patience, and after forcing his way to the bottom of the pole, raising his cane in an act of rage, he broke it against it. "Come on you bunch of cowards!" He shouted turning angrily toward the other competitors. "Give him a hand, don't be so mean. After all he is offering you half of the prizes, and I believe half is better than nothing."

The last two contestants were the two brothers, and they were the ones that were doing all the talking and arguing. "Why should we help him out? If he can't make it to the top, he better come down. After all we have not tried our luck yet." And turning to the unsuccessful rivals, they added: "If any of you intend to help him, you are free to do so. We want no part of it." Walking away and laughing among themselves.

The two brothers were playing it safe now. If someone decided to go up, which was quite a way, and failed to reach the shepherd, they both had to come down, the pole was almost clean to the top, and between the two of them, being fresh and experienced, they would have an easy job and the prizes all to themselves.

You could not blame them, it was actually good thinking on their part, but as it is usually said: "Don't count your chickens before they are hatched."

As I was wishing, the tall guy with the red toque, still dirt but fresh and eager to get a second try, did not waste any time. He picked up a double bag of sand and up he went, getting a big ovation from the spectators as their sign of approval.

This time the pole was not as greasy and slippery as it was at the beginning, and the toque guy with giant strides, in no time was up there, handing one of the bags of sand to the shepherd, that up till then, was resting his long arms and legs around the pole, and had given the impression to be as comfortable as a king sitting on a throne.......... From then on, the task seemed very easy. Using his companion's shoulder as a rung on a ladder, the shepherd reached the crossbar with his hand, then when the prizes were touching his head and nose he stopped.

The tension among the crowd had reached a fever pitch, but suddenly the shouts of incitement died out, because for the first time the shepherd was showing signs of tiredness and exhaustion, and once again, words were whispered from mouth to mouth: "What is wrong now? Why doesn't he move anymore? Gosh he is so close now, will he be able to make it?"

But it was just a moment to regain his strength for the last and decisive fight, and while everybody was holding their breath, with a final effort, he threw a leg over the crossbar and sat on it.

A roar of cheers and " Hurrah. Hurrah. He made it," exploded from the happy crowd as he waved at them. Almost immediately, he was joined by his partner, and that made the pole sway from side to side. They shook hands, they split the hundred lire and laughing heartily, they tackled the big fiasco of vino, passing it back and forth to each other, until there was not a drop left in it, then having no further use for it, they threw it down. The fiasco broke on the pavement with a loud plop, muffled on the straw cover, and just missed one of the two brothers, protesting vigorously but in vain, the unfair victory of the little shepherd.

How did they do it, I will never know, I kept repeating myself. Only looking at them made me dizzy, and yet they seemed to be completely at ease.

As they came down, they resembled two chimney cleaners rather than prize winners. All black and dirty, with salami, hams, mortadelle, bottles of liquor, cans of olive oil, a box of spaghetti, and cartons of cigarettes and cigars, all tied to their waist, hanging from their shoulders and neck.

Looking at all those goodies, no one would have ever thought that there was a war going on and everything was rationed.

I have always been afraid of heights, and walking away, I consented to papa': "They must have a lot of courage, but as far as I am concerned, it is not worth all the trouble and risk they took. I would starve rather than repeat that dangerous operation."

"Hahaha." Papa' couldn't help laughing. "In sport you never think of the danger, besides if you stop and think just for a moment, even in everyday life there is a danger of one kind or another, and you can't stop and analyze the consequences, otherwise you would never do anything. Courage and persistence will always succeed in the end. Remember now, you still have a lot to learn yet, on some occasions you will find yourself in a bad spot, things will look impossible, but that is the time when you will need all the confidence and courage you hardly realize you possess. Don't you ever be afraid to take a chance. Take the story of the little shepherd as a good example, and don't forget it, ever."

Gradually the daylight disappeared and the moon took over. The musicians stopped playing and walked away from the bandstand to take a rest and have a bite to eat. They were immediately replaced by four men carrying an empty drum placed on two wooden horses, and as they were all set and ready to start, one of them, holding a megaphone to his mouth began calling: "Ladies and gentleman. Your attention please."

But his words vanished in the air. It was as if he had spoken to a solid wall. The noise, the sound of trumpets, the shouting, the singing and laughing, kept on going as nobody was paying any attention to him.

"Ladies and gentleman" Please be seated, get your cards ready. He called time after time, with growing signs of impatience showing in his loud voice, but trying to rush things, didn't get him anywhere, not with this disorganized crowd anyway. Finally, when in their own good time, they were ready and order was established, the "Tombola" (Bingo) got under way.

Papa' bought a stack of cards and lined up on one corner of the bandstand, and at the beginning Carmine and I helped Mario and Maria to mark the numbers called on their cards with anything that you could think of, white and red beans, lima beans, chick peas and little stones, but after a while it got to monotonous for us.

Knowing how much there was to do and see on an evening of fiesta, we left them to their tense occupation and moved towards other games, and into the exciting unknown darkness beyond the fringe of the square.

Struggling our way through the closely packed tables and chairs, in an effort to get out, suddenly I thought I heard my grandfather's voice. It was impossible, it couldn't be him. I stopped, and looking toward where the sound came, I listened carefully, and distinctly there it was again. I couldn't make out what he was saying right away, because somebody tapped on my shoulder and asked me to get down or get out of his way. I was quite positive that it was him alright, with some friends of his. In fact one of them could be heard saying: "Agostino, give me some more beans."

"Here" A wine soaked voice replied. "Take them all and make sure to mark mine right.

It was nonno alright, there was no doubt about it. Waiting at the end of the tables, impatiently Carmine asked: "What's keeping you, Come on"

"Just a moment," I said walking toward him. "Look over there." Pointing with my finger. "Nonno is playing Tombola."

"What? Are you dreaming? How can he play Tombola if he does not even know how to read or write his own name?"

"I know. That is what I thought myself, but he has somebody with him marking the cards. There he goes again. Listen"

"Hey you up there with the big funnel," nonno yelled. "Take it easy, you are calling the numbers too fast, and we can't keep track of them."

"Pipe down" Called an irate player at a neighboring table.

"Leave him alone," A woman's voice whispered loudly. "Can't you see that he is drunk?" "Why doesn't he go home then," the irate player answered. "He is making a nuisance of himself and at the same time spoiling the game for everybody else."

At this point, Carmine climbed on a chair occupied by a boy and gave a quick look trying to locate him, but it was too dark and too far, besides, there wasn't very much we could do about it even if we did, and before someone jumped on us, we looked around for the shortest way to take and without much trouble we found ourselves behind the stage and nose to nose with a donkey.

"He must be the prize for the Tombola winner" Carmine said. "See how cute he is?"

"The hell with him and the prize." I shouted, holding my nose to block off the stink coming from a steaming hot pie that I had just stepped in.

"Damn it! What a short cut." Looking around to find some grass but there wasn't any. "How do you expect to find grass right in the middle of the town square?"

"Come on," I shouted in bad humor and heading for the fountain. "I have to clean my shoes."

The Bocce Tournament held in the open, had just ended when we got there, and having nothing else to do we went down by the church of Sant'Arduino, where its door wide open, showed the inside all illuminated and the people knelt in prayer.

For a second, I was tempted to enter it, but just then, a look of recognition came over my brother's face, as he spotted an old acquaintance of his.

"Hey there goes the daughter of the druggist," he exclaimed with joy. "Come on hurry up, I want to talk to her. She is quite a girl you know? I met her last year when papa' and I came here to buy the olive oil. Remember?"

"Yes," I replied playing dumb. "I remember the oil part, but I can't remember her."

"Oh come on, don't get smart all at once. If we don't move fast, we might lose her from our sight. I bet she must be going home."

Entering the bridge over the river that unites Ceprano with the Casilina Highway, we were able to catch up with her. As a matter of fact, to be exact, he did, not me. I was still ten feet behind, and as they were walking side by side, I heard the voice of my beloved brother, like if he just fell from the sky ; saying: " Hello Tina........ Mind if I join you on your solitary walk?"

"Bull" Listen how romantic he is, I said to myself.

Hesitantly turning her lovely black head toward him, she looked and recognizing him, she stopped and: "Carmine. How nice to see you. Oh my what a surprise. It has been so long. Where have you been all this time?"

At this crucial moment, I was lost, I didn't know what to do, but not him. Signaling frantically with his hand behind his back, as if he wanted to say: "Go away. Go away" but I couldn't. She must have heard my footsteps coming, because she glanced over her shoulder and I decided that it was too late to turn back. Indifferently I walked past them as though they were complete strangers, and again, without intending to eavesdrop. I couldn't help over hearing her: "Caro Carmine. You remember the good time we had last fall? How come you never wrote? You promised you would. Remember?"

By then I was too far to catch his answer, and really it didn't matter, because the only thought of what he might have said, made me laugh. Poor Tina. She didn't know, how little a promise to a woman meant to him. If she ever knew. Maybe the several girl friends he had in Rome. Could tell her what kept him so busy.

Once I reached the other side, I looked back, and from as much as I could see, they were stopped against a column of the bridge, kissing and necking.

That was a very good spot for it, dark and nobody around, but what about me? The way back was closed for the time being, I was stuck, knowing as I did my dear brother, I knew that it would last for a while, so I made myself comfortable, and when finally they decided to quit, I was fed up from waiting. After her departure, I rejoined him, and before he had a chance to excuse himself I gave vent to my feelings, but it was like I was talking to a stone wall.

As we got back to the main square, the band was playing again, which meant that the Tombola was over, so we wondered around to find our family, and there they were, behind a huge pile of watermelons. Papa' held one up, while the owner, with a pointed knife, cut a triangular hole in it, and pulled out the red piece, handing it to him to sample it, and after papa' had tasted he asked: "You liked it?"

"Bah... Not too bad." Papa' managed to answer with his mouth full.

The whole family was all eyes for the watermelon and my brother Mario realized our presence, all excited shouted:

"Armando. Carmine. Do you know that nonno Agostino won the donkey."

"No, really?"

"Sure, sure he won it at the Tombola."

"Good for him, where is he now?" We both asked.

"Where else? He is in the pub celebrating. As if he needed an excuse," mamma remarked quite bitterly.

"Come, come with me, I know where he is," went on Mario pulling my arm.

"You stay right where you are," Papa' commanded. "He knows where to go when he comes out. Come on now. Let's eat this watermelon."

We borrowed a knife from the owner, and using one of the tables set there for the sole purpose of accommodating those who liked to eat them on the spot, we stood around and helped ourselves to the red succulent fruit. I was just about to tackle my fourth thick slice, when I saw nonno Agostino walking backwards and pulling the docile little donkey by a rope tied on his neck. As he approached, he sure made a comical sight, and we couldn't help but burst out laughing.

"Here, have some watermelon daddy," said mamma offering him a piece.

Seeing him with his hands full, Mario asked eagerly:

"Do you want me to hold the donkey nonno?"

"Sure. Here. But don't go away." Said nonno passing him the rope.

"Hey you! Get that beast away from here," shouted the owner of the watermelons, but just then, the fireworks started with a tremendous bang, which startled the poor donkey, who let kicked with his hind feet, and catching the edge of the table sent it crashing into the neatly piled watermelons, that came toppling down and rolling in all directions, smashing and breaking when they found obstacles.

One of them, rolling at full speed, landed right into my grandfather's already unsteady legs, throwing him heavily on the, hard cobblestones.

I had never seen my father move so fast, at the same time the terrified donkey started to take off, he dashed for the rope that Mario had dropped, and propping his feet on the ground, doing his best to hold tight the fidgeting animal at bay.

All this happened much quicker than, it took to write about.

"Jesus, Mary and Joseph," exclaimed the proprietor gesticulating wildly with his arms. "Look at all my watermelons! I am ruined. Poor, poor me. What am I going to do now? What am I going to do now? Who is going to pay for all this?" He shouted, but the shouts were lost in the bedlam created by the fireworks.

"Damn it. Damn it." Pointing his finger at my grandfather, who was having a hard time standing on his feet, holding his back with both of his hands. "I told you to get that damn beast out of here. Now who is going to pay for all the damage that has been done?"

"Ah. Calm down you crazy fool," replied nonno, "Is it my fault if the donkey got scared and went wild?"

"I don't care whose fault it is. That is not my problem. I do know, however, that half of my watermelons are lost, and I want my money, understand?" Raising his hand as if he intended to strike nonno, but promptly putting himself between the two, and handing my brother the rope, papa' said: "Here Carmine, hold this poor animal steady," then turning to the merchant; "Hey compare! Keep your hands in your pockets. This is not the best way to settle the problem, if you intend to come to an understanding, lower your tone and calm down."

But the irate merchant didn't seem to understand that the accident was purely unintentional, he was out for blood, and it was a good thing that at this point, two Carabinieri arrived on the scene and immediately took over.

"Come on. All of you move," they commanded to the people standing around, then turning to the complainant: "What is going on here, what seems to be the trouble," after they had heard both sides, and things had quieted down considerably, both parties agreed that it was an accident, and to make the unhappy merchant feel better, papa' slipped twenty lire in his hands for the damages suffered and the incident was closed.

Naturally that was the end of the festivities for us, and on reaching the outskirts of the town, being tired, nonno decided to ride the donkey, but what a big mistake that was. The stubborn beast was still frightened, and the very moment my grandfather sat on him, the inevitable happened. "Hoo. Hoo. Ferma. Ferma." Nonno yelled. Stop damn you," as the donkey let go with his hind legs. Holding desperately to the short rope tied to the donkey's neck, and bouncing up and down like a rubber ball, he kept shouting helplessly: "Ferma. Ferma per la Madonna." Then, "stop him" he begged, "before he kills me." But the more he shouted, the more the poor animal got excited, and savagely kept kicking and jumping harder and harder.

It all happened so quickly, and it all seemed so funny, that even the angels in paradise must have been laughing, and at that particular moment, no one thought of the great danger to the old man, until papa' ran to help him, which unfortunately was too late for anything, but to give him a hand to get up from the hard cobble stones, and inquire if he was hurt.

"No. No. I don't think so," answered nonno, while gingerly he explored the lower part of his back with his hands and a grimace of pain showed on his face, then walking slowly toward Carmine and the quadruped, who by this time had calmed down, once again he picked up the rope, and muttering between his teeth he patted the beast gently on the head saying: "Don't worry, I will get even with you old pal." Then giving a yank to the rope: "Come on you old bastard. Let's go."

The way back to the farm, was a real long one because between nonno and the donkey, it was hard to say which one was the most troublesome.

For a while, with any means, including candies and green leaves, he tried to make the donkey move, but at last the stubbornness of the indignant little beast prevailed, and dear grandpa, overwhelmed with fatigue and the wine, had to give up. After that, if he could have had his own way, I bet he would have laid on the soft grass, and slept it off right there.

As for the donkey, well.... pulling, yelling and dragging, we all had to take our turn to the rope, and at last when we arrived at the top of the hill, believe me, it was all we could take from him. We were exhausted.

As we turned toward the house, barking and waving his plume like tall, we were greeted by Barone, who in giving us the warm reception, almost got us in trouble again with the donkey. Who seemed to dislike his barking manners.

Nonna got up from the front steps, where she must have been sitting all evening, and with a threatening manner started toward her errant husband, who holding up both bands, as if to ward off a blow, and taking a couple of steps backwards, hiccupping loudly and covering his mouth hurriedly in an attempt to smother it, he said: "Now. Now Teresa, wait a minute. Don't get excited, I am not drunk, and before you blow your cork, look what I have for you," pulling the rope away from Carmine's hand and proudly displaying his new possession. "Look Teresa, look. He has a one track mind, but he sure is a cute little thing, isn't he Teresa?"

"Oh no. What have you done now?" She exclaimed frightened, raising her arms up in the air. "Sant'Arduino mio, give me strength and faith, before I kill him with my bare hands. Where are we going to get the money to pay for it?"

"I won it Teresa. I won it." He replied proudly. "If you don't believe me, ask them, they will tell you," opening up his arms widely and hitting me right on the face with the back of his hand, as he made an effort to get us into the conversation.

"You won it?" She said incredulously. "How? Where?" talking to him and looking at us, waiting for an answer to confirm the words.

"That's true," mamma said quietly, nodding her head. "He won it at the Tombola."

"Really?" Nonna said, still a little doubtful, then, throwing herself into his arms, crying and laughing at the same time, lifted up a corner of her apron and after she had wiped the tears coming down her cheeks she said: "Oh Agostino mio, it took us forty years to get it, and I don't care how we got it, but finally we have our own donkey, and I don't have to beg anybody anymore. Thank you."

Immediately knowing that the worst was over, nonno thought of taking advantage of the situation and started bragging: "You see dear? I am not as bad as you thought I was from now on," pointing at the donkey, "he will carry all the water you want, and save your little head from a lot of hard work. And you know what?" He went on excitedly: "I am going to repair the old two wheeled chart, so when we go to town he will take us. What do you think of that eh Teresa?"

"Yes dear, yes" answered my grandmother in a sarcastically flat voice. "At last you have the companion you need, so when you get drunk, he will find the way home for you!" And sharply becoming herself once more, "come on, take the donkey to the barn and stop yakking. I don't intend to stay up all night and listen to your nonsense."

Hurrying into the kitchen and coming out with the kerosene lamp: "Come on," she shouted once more, and holding the lamp up to light the way, lead the trio that disappeared around the house and into the barn.

For the next few days, we talked and laughed about the good and the bad things that happened at the fiesta of Sant'Arduino.

At first Barone did not accept the idea of having an intruder and a competitor around us, but when he noticed that our attentions were equally divided between him and the donkey, baptized by nonno with the name of "Testardo" "Stubborn", he became reconciled to the new addition, and with the two together, we had a wonderful time.

Unfortunately, this couldn't last forever, for me the vacations were over, and next Sunday morning. Heartbroken, leaving Maria and Mario to our grandparents care, we took the early train back to Rome and the old city life.

Chapter 9

I found it very strange that while I was away, and only a short distance from the Eternal City, capital of Italy, something of great importance, had happened to change the whole political structure of our government, yet at the farm, no one had even mention it or cared to talk about it.

After reigning for over twenty years, the night of the 25th of July, only six days after the American bombardment of Rome, the Fascist Government was dethroned from power. Benito Mussolini and many of his followers had been imprisoned, and all signs of remembrance of the past dictatorship, had been destroyed or torn down by the tired and angry population, who were happy to be free from the old regime.

Hate and bad feelings were running very high among the once oppressed people, and with some of the fascist tyrants still at large, a ruthless hunt for them was going on daily, yet so far, no big incident of reprisal had occurred. The curfew imposed by the new government, in order to avoid any possible trouble, had been removed almost immediately.

But heavy armed groups of police and soldiers, were still patrolling the streets.

There were rumors spreading around the whole country that the new government, had already approached the High Commands of the Anglo-American forces for a truce talk between our nation and theirs. But they were just rumors, nobody could tell how much truth there was to it.

Most of our neighbors never came back after the massacre of that Black Monday. Of the several friends we had before, we couldn't find any, and our street had become as lonely as a solitary mountain road.

Viano was out of the hospital and in fairly good condition again. He had moved with his parents to another part of the city, and to be exact, near St. Peter Square, where, being so close to the Vatican City and the Pope, they thought there wouldn't be any danger of being bombed.

One day I went to visit him, and I couldn't believe my own eyes. His whole body and face, were completely covered with little black holes, full of sand, pebbles, coal and shrapnel's, and where it was possible, some of them, were gradually removed.

On the way home, I felt a sense of the old guilt bothering me again, and somewhat responsible for his misfortune. Had I been sober on that Monday morning, what had happened to him, could have very well happened to me, and that is when for the first time, another thought passed through my mind. "Why it happened to him and not to me? Was it plain coincidence or was it something called destiny, fate?" Anyway, whatever it was, somebody up there was looking after me, and I thanked Him with my whole heart.

The alarm sounded frequently, two or three times a day maybe more, but it was always the usual reconnaissance plane, that it seemed, came to take pictures and went away undisturbed,

The few families still left, mostly women and children, like us when we were around, spent the day running back and forth for the shelter of the Nuns, on Via Casilina, almost a mile distance from where we were. To be accurate, it was not a regular shelter built for air raid protection, but merely a cave, about two hundred feet long and with a sole entrance. It was part of an underground pit of Pozzolana (A sort of special earth found only around Rome, which came in different colors, reddish brown, gray and black, used by builders and mixed with lime instead of sand) used many years ago and long since closed, when there was no more pozzolana. It was located on the property of the Convent of the Nuns, which it explained why it was called "The Nun's Shelter".

Almost daily, the good nuns, came out with huge pots of soup, and fed the hungry and homeless, besides taking care of about hundred war orphans, that in the convent, found a new home and sometimes new parents.

Since papa' had forbidden me to go back to my old job at the railway depot, I had to start looking for some other work. With the help of a letter from my uncle, introducing me to an old officer of his, whom he had served under the Abissinian war, and who was now owner of a big construction company, I was hired as a blacksmith helper. The housing development under construction, was about four or more miles outside of Rome, just off the Appia Highway, called Borgata Spinell or Statuario. At the end of this huge properly, ran the railway tracks and behind them, there was the same Concentration Camp with the main entrance on the Tuscolana highway, where last spring, I had taken a parcel to an English prisoner friend of Signor Spizzichino.

Due to the scarcity of laborers, some of the prisoners were working with us in different departments, and for the first time, with my big surprise and curiosity, I met someone who was the so called "Enemy".

The one assigned to the blacksmith shop, looked after the electric saw machine, and all he did, was cut pieces of steel into different lengths and other little jobs. Strict orders from the main office, were not to fraternize with the prisoners, and naturally being new on the job, and afraid to lose it, I obeyed the rules. For the first few days I was content just to look at him, and to be frank, I liked it that way. I had heard so many bad things about them, and I was a little diffident, I didn't trust them. This one, seemed to be different from the others I had seen around, and in spite of myself, I couldn't take my eyes away from him, even though I didn't dare talk to him. He never spoke, but I had the feeling that he understood every single word we said.

Every day at ten to twelve, he went out to join his friends waiting on the center of the road, there was sixteen of them all together, tall ones, short ones, medium height, fat and skinny ones, but they all looked alike to me. I never missed watching them, as they went down the dirt road toward the barracks to have their lunch, accompanied by an Italian armed guard.

Lately, something was happening inside me, I began to ask myself questions and looked for an answer that didn't come. They were men made of flesh and blood like me and the rest of us, still, we were free to do anything and go anywhere we pleased, but them. They were not. I began to feel sorry for them. Yes I did.

They followed the same routine like clockwork day after day. At one o'clock they were back, and on the third day entering the shop, our man saluted me. Won by his friendly smile, I couldn't help smiling back.

Sandy was a tall well built guy in his middle twenties, with very thick dirty copper red, curly hair, two deep brown eyes widely spread by a large hook nose, with lots of freckles on his fattish round face. Orders or no orders, I still had to work with him, and once the ice was broken, I found it impossible to resist his sympathetic manners, and we began to communicate.

The three years spent in school and the twice a week of English lessons I had taken, now came in very handy. We didn't miss any opportunity to have small conversation together, and when we ran into difficulties, we used sign language or drawings. We soon became good chums, and to show him a sign of my friendship, one morning, I brought a little sample of our white wine from Frascati, and when the two blacksmith went out to take some measurement, I gave him the bottle.

Sandy was really thrilled, immediately he put the bottle away in his haversack, than to repay me for the favor, he offered me a cigarette. "No, thank you, I don't smoke," I told him. "Come on, take it." He insisted. Afraid to hurt his feeling, I accepted and lit it, but poor me, I wished I hadn't. At the first puff, my head got dizzy, my eyes got watery, coughing and choking, I was ready to throw up any minute, and the temptation to throw away the cigarette was big, but the hilarious laugh of Sandy, stopped me from doing it.

"He must think I am a sissy," I told myself. Well, I am going to show him that I am not as delicate as he might think "With a great effort, I pulled myself together then puffing gently, gradually got used to inhaling the smoke, and by the time the cigarette became a butt, I was sailing along like an old veteran.

Honestly, I wished I had never done it, because from then on, I have acquired a new vice "Smoking", at the same time, I also acquired a new friend: "Sandy".

Sandy was a very polite, bright and intelligent young man and gave me the impression to be very well educated.

To the contrary of me that had a very poor knowledge of the language, when he spoke, his English was very clear, nevertheless, there was a certain accent in his speech that became more noticeable especially when he spoke with his friends. What I appreciated the most from him, was the fact that when our conversation became too complicated and I was completely lost, with the utmost patience, he explained it to me in so many other ways that it was almost impossible not to understand. Once again, I am going to mention it, and I could have been dead wrong, but somehow, something deep inside me, was telling me that he understood Italian. I don't know why I am saying it, but usually when Giocondo the master blacksmith, made some dirty remarks about the young female cook, or complained vigorously about our employer being very stingy with his money, or complained about the English people, that were allowed five meals a day, while we Italians, couldn't even get a decent one, more than once, from the corner of my eye, I caught Sandy smiling. Besides, several other considerations had influenced my doubts. For example just to mention one, neither Giocondo nor his helper Alberto, could put together more than ten English words, yet, when they gave him an order, either to do a job, or get something, or go somewhere, he never answered back, argued or question it, but by the same token, he never made the wrong move.

If he spoke our language, why did he not say so? Was he ashamed, or afraid we might tease him? Why was he keeping it a secret? What could he lose?

Personally, I thought that it would have been more advantageous to him than to us.

I confess that at the beginning, it was really bothering me, but after a while, I got used to the idea, and never questioned my mind any more. After all it was his privilege to do as he pleased, to me, what did matter the most, was that he was a real nice guy, easy to work and get along with, the rest didn't count much, after all, he was not only a prisoner of war, but an enemy of my country.

All I knew about him is that he was originally from Warsaw, Poland, where he was born, but was living and studying in London England, when the Germans invaded his homeland. Not too long after, he had joined the British army, where he became a radio operator. Soon after, his regiment was shipped to Egypt and the front line. The first time he went into action, his tank was hit and destroyed by the flames. Luckily he came out of it only with a few superficial wounds and taken prisoner.

Since he was one of the first English soldier to fall in to the hands of the Italians, he was brought to Rome with a group of Australians and south Africans, loaded on open trucks and paraded on the main street of the capital, to show the people who their enemy was.

He was twenty three when he entered the concentration camp, now he was twenty five, he had already spent two long years in captivity, and although he had no complaints about his captors, he was still a prisoner, he was not free.

During that period, he had no news whatsoever of his parents and brothers and sisters. He had tried more than one channel to get some information, but at last, not even the Red Cross could find out anything about them.

Were they dead? Were they alive? Poor Sandy. When he spoke of his family, he sure had a sad grin on his face. For his and his parent's sake, let's hope for the best.

Time went by, and another big holiday was approaching. The fifteenth of august is the feast of Our Lady of Assumption. This religious event, is considered everywhere as important to us as Christmas or Easter.

A year ago, at this time of the month, everyone was making plans as to where to go, to spend the weekend, but not this year. What a change, everything around us was dead. Never before had our daily routine seemed so monotonous, work, eat, and run to the shelter, as the alarm sounded more often than ever.

Oh God. What a life.

The only exciting thought that kept our minds occupied, was that maybe my brother Peppe, might be with us for the following Sunday. At the table, no matter what we were talking about, he was always the center of conversation, one way or another, his name was always on our lips.

Easter of 1941 was the last time he had been home, with tears in her eyes, mamma kept constantly reminding us of this. Poor mamma. She sure missed him, but she was not the only one, only God knew how much I missed my oldest brother.

The last time he came home, wherever he went, I went, as a matter of fact, I made it a point to go with him, walking beside him was quite an honor and a treat for me. More or less light complexioned, we all had blondish curly hair, but while Carmine and myself had papa's blue eyes, the rest of them, had mamma's brown eyes.

Of medium height, Peppe had a beautiful head of hair, straight and wide shoulders like papa' and an elegant deportment, I thought that when he dressed in his blue sailor uniform, he was the most handsome guy walking on Via Marmocchi, and I was very proud of him. I bet after spending almost two and half years at sea, his face would be real tanned now.

I was certain that his coming home, would bring us back to normal, his presence would be like a tonic to everybody, and boost our depressed spirits and moral.

Day after day, every evening on the way back from work, I thought of him, expecting to find him home, but so far, my wish had not been fulfilled, and I kept on hoping and praying as the days went by, but the chances to see him were becoming dimmer and dimmer.

It was Friday the thirteen, and papa's day off. He always remained in bed as late as possible, especially those last couple of weeks, because of the alarm that had kept us constantly hopping in and out of the shelter, and we never got a full night's rest. That morning though, something was unusual, he was already up, and when I asked him if he had some special places to go, he answered: "No, no. I can't sleep. Last night I had a bad dream, and I can't shake it off my mind." Rubbing his hand on his forehead over his puffed eyes, "I have already told your mother, but she won't believe me"

"What is it papa'? Tell us will you?" Carmine and I inquired.

"Oh doesn't matter. Maybe you will laugh at me just as your mother did"

"No, no, we won't papa'. Tell us"

"Well," he began, "Our Lady of Assumption appeared to me in my dream, and told me to go away from here today, because something very terrible is going to happen. She made it very clear, go away from here. Now please yourselves, but it is God's truth." Bringing his hand over his heart and crossing himself.

"Go on you and your dream's, go back to bed," mamma yelled picking on him. "And don't delay them any longer, otherwise they are going to be late for work." Then picking up the lunch on the table and handing them over to us, while pushing us toward the front door she said: "Go on you two, and don't pay any attention to your father's dream, he is still asleep." And before we got out, "don't forget to sign yourself. Good bye."

"Ciao mamma. Ciao papa."

Impressed by papa's words and his strange dream, silently we walked together to Via Prenestina, we boarded the street car and after four stops Carmine got off.

I saw him disappear through the Officine Centrali's gates among many of his fellow workers, then left by myself and my thoughts, I moved behind the motorman and stayed there till Viale Manzoni, where I got off and waited for the Tranve dei Castelli that took me to the Statuario and my work.

Along the way to the shop, I couldn't resist the temptation, sneaking under the wire fence and into the field, I filled my pockets with fresh tomatoes and cucumbers, still wet with the morning dew. By the kitchen, where we received our daily soup, I got some salt from the cook, then as happy as a bird, whistling and singing, I entered the blacksmith shop, saluted everybody and got busy.

Around ten o'clock, taking advantage that the other two were out on a job, I stopped and winked at Sandy, who immediately joined me, then with both of us seated behind a pile of iron pipes, we shared one of my sandwiches and a good part of the stolen tomatoes and cucumbers. When we had finished: "Here Sandy, take the rest of them with you, there is a lot more where these come from. Tomorrow…" I didn't get a chance to finish my sentence, as the foreman looked inquiringly through the door, and Sandy rushed back to his electric saw.

Good old Sandy. Even if he was always smiling, it was quite obvious that he was not happy. His smile was a sad one, a forced one. Lately, since Giocondo and Alberto were away most of the time, the two of us had more time to ourselves to talk and joke around. On a couple occasions, especially when we were fooling around, suddenly he would stop, giving me the impression that he wanted to say something important, but then he changed his mind again and nothing. I couldn't exactly know what it was, but definitely, something was bothering him.

At times, he looked like a lion in a cage, and often I wished I could have done something to help him out. How though? His was a problem that could not be solved, not by me anyway. What he wanted was freedom, but how could I give that to him? Nothing could be done about it, not until the war was over, in the meantime I would try my best to alleviate his boredom and promised myself that the next day I would bring him another bottle of wine and steal enough tomatoes and cucumbers so that he could give some to his pal Bill too. That I would do, and nobody could stop me.

Busy with my work and plans for the coming day, I didn't even bother to stop, when at eleven o'clock the alarm broke the morning silence. It was the usual reconnaissance plane, and very shortly everything would be back to normal.

Out here we had nothing to fear anyway, there were only a few scattered houses going up, all around us was plain country land, and to make it more safe, the Concentration Camp where the English prisoners were kept, was only a whistle away, and I was sure that no enemy airplane would ever bombard the camp.

To my disappointment though, it didn't look at all like the usual routine, a clear and distinct sound of many planes roaring in the sky were approaching, and that couldn't be mistaken. I knew them all too well by now.

Dropping what I had in my hands, I rushed outside and tried to spot them. There they were, flying in the same formation as they were flying on the 19th of July, not as shiny though, because the fog was still thick up in the air. Oh no. They were heading straight toward the same area they bombarded the last time, and suddenly thinking of my family, a very cold chill ran through my spine. It can't be, they are not attacking the same place again? There is nothing over there standing up worth bombing. What is the matter with them? Have they gone mad? Oh my God. It's impossible to believe.

Suddenly under my terrified eyes, I saw hundreds of bombs dropping from the planes, immediately followed by tremendous explosions that made the ground tremble and every window and door of the shop rattle. "Our lady told me to go away from here, because something very terrible is going to happen, go away from here." As if hearing them for the first time, papa's words echoed distinctly through my mind. Oh Madonna mia. Did they go away? Did they listen to you? Did mamma believe in the warning you gave to papa. Have they done something about it, or have they remained at the house?

Struggling with this excruciating thought of uncertainty, like in a nightmare, I saw Sandy and the rest of his friends brought out in the open and assembled by the shouting guards, then hurriedly taken away toward their camp.

At this moment, as the hot blood rushed through my veins, almost blinding me, I felt a strong sense of hate and rage. And looked at them, not as poor Sandy, poor Jim, or poor Bill, but as my country's enemy, my enemy.

Presently it maybe they couldn't do any harm to us, but they must have had their share of shooting and killing before they were taken prisoners. I didn't feel sorry for them anymore, as a matter of fact, I hated them, yes, I did. I hated them as much as I hated their companions in their damned planes up there in the sky that kept on coming and coming, with their infernal loads of death and destruction. Oh God. What a torture this was.

Being bombed, praying and begging for my life to be spared as I did the last time, it was bad enough, but standing here, watching helplessly, only hoping for the best, unable to open my mouth and shout loud, or even cry, or do anything, it was an unbearable situation. How much pain and anguish could a mind endure?

How long did it go on, I had no idea, but surely for more than two hours, and I felt that if those plane didn't stop coming, I would lose my mind. I turned around hoping to see somebody that I could talk to, but the place was deserted, no one was in sight. Where they all disappear to, I did not know.

All at once, the thought of being alone, frightened me, and unable to stand still any longer, I started walking toward the Appia Highway, and when I got there, seated on a rail track, watching the giant clouds of smoke rising toward the sky, waited for the end of the air raid and the street car to take me back to Rome. After a while though, suddenly realizing that there wouldn't be any street car, not for hours anyway, as if I had a spring under me, and determined to go home at any cost, even if that meant walking all the way, I got up, and under the protection of the trees, began moving toward Rome.

After maybe fifteen, maybe twenty minutes, there were no more planes in the sky, the humming of their motors had vanished, lost in the distance where they came from. The sirens hadn't sounded the all clear yet, and the highway was still deserted. I hadn't gone more than a mile, when from, behind me, I heard a vehicle approaching. I turned and looked, it was a truck, a truck from the Italian Air Force, possibly coming from the Ciampino Airport. Moving to the centre of the road, lifting up my hands in the air, I began shouting.

"Stop. Stop, please stop."

Startled, the driver slammed on the brakes and slowed down, then changing his mind continued on his way.

"Dirty bastard," I yelled in frustration. But I couldn't let such an opportunity vanish as easy as that. His slowing down was plenty enough, it was just what I needed. Inspired by determination, desperation and indignation, I ran after him, and in a matter of seconds, reached the tail gate and with a jump, threw myself into the truck. No matter what I would have done or found, this was the fastest way to get home, even faster than any street car.

Satisfied with my success, I got comfortable , and only then, I noticed that one of my shoes were missing. Too bad. One way or another, I had to pay for the ride.

The danger was over. While at high speed, the truck entered the outskirts of the city, one after another, the sirens began singing at full blast.

All along the Via Appia, everything was the same as it was when I went by earlier this morning. Once in a while we passed a street car stopped along the way, with their personnel and the passengers on the ground, waiting for the electricity to come back on. At the entrance of San Giovanni Square, going through the narrow arch of the big doors on the old Roman walls, the truck had to slow down, and taking advantage of it I jumped off. Here too, everything was normal, no destruction, or signs of it, only the people appeared to be different, as they moved hurriedly, nervous with excitement. Following the road along the high wall, in no time I was at Porta Maggiore, where the signs of the bombing was immediately noticed. The traffic was completely paralyzed and confusion and chaos were at their peak.

An aisle of the Panatela's Flour mill was demolished to the ground, with flames raging on in the rest of the building, with the firemen trying their best to put the fire out but with very little success. Across Via Prenestina, almost below the subway, where the road narrowed forming a tunnel, a street car with its trailer were laying on their side across the road. Here too, a crew of firemen and mechanics of the company were trying to remove them and put them back on their tracks, while soldiers and ambulance people were picking up bodies of dead and wounded, scattered all over.

In the meantime, all traffic was switched toward Circonvalazione Casilina, a beautiful wide road built only a few years ago, on a brand new housing development, with rich apartment houses, ten, twelve stories high, were now, nothing but a pile of mangled cement and steel debris. Great big craters all over, and countless dead bodies laying along the sidewalks, covered and waiting to be picked up by the soldiers, which gradually were loading them into army trucks. If their bodies were still in one piece, but had not been identified, they were taken to the morgue, but if they were unrecognizable, or just remnants of arms and legs, they were taken directly to the incinerator of the cemetery and immediately burnt.

A few hundred feet from the overpass of Ponte Casilino, something very unusual attracted all the passerby's attention and curiosity. Of a tall apartment building, only a part of the facade was left standing up, and on that wall, hanging from a nail, was a crucifix, and the big question going from mouth to mouth was only one: "If the rest of the building collapsed, why was that wall still up?" Many called it a miracle, someone less religious, or less superstitious, attributed it to a mere case of luck and circumstances, but the majority of the people were impressed. As for myself, I didn't know what to say, but it sure was a sign of God's power, and it must have meant something.

Before entering the bridge, on the left side, another flour mill, Agostinelli's had been severely damaged, as well as the Viselli Company across the street, where ninety per cent of the city garbage trucks and most of their garages and equipment had been destroyed or lost in the fire.

On the other side of the bridge, the Istituto Serono, a big medicinal plant, had been hit very hard by the falling bombs, and nobody knew as yet, exactly how many girls had been killed because they were still digging them out, but gathering from the commotion around the place, the number of casualties must have been very high.

On Piazza del Pigneto, the dry cleaning plant, where hundreds of women were employed, was another sad sight. Gondrand, known as the largest transport company of Rome, the street car depot where papa' worked, and many other places had received the same treatment. Destruction.

Via Del Pigneto were the daily open market took place, looked like an inferno. The fruits and vegetable stands, the meat and fish counters were scattered everywhere. Scales, fruits, vegetables, meat and fish, arms and human legs, were hanging or resting on doorways, windows, walls and roofs, mingled with cobble stones, bricks, wood and the rest of the debris.

Via Macerata, Via Ascol il Piceno, were white with a foot deep of plaster and stucco dust. The few apartment houses that were still standing, and the Aquila theater that had partly survived the big blow, looked bare and lifeless.

Wherever my eyes rested, saw dead bodies, but the sight of them didn't affect me the way it used to. I had become accustomed to them. What tore my heart to pieces was the inhuman cry of the wounded that were being carried away on stretchers, hand carts, willow bars, bare planks and blankets. Oh Lord!! What a gruesome sight.

Walking on my bare feet over the piles of debris, was like walking on a bed of nails, my feet were bleeding and aching so much that for a while I forgot almost everything and everybody around me, and my only concern was to select the most leveled spots to step on. And finally when I set foot into the Officine Centrali were Carmine worked, I was exhausted.

The gates were wide open, so was the office door of the little building that after two bombings, was miraculously still intact, but there was no sign of life or activity anywhere. Everything seemed dead, everything was so silent. Two street cars completely charred, piles of contorted steel beams and debris everywhere. The big electric clock hanging on the corridor wall had stopped with its two hands marking ten past eleven. That must have been the time when the electricity was cut off. In the hall four workers were having coffee, and even though their faces were covered with black soot and their clothes torn to pieces, they looked familiar to me, but I didn't recognized anyone in particular. Hesitantly I paused under the doorway.

"Don't stand there looking at us as if we were ghosts, come right in," a little gray haired man shouted at me, getting up from the bench where he was sitting, and shaking the last drop of liquid on the floor, refilled it with hot steaming coffee from a big thermos bottle, and handing it to me he said: "Here boy... Sit down and drink." Pushing me toward the nearest bench.

"Thank you," I whispered without moving. I couldn't sit down. Only God knew at that moment how much I would have liked to, give my aching poor feet a chance to rest, but first things first. Until I had found out what had happened to my brother, I wouldn't be able to swallow a single drop of coffee or even relax.

"Has any of you seen Carmine Viselli?" I asked with a lump in my throat. "Who? Carmine? Have no fear, he is alright. We were all together in the shelter," replied the little man. "Then you are his younger brother. Aren't you? I have seen you many times walking with him when you used to work next door for the railway. Believe me, you certainly made a wise move when you quit that place. Poor guys. They sure got it again today, just as bad as the last time."

Feeling better instantly, I flopped on the bench and with my feet still touching the cool and smooth cement floor, I began sipping the hot coffee, but with a sudden doubt in my mind I asked again: "Excuse me sir. If you said that he is alright, how come he is not around?"

"Oh. Relax will you? He will be back soon. He and Dante went down to the shelter to bring some food and water to Lilla and her puppies. The old bitch won't come out, she is scared stiff."

"I don't blame her a bit," said one of the workers talking for the first time.

"If they gave me permission," he went on, "I wouldn't mind moving all my belongings down there, and make it a permanent residence myself"

"Ha ha ha. Cut it out will you? You wouldn't last a day down there. The rats would have a few good meals out of your fat belly," retorted someone else.

Everybody burst out laughing, and I couldn't help joining myself. Right then, Carmine appeared through the door with his friend behind him, but it took him a second or two to notice my presence. And when he did: "Armando how on earth did you get here so fast? You didn't work today?" Then looking at my bare feet "What happened to your shoes? Have you been home?"

Bombarding me with many questions and without giving me a chance to answer, impatiently he asked again: "Well, have you been home?"

"No I have not." Quickly rubbing away the tears that in spite of myself began streaming down my face.

"Hey. What is the matter with you? Is something wrong?" He asked again, now with fear in his voice.

"No, nothing is wrong. Just seeing you made me cry."

"Come on you big baby, let's get out of here." Then patting me on the shoulder and turning to his fellow workers: "Well, no use hanging around here any longer." And leading the way to the outside door "Arrivederci a domani." At which, somebody answered back: "Don't be so sure. I am getting fed up with this damn place." "Where you scared down there?" I asked him on the way home.

"No, not much. For us it wasn't as bad as the last time. As you know, there is not much left to be destroyed here, that is why for us and the scalo San Lorenzo they used mostly incendiary bombs. But I understand they sure made a pizza pie of the Tuscolana Station though, they got the full blow this time. So have the Villini del Ferrovieri and Via Casilina. In fact, they were saying that Via Casilina and the adjacent railroad tracks, looked like a slaughter house. Those dirty assassins caught a train coming from Napoli with over a thousand passengers aboard, exactly right between the Subway del Mandrione and the Church Of Sant Elena. Can you Imagine what must have happened at that particular point?"

With high walls on both side of the road, they had no chance, no way of escape, trapped like rats. In fact, as the first bomb hit the locomotive, the convoy stopped, and as people tried to abandon the train and take cover, not satisfied with just hitting the train, the dirty bastards began flying over very low, and with their machine guns, they shot down everything in sight, as though they were having target practice.

They even killed Father Faloni who came out from the church to give the last rites to the dying victims. Poor Father Faloni. After he had been hit twice, he refused to leave the scene and kept going bringing God's word and administering the Holy communion as many as he could, till the bullets put an end to his holy work.

As we proceeded, it was the same sad scene a thousand times over, and over, everywhere death and destruction. Finally when we got home the house was still up, and besides lots of small debris all around us, nothing serious.

As though nothing had happened, nonno Edoardo was enjoying his usual afternoon nap under the apple tree, and when we asked him about mamma and papa', all he knew that they had left the house early this morning. We couldn't find out much from the few neighbors either. Nobody had seen them or talked to them. Besides, they didn't pay much attention to us, because they had enough problems of their own, as many of them were crying with despair. My friend Pino's family had been severely hit. A sister and his mother had been killed, while two of his sister's mother had been taken to the hospital so badly wounded, that it was doubtful if they would live.

Bruno's seven year old sister, a little doll with long blonde hair, was brought to the hospital with her left arm neatly cut off at the shoulder by a machine gun bullet. Mrs. Ersilia, a big woman, almost six feet tall and weighing more than two hundred and fifty pounds, had just been found under the ruins of the drug store, at the corner of Via Casilina. The firemen found a leg belonging to her body, the only remnant left for her husband to identify, and declare her dead. It was presumed that she tried to run for the Nun's Shelter, but didn't quite make it. Even if she had made it, maybe it would have not made much difference, because the Nun's Shelter was bombed too, and the only entrance was blocked, killing two Carabinieri and five civilians, while the rest of the people who took refuge in it, almost died of asphyxiation, until from outside, a crew of volunteers working for more than three hours, were able to dig a hole and let some fresh air go through.

Hearing all sorts of bad news and seeing death at every corner, was not very encouraging, nevertheless we kept inquiring and searching for our parents, always hoping for the best, and finally around three thirty, when we had almost lost faith of finding them, a ray of sunshine brought us back to life.

There they were, the two of them, coming around Via del Pigneto, shouting and waving their arms. Mamma's voice could be heard a mile away. The reunion, was nothing but tears and hundreds of broken words, as the joy to be together again, felt like the beginning of a happy new life.

At last, mamma also believed in the dream that papa' had the night before, and it certainly paid off. In fact around nine o'clock they both left for the shelter of Piazza Vittorio, therefore they heard very little when the music began.

Thanks to our Lady of Assumption, my parents were safe, and for the rest of my life, I will never forget it.

It might not sound possible, but this was the second warning that papa' had from our Lady. In fact he had a similar dream twenty five years ago, when he was a soldier in the first world war of 1914-1918. That night, it was our Lady of Carmine that appeared and warned him. She told him not to worry because his mother was praying for him. The same morning, as they attacked the Austrian lines, the whole platoon was wiped out, as his friends fell on both sides of him. Of thirty six men, that took part at that action, only my father and two other soldiers came back alive. Papa' came back with a little wound below the knee, that left a scar still visible after so many years. And that is why my older brother got the name that he has got, in devotion to our Lady of Carmine.

As I said, the house was still up, but the floors in the rooms were covered with plaster and broken glasses. The ceiling full of new holes made by the machine gun, looked like a colander, in fact through the countless holes, about the size of a big orange, we could see the blue sky again.

"Well ... This is it," said papa' looking around once more thoroughly disgusted. "I am afraid this place is not fit to live in anymore. Besides.... They might come back again, and I wouldn't try our luck too many times. We have been very, very fortunate so far. Come on. Let's pack and get out of here. Nonno, are you coming with us?" I asked as he didn't make any effort to get up from his stool.

"Who me? No. You are young, you go ahead. The roaming days are over for me, now it is your turn. Yes, I had enough, besides, when our last call arrives no matter where we are, we will get it, and if anything is going to happen, believe me it will. Me, I would rather die here. I spent too many happy days in it and .....", tears coming down his face and his voice failing him: "Somebody has to remain here to make sure that no one steals anything, and I believe I am to be the right candidate." So getting up, with a wide grin on his face, and a mocking tune on his tired voice, "go on now, go, and don't feel bad about leaving me alone. A good glass of wine will keep me company for a long time."

Without any delay we picked up the most valuable and necessary belongings, then like thousands of others, we joined the long procession heading for the open country, away from the city, the railway and the industrial centers.

If we had followed the endless line of human derelicts, that was slowly crawling along the Casilina Highway, it would have taken us the rest of the afternoon and maybe part of the evening, instead, at papa's suggestion, taking a few gravel roads, and crossing the railway tracks at different points, before sunset we reached the Appia Highway and the farming district.

"We better camp up there," said papa', pointing at a wooded area to our left.

"What? Up there on the Tombe La tine among the dead? No papa', not there," I tried to argue. I have always looked at cemeteries like a sacred place, and somehow I was kind of a bit scared.

"Come on, come on. Never mind the nonsense, that is as good a place as any, besides I am getting tired," he said a little annoyed. "We will not be alone up there anyway. Look at all the people. And as far as being afraid of the dead, don't worry your little head, they won't bother you. Once they are gone from this world, they won't come back. It is the living one's that you have to be afraid of, not the dead."

We stopped at the foot of a big pine tree and looked around. The place was practically invaded with improvised campers spread in every direction, under the hundreds of umbrella like pine trees, tents of any type and color, inside the old Roman chapels, the Roman tombs and any other ruin that offered a little privacy and a roof over their heads The place resembled more a fairground than a cemetery. What a difference from the last time I saw this place. War is a cruel thing, it doesn't respect anyone nor any place.

In peace time, thousands of visitors, tourists from all over the world, used to come here to see the old ruins of this well preserved Roman Cemetery.

Only a couple of years ago, at the gates, there was always several drivers with their traditional horse and buggy, waiting patiently, while their customers toured the place. There was an attendant at the entrance, a guide. And the usual old policeman. Not now. The thousands of tourists, the attendant, the guide, the policeman and the drivers, are not here anymore, they are gone, gone forever.

Only two years ago, in this very place, on this very ground, under these very old pine trees, and inside the ruins, all these people met and spent many happy moments together as friends. Now .... Very likely, they are meeting again, only in different places, wearing a uniform, fighting and maybe killing each other for a reason unknown to me, and I bet to them to.

It doesn't seem possible, does it?

We were just ready to spread the blankets on the grass and get settled for the evening, when a tall dark haired man, called my parents by their first name.

"Oh my God." They exclaimed, looking startled at the man. Then "Paolo, what are you doing here?" And turning to us mamma said: "Armando, Carmine? Do you remember him? He is your cousin from Ceprano. You met at the fiesta."

Frankly I had met so many people when I was there that it was quite hard to remember them all, but it is always a pleasure to meet a member of the family, especially under such conditions.

Hundreds of questions were exchanged before he finally invited to pass the night at his house, and believe me, he didn't have to twist our arms, and we gladly and gratefully accepted his invitation.

The offer couldn't have come at a better time, and once repacked we moved out.

At the end of the cemetery, we crossed a dirt road running along the edge of a cliff, suddenly giving us a beautiful full view of miles and miles of the country below and in front of us.

"There is the house" Paolo said loudly in his baritone voice.

Standing right in the middle of nowhere, without a single tree around it, the house looked bare, cold and unfriendly, resembling more a warehouse or a modern barn than anything else. Facing it, and almost under our feet, there was another big building extending all along the cliff's edge and standing on brick pillars that were holding up an endless tile roof.

As we descended, we noticed piles and piles of manure, stored underneath this huge hangar, and as we got closer, an horrible smell caught our nostrils.

"Hey Paolo. What is all that manure for?" I asked.

"Oh. That. We use as fertilizer for the mushrooms," he replied with his sympathetic smile. Showing a double row of beautiful white teeth.

"Mushrooms? Are you kidding? There Is nothing around here but brush and stumps."

"Ha ha ha. Not up here, down in the grotto. That is where we grow them. They have to be in the dark all the time, otherwise they won't grow."

"You mean they have to be cultivated underground?" I asked again, just to make sure that I understood right.

"Certainly. They are the artificial ones, but they don't grow by themselves" he went on explaining, at the same time laughing at my ingenuity. "It takes a lot of hard work and care to grow them. Believe me, it is something worth seeing, and if I have the time and the boss's permission, tomorrow I will take you down the grotto."

Entering the house, black pots and pans hanging from a board nailed to the chimney over the fireplace hit our eyes. A solid wooden table in the center of the floor, with a bench on each side of it, was the only furniture in the small kitchen. The immense bedroom was not much better furnished.

"Don't be surprised if the place is in such a mess," Paolo excused himself. "The men left right after the bombing was over, and didn't have much time to clean around. Every weekend, we all go home but one, and this is my turn to stay. Every Saturday morning, the mushrooms have to be picked up and loaded on the cart so that Nino the foreman can take them to the market and sell them.

"Well, folks, don't expect me to tell you what to do, make yourselves comfortable there are lots of beds and room for everyone."

He was right. There was lots of everything, dirt and all. Lined up on each side of the bare walls, there were many beds, all undone, wet towels and dirty clothes on, dirty sox, shoes and clothes scattered all over the brick floor.

The air was heavy with manure and perspiration smells, and on top of everything, the little window with the iron bars, gave the last touch of beauty to the room.

Wow. What an inviting place that was to spend a night, but beggars can't be choosers, and we had to make the best of it.

Wow. How generous it was on our part. That shows how incomprehensible, fussy and ungrateful the human being is. Half an hour ago, we were ready, and more than happy to lay down on the grass, and spend the night with only the stars and the moon above us, yet, this man offers us a roof over our heads, and all kinds of beds to sleep on, plus many more facilities, and just because the place it is a little bit untidy and dirty, right away we become snobbish.

Anyway, helping mamma, we all pitched in and in no time, order was restored, after that, even though the atmosphere and surroundings were still not too appetizing, our bellies began crying out loudly, so we prepared for supper, and with what little we had brought with us, and what Paolo offered, we managed to satisfy our hunger while we were eating we found out many things.

Besides the one apartment we were staying, there were two more in the same building. One was occupied by a family that at the present time were away on vacation up north, and the other one was empty. We also found out that the grotto, plus four big farms all around here, belonged to the same person, Mr. Spinelli, the same person who owned the big housing project at the Statuario, where I was employed as blacksmith helper.

Putting two and two together, the next morning, papa' and I paid a visit to Mr. Spinelli, and for three hundred lire a month, we rented the apartment.

On the way out from his office, papa' was furious, "Dirty thief, scoundrel, rascal. They should shoot him. Three hundred lire for that lousy dump. He kept complaining. "No wonder the bastard owns so many properties."

We actually slept on the floor for the next week, until papa' and Carmine were able to borrow a truck from the A.T.A.G., the street car company for whom they worked, and transferred what was left unbroken of the old furniture to our new residence.

When we were in Ceprano at nonno's farm, it seemed natural to have an outside toilet, and to go downhill to the well to get the water, and to cook on the fireplace, but here, we all found it very hard, we couldn't get used to it, because it seemed that everything was in the wrong place. Mind you, we were grateful to have found a place to stay, far away from the city and all the dangers, when there were still thousands of families without not only a roof over their head, but without nothing, zero, still, we didn't seem to get adjusted.

The kitchen was too small, long and narrow, with just enough room for the table set against the wall and the chairs around it, the bedroom was nothing but a long room, intended to be used as dormitory for the workers. With no stove to cook on, no sink, no water, and the kitchen so small that we could hardly move around, when mamma cooked the house was full of smoke, and in order to keep the smoke out of the bedroom as much as possible, she kept the door closed. Even with the little window and the outside door wide open, it got so hot, that by the time the meal was ready, and before we even thought of sitting at the table, we had to put the fire out and wait at least half hour to give the room a chance to cool off. By then, the pangs of hunger were gone and we hardly touched the food.

"There will be more for your lunches tomorrow, and also this is a good way to save money and food." Half smiling and half disgusted, mamma told us one day, but it took a while to get organized and finally we came up with the solution.

As the evenings in August were nice and warm and it was a pleasure to stay outside, we scraped together a few planks and built a picnic table, and once again we enjoyed our meals. Another big problem was the bedroom that Carmine and I had to share with our parents.

Once papa' went to bed, he didn't like to be disturbed, not even with the slightest little sound, therefore either by ten o'clock we were all in bed, or we had to be very, very quiet, which was impossible. When he got up at four o'clock in the morning to go to work though, he didn't care how much noise he made, and as a result, we exchanged a few words, while poor mamma stood in between us to act as a peace maker.

Shopping was another headache. All the stores were at least two miles from here, and mamma couldn't go to the market every morning as she used to do. Only the bakery shop was on the other side of the cemetery, where every blessed morning just like clockwork, and before we went to work, either Carmine or myself, had to go for the earthly walk to get those miserable nine hundred grams of bread.

As for transportation, I was the only one that had gained on the deal. How I caught the Tranve del Castelli on the Appia Highway, that was not even a thousand feet from the house. In fifteen minutes I was on the job, where before it took me at least one solid hour. For papa' and Carmine, it was the opposite, now it was their turn to leave the house an hour earlier than they were used to.

The street car stop was exactly across from the property and pub house of Mr. Oliva. The building itself, erected right at the corner of a very busy intersection, was precisely where the unfinished dual highway ended, at which point, the highway became again a single lane, forming a tunnel, very dangerous for any speeding vehicle.

From that point, another road began leading to an old fort, occupied by some Air Force soldiers, and to the real ancient Appia way, built by the early Romans. This road, called Via dell'Acqua Santa, (Road of the Holy Water) because of the several wells of a special type of water, found abundantly in the vicinity. As a matter of fact, there was no specific name for the place where we lived, and everybody knew it as "Acqua Santa." Also from here, that same road, unpaved and narrowing considerably, continued on the opposite direction, following the Tombe Latine and ending at the Arco di Primavera on the Tuscolana Highway.

Along the Appia Highway, besides the street car tracks, there was nothing but farm land, until a mile going south, exactly around the big bend, there was the Golf Course and the Club House. From here on the left side, and making a complete three quarters of a circle, after serving all the houses and barns of the farmers, turning and cutting through the fields, came back to the secondary entrance of the grotto, and our house, proceeded along the manure hangar, then, making a sudden sharp turn, entered a short canyon and died again at the Appia.

Before entering the canyon, up high on the left hand side, there was the "Pump House". Whereas on the right at the end of the canyon, there was the main grotto entrance, with its two big doors always kept closed, and very next to it, a very tiny building known as the office. With the only telephone in the whole area, and Nino the foreman kept the keys.

Next to it, there was another low and long building, with a wide cement sidewalk right in front of it. The brick building, had been divided into two apartments, one was occupied by, a middle age couple, Mr. Ferrari, his wife and their blonde sixteen year old daughter, the other by Nino, in charge of the grotto operations, his lovely wife Elena and their three year old son Fausto.

Further down, still facing the dirt road, lived the cart driver Ruggiero with his wife Derna and a dozen children of both sexes, ranging from nineteen to four years old. Next to them, but facing the Appia Highway though, not more than two hundred feet from the street car stop, there was another pub, owned by his Excellency Mr. Fano and his family.

This stupid imbecile, the third time we went to purchase some wine at his pub, almost caused an incident. Not because Carmine is my brother, but he sure is a handsome looking young man, and the girls are crazy about him. This day, while I was getting my fiasco filled with wine, Lucille, Mr. Fano's daughter, called Carmine aside and began talking to him. Suddenly, for no reason at all, her father, in the rudest way, called her to his side. Slapped her on the face, pushed her into the kitchen, and forbade my brother to speak to her again.

Needless to say that from that day on, he lost our business, and even though we had to walk a little father, we became steady customers of Mr. Oliva, owner of the other pub, located at the corner of the Appia and Acqua Santa roads, very fierce enemy of Mr. Fano, who had better wine (with less water in it) and better manners.

All these people, plus the gang of workers with Paolo living next door, were our new neighbors, and so far, with the exception of Mr. Fano, everyone of them had been very nice to us.

Chapter 10

Because of shortage of material, at the Statuario, the construction had slackened considerably, and everybody on the job was expecting to be laid off.

The English prisoners didn't come to work anymore, I was told that they were taken daily at the Pirelli factory which had been hit very hard, and they were there to help clear up the mess, therefore I hadn't seen Sandy or any of his friends since the day after the bombing.

Only two weeks before, right after that unforgettable Friday, I could have sworn that I hated Sandy and the rest of his companions. It doesn't seem possible that in a moment of rage, a person can get and think as low and as mean as I did. My heart was full of hate and revenge. Now, in the blacksmith shop, looking at the corner where Sandy used to work, I kept expecting to see him, but his smiling freckled face was not there anymore, and, you want to know something? I missed him. Yes I did. Poor Sandy. What will become of him? I bet his mother and father far away in Poland, must be thinking of him and wondering how and where he is.

I am sure they would pay anything to see and talk to him, even if it were for only a few minutes, just as much as I would have liked to see my oldest brother Peppe. Yes, dear Peppe. God knows how many times he has written to us that soon he would come home, but so far, the promises, have been nothing but promises. We are still waiting and hoping that he would come someday real soon.

Finally and not very welcomed, Carmine had received the red card, which means that he is being drafted into the army, and he is due to report to the barracks of the Cecchignola by the first of September. Cecchignola is an army center about seven kilometers outside of Rome, half way to the small resort town of Ostia on the Tyrrenian sea.

Before he reported to the army, papa' sent him to Ceprano for the weekend to say good bye to our grandparents and at the same time to bring back my brother Mario and my sister Maria it was not even a month since we had left them in Ceprano with nonno and nonna, still it seemed such a long time.

Monday morning came and here they were. How nice to hear their voices again. They both looked real well and we were all pleased, and it didn't seem possible that in such a short time, they had gained weight and grown.

On their arrival, we tried to put up another bed in the already crowded room, but it didn't work, and with only three beds and six people, it was not going to be all roses, not until Carmine left anyway, and, for the time being Mario and I shared the same bed. He slept at the head and I slept at the foot or vice versa, and that is when the trouble started.

During the night, silent war went on between the two of us. He kicked me and I kicked back, he pulled the blankets over himself, and I in return pulled them over myself, but in the end, nobody won. When dawn came, we were both uncovered with the blankets on the floor. Thank God it was summer.

Wednesday morning mamma and papa' were crying at the street car stop, while with a lump in my throat, standing beside them holding the little wooden suitcase, I listened to papa' giving some last words of advice to Carmine: "Let us know as soon as possible if they are keeping you there or if they are sending you away. If they do, don't forget to phone or write to us. Be prudent and take good care of yourself. We won't be there to guide you anymore, but as long as you use the good senses you were born with and remember what we always tried to teach you, you will be on the right road. Capito? Pay attention to your superior officers, and don't be an empty head. Understand?"

The street car arrived, he kissed us good bye, jumped on the moving tram, waved at us and was gone. Yes. Just like that.

"It doesn't seem fair, does it?" Mamma said, wiping her tears, " it takes the best years of our lives to bring our children up, and when they become old enough, when we feel we have accomplished something, and are proud to have them around and be able to say: "Those are my sons, and the government comes along and takes them away from us just like that." She went on snapping her fingers. "Who gives them the right anyway? Nobody. They just do as they please and take them. They already have a son of mine that I haven't seen for two long years now. Isn't that enough? No. They had to get this one too. Why? Why? Why does it have to be this way? Why is it that a few irresponsible people should have the power to throw millions of innocent boys into this endless bloodshed? What are we gaining out of this war anyway? I know what we are gaining. An ocean of tears, destruction, hunger, misery and poverty all over the world for many years to come. That is what we get." She went on bitterly. "Why doesn't the Almighty God see these things and strike then dead? We could get along very well without them." Then, as though regretting what she had just said, "Oh Lord. Forgive me for blaming this on to you. This is man's doing not yours."

That same evening, we got a reassuring phone call from Carmine, that instantly put papa' and mamma in a better mood. He had been assigned to an infantry battalion and, as long as they were in training period, there was no danger of being transferred. We hoped it would last for the duration of the war.

Three days after that, he came home and at first sight we were shocked.

"Oh my God," cried mamma. "What have they done to you?"

The pants were much too big for him, they were hitched up almost four inches above his waist line, and so long, that they dragged on the floor and we could hardly see his army boots. The shirt was the opposite, the sleeves too short, the collar too small and so tight around the shoulder and chest, that we expected to see the buttons fly off into the air any minute. The heavy winter wool service cap, resting on his ears, completed the picture.

Papa' was furious. "Christ almighty," he exclaimed. "Is that the best they had in stock? What is the matter with the Italian army now-a-days. Tell me. What is that uniform suppose to represent? I Pagliacci?"

"Oh, never mind the uniform papa," retorted Carmine angrily, throwing the hat in the air in disgust. "Look at this masterpiece. How do you like my new hair style?"

"The dirty bastards, the dirty rats," shouted papa', by now redder than a cooked lobster. "They still do it? I thought that was abolished a long time ago."

"Yes. Perhaps it was abolished, but that didn't help any of us. The last three days, the barbers have been busy cutting hair to all four hundred of us, and until that was done, nobody could leave the barracks."

The way Carmine said it, sounded like a joke, but believe me, it was not a bit funny, There was not a single hair left on his head, and it was so shiny, that I bet, in the dark we could have used it as a light bulb.

When we finally reconciled ourselves with the idea, we sat around the table, and while chewing at some fresh dried figs that nonna Teresa had sent us, we talked a little of everything, included politics and the latest events of the war.

The Anglo-American troops that had landed in Sicily, had advanced so rapidly that the whole island was practically theirs, meanwhile the situation was getting worse daily, and it was rumored that a lot of Italian soldiers were deserting or giving themselves up as prisoners, rather than fight. Everybody we talked to seemed to say the same thing. Suddenly everybody knew the score, a few more days and it would be over, and these were the gossips whispered in the bars, cafes, theaters and everywhere else.

Some very important representatives of our government were already behind the Allied lines and the Armistice had already been signed. Very soon the Allied will land near Leghorn on the Tyrrenian Sea and near Venice on the Adriatic. The Germans to which we have been allied since the beginning of the conflict and who have sent troops and material into our country, will have no choice but to leave Italy, and in a matter of days, the war will be over and completely forgotten.

We had heard so many bells ringing, that at last, we hardly paid any attention to what was said anymore. No one knew the real story, and our guess was as good as the next one.

"But where there are rumors, there is a certain amount of truth, and if we live long enough, we will find out," claimed papa', who didn't seem too happy. "I hope that what I am predicting is dead wrong, but our problems are very far from being over yet, because even if we do surrender to the Anglo-Americans, we would still have the Germans to deal with. I am almost positive, for I know them too well, the idea of being double crossed wouldn't sound too appealing to them and I could bet on it, that before they left Italian soil, Hitler and his generals would make us pay very dearly for it. Don't forget," he kept saying, "that there is still many Divisions of Fascist troops that have been incorporated into the regular army, but their ideas are still the same, and it would be difficult to know what they would do in such case. The Fascists, were the only ones who wanted this lousy war in the first place, and would very likely create an unpleasant incident before they accepted the facts as they were. Anyway this is only my personal opinion," continued papa'. "I have been wrong many times, and for our sake, let's hope that I am wrong again. So let's change subject, shall we?"

"Yes. You are so right papa! Hey Mario come here," Carmine ordered my younger brother, and pulling out his wallet, "here is some money, go get some wine, and make it fast. I want to celebrate my bald head." Meanwhile, time went on, so did the war.

We had known for a long time that many German generals and a whole armored division had been hiding for months among the trees in the woods of Frascati, a small town up in the Colli Albani, and only a few miles from Castel Gandolfo, but not even once, had they been molested by the Anglo-American airplanes, surely their high command must have known for some time that the Germans were there.

It was only a couple of days that Sandy and company had rejoined us, when that morning, the two of us were cutting a steel beam on the electric saw, when the unmistakable humming noise, sent a cold chill through my spine. We both stopped and rushed outside to see what it was, and there they were again, formation after formation, same pattern, same routine flight, with only one difference. This time they were going in the opposite direction of Rome, straight on toward the Colli Albani. As the Italian guard shouting and yelling began assembling the prisoners in the middle of the road, very loudly and vulgarly while pointing at the planes in the sky, one prisoner made a smart remark. I didn't catch what he said, but it must have been very funny, because everybody burst out laughing.

I don't know why I should have resented his remark, but he enraged me so much, that if it is true that a person can kill with his thoughts, then at that very moment, I was guilty of having committed such a grave sin, because I had just killed that same man with my bare hands and if so, please God forgive me.

Once again, it was the usual tremendous show of destruction, useless, brutal killing and crying, where another eight thousand innocent people, were reported to have lost their lives, in one of the bloodiest massacre ever witnessed in history.

But the carnage of Frascati, didn't surprise us any more, it was one of the American specialties that was becoming more popular every day. They were getting better every time, and we had to give them credit for it.

What puzzled us, is that thousands and thousands of bombs were dropped on this little town but all for nothing. Because the Americans were late for the appointment. Not a single German was hurt or killed during this raid. Only helpless civilians.

In fact, bright and early the same morning, the villagers were awakened by a thundering noise that was making the earth tremble. Surprised, they looked outside to see what it was, and there they were, the Germans and their armored tanks, were finally leaving, they were moving out, and they were glad to see them go. Everybody was still talking about them, when suddenly the sky above them darkened and the end of the world came, as hundreds of the well known American "flying Fortresses" appeared and began to seed death below them.

Were the American big generals aware of this colossal error? What kind of espionage system did they have? Why they had not taken action before? If that was not possible, why at the last moment this outrageous mistake was not avoided? If this was not serious enough, how could they explain this second horror?

The echoes of the falling bombs over Frascati, was still sounding in our ears, when the newspapers with big headlines, announced the end of hostilities between Italy and the Anglo-American nations. Surely the American Command must have known about the cease-fire before our newspapers. Why then the planned raid over Frascati had not been cancelled?

At work, nobody had done very much since the eleven o'clock raid, and when late in the afternoon, we received news of the armistice, we quit all together. For a few minutes, I was undecided, I didn't know what to do, if I went home now supper wouldn't be ready for a couple of hours yet, and if I stick around here, I might learn something. The prisoners had not come back at one o'clock, the bosses were not around, and the majority of the workers, were heading toward the barracks of the P.A.I. (Italian African Police), where a large group of this special militiamen had been stationed for years.

This was a new corps, founded after the Abyssinian war in 1935-36, composed mostly of young fascist screwballs, which spent their time parading up and down the street of Rome during the fascist holidays. I had heard so much of them and their place that I didn't hesitate too long in making up my mind, and before I realized, found myself following the rest of my excited companions along the dirt road.

As we passed by the Concentration Camp, where the english prisoners were kept, we noticed a lot of confusion, the Italian sentries had abandoned their post, thrown away their rifles, opened the gates and let the prisoners free, who were leaving in groups of two and three, carrying with them their essential belonging, and spreading out in every direction.

Sandy came to my mind, but unfortunately, even if I did find him, there was very little I could do to help him, besides wishing him good luck, so I kept going with the crowd toward the barracks, and when we got there. As expected, the place was deserted. The militiamen, had abandoned the premises, consisting of twelve bungalow type buildings, with everything in them.

Screaming and shouting like wild animals, we joined the already big crowd of people invading the rooms one by one, and the looting began. The best supplied was the food store, where there was lots of everything we could think of. Wow. There was maybe one or two thousand kilos of hard Romano cheese, neatly piled up in one corner, a huge stack of spaghetti cases, barrels of oil, barrels and barrels of wine, cases and cases of dry biscuits and crackers, bags of sugar, cognac bottles by the case, bags of potatoes, oranges and apples, and several cases of different kinds of meats and dried fish. As I said, there was a lot of everything, but it was disappearing so fast under my eyes, that I could hardly believe I had seen them. Where all the people were coming from, was a mystery, but they were coming and kept coming. They were like ants that move as quickly as flies, and when they went, everything went with them.

At this moment in particular, this scene, reminded me of the barbarians that centuries ago, invaded and sacked Rome. There couldn't have been too much difference between the old one and the new ones. I bet they all looked like a bunch of starving wolves attacking a herd of docile sheep.

How true it is when they say that the eyes are bigger than the mouth. In fact many of them overdid it, they accumulated so much in front of them, that when they were ready to leave, they didn't know how to carry it away. So they picked up what was most valuable and left the rest to the next dozen guys, who were ready to grab, and if necessary, fight for it. Others were not so easily discouraged though.

They fought so hard to get it, that a little problem like that, was not going to stop them. In a matter of seconds, they tore a door down and once loaded, they departed, still looking around, feeling frustrated at having to leave so much behind them.

All, all for free. Come and get it. My o my what a sight.

Some others were more practical. Why tear the building apart when there is a much simpler way? Here, let's not waste any time eh? So they carried the entire beds with one or more mattresses, without forgetting to grab a few spare sheets, blankets pillows, then, why not, army boots, uniforms, bags of potatoes, and a whole side of beef. Naturally they forget that the whole bed wouldn't go through the door and when they came to that, struggling, sweating and cursing, they had to unload and reload before they could take off for good.

Then, there was the mechanized type, the more ingeniously that came with willow bars, hand carts, baby buggies, and some actually came with a regular horse and cart.

Things that couldn't be carried, were rolled away, such as barrels of oil, wine and those great big wheels of Romano cheese. Window, doors, chairs, tables stoves, and pipes, fire wood, plumbing and every damn thing nailed, or not nailed, was hauled away, as the looters were becoming more and more numerous and the loot was getting scarcer. Nothing was left standing up, even the walls were coming down now, as the new comers, in a mad rage, were tearing and breaking everything in sight.

As I looked at them running wildly, I couldn't believe my own eyes. In school, I was told that we Italians were one of the first civilized nations in the world! Up to now, I believed it. Not after this afternoon though.

That we have had hardship for many years, that we had and still have ration cards, and that we got very, very little with them, it is all true, that people have been starving, nobody can deny it, and if they were stealing food or clothes that were actually bought with their tax money, it was understandable, but their vandalism was not, and what they were doing was inadmissible. After all the war was over now, soon we will have to start rebuilding what was destroyed. Damaging what was still standing up, it is a crime and should not be permitted. The law should prevent such things from happening. But where was the law right now? Disorganized as was everything else, and nowhere in sight. In fact I am quite certain, that they were afraid to come out in the open and interfere with the enraged people, who, at this very moment, wouldn't think twice of turning against them.

Behind all this raving madness, there was only one explanation, and only one reason, it was the result of keeping the population oppressed too long.

More depressed than disgusted, I left the scene and slowly walked to the street car stop. At the Acqua Santa, getting off the tramway I had the biggest surprise of the day. Not only a road block had been erected, but armed soldiers were everywhere. Four of them, helmets on and rifles leveled, were placed two at each exit, of the street car, while a young lieutenant came aboard, and walking directly toward the only two German soldiers, politely asked them to descend and follow him to Mr. Oliva's pub, which being the only building around, was used as temporary headquarters by the Italian Command.

An infantry captain, helped by an interpreter, questioned them, asked them to surrender their weapons, and without too many ceremonies, ordered them into the big pub hall, already crowded with other German soldiers picked up earlier.

German cars and trucks, going in and out of town, were stopped and searched, and while the occupants were taken into custody, the vehicles were parked on the graveled back yard. None of the German soldiers offered any resistance, nor tried to start an argument, and even if they had, I don't think it would have paid them, they were outnumbered ten to one.

Driving a brand new Italian Fiat, a couple of high ranking German officers, seemed very annoyed when stopped, but after the Italian young lieutenant had spoken to them, they got out of the car and joined the rest of them without causing any incident. It seemed that the majority of them, learning that the war had ended for our soldiers and cur country, liked the idea quite a bit, in fact more than once, we heard them explode with words of joy: "Good. Good." They said. "Maybe soon we will go home too."

From an artillery man, seated on the ground chewing at something, I tried to get some information.

"Well. This is for their own good!!" He explained. "Our Command is doing it in order to avoid any incident or misunderstanding on their part. Once they have reached a certain number, we will form a column and vehicles and men will be escorted north and to one of their own centers, among their own people. That is the easiest and quickest way to assemble them and get them out of Italy."

"Is that all? " I asked doubtfully. "You make it sound so simple. Then, why did you guys dig those antitank holes in the pavement? And what are all those wooden horses loaded with barbed wire across the road for? And how do you explain the presence of those pieces of artillery right in the middle of the highway and what about all those soldiers up on the Tombe Latine? Are they on a picnic? Come on man, tell me the truth, what's behind all this?"

"Don't ask me brother. That is all I know, and what the officers told us. Anyway, there is nothing to worry about, and soon everything will be over. You will see"

After supper, I joined papa' and many of our worried neighbors who were standing by the little office near the grotto entrance, discussing the day's events, and waiting to hear the news from Nino's radio.

At eight o'clock, besides repeating what we already knew, the authorities, were warning the people to stay off the streets as much as possible, and to avoid any confrontation that might occur with the German soldiers, that from now on, were considered enemies of our country.

Later, due to the circumstances, and at papa's request, Nino made an exception to the rules, and left the door of his office open for us.

Quietly, we waited and waited but in vain, for Carmine's usual phone call, till papa' broke the silence, saying: "I wonder what has happened," looking for the hundredth time at his pocket watch. "It is now past ten o'clock, and if he hasn't called by now, we can forget it."

"Papa', he could be on duty" I suggested.

"Maybe he is. Who knows. Anyway we better not bother these people any longer" Getting up and locking the door behind him.

The house was in complete darkness, my sister and brother were already sleeping, but mamma was still awake, and with anxiety in her voice, she asked: "Did Carmine call?"

"No. He did not. But don't start worrying now, because even if you do, it won't help anything," papa' replied angrily, then talking aloud to himself: "Maledetta la Guerra, Damned war."

Slowly finding my way in the dark, I reached the bed and began undressing, when suddenly in the distance, I heard a thundering sound. It's funny, I thought the sky was nice and clear. Bah. Maybe a storm is coming. I said to myself, as I proceeded to unbutton my shirt.

But the sound became more and more distinct, and realizing that it could have not been the thunder, with fear in my heart I called: " Papa', papa'. Did you hear that?"

He didn't answer me, instead he got up, ran to the kitchen, opened the door, and holding his pants up with both hands, stepped outside and listened carefully.

"By Jesus " He exclaimed. "Those are pieces of artillery firing. Yes. I heard them too often during the first world war that I can't be mistaken. Those are the seventy five millimeters cannons."

In a very short time, we were all outside, running toward the grotto entrance, already crowded with most of our neighbors, half dressed, or wearing pajamas and nightgowns, anxious as much as we to know what was going on.

For the last ten minutes, Nino had been trying to make a phone call, and finally when at last he succeeded, it didn't take long to learn the bad news. At the Cecchignola, the Germans had attacked our Grenadiers, and the fight was rapidly expanding all over.

"At the Cecchignola? That is where my son is," exclaimed mamma in a terrorized voice. "Madonna mia," she went on. "Please help him. He is so young, only nineteen years old. I bet he is not even able to hold a rifle in his hands. Please our Lady of Carmine, I beg you, keep an eye on him." Bringing both hands up and wiping her face wet with tears.

As the night went by, the incessant pounding of the cannons delivering their deadly messages increased, so did the rattling of the machine gun fire and the musketry, that could be heard only when the wind blew toward our direction.

Dawn found us walking up and down the dirt road beside the grotto entrance, wrapped in blankets and winter coats to protect ourselves from the heavy fog that had fallen during the night.

Nino had constantly been on the phone trying to get more news, but nothing of importance had developed. On the radio, at seven o'clock, they announced the Departure of the Royal Family and the Government for an unknown destination, adding, that they were evacuated from Rome for precautionary measures. As for the fight that was still going on at the Cecchignola, they claimed that there was nothing to be alarmed about, because everything was under control.

The Germans had been asked to surrender to our forces and leave the country immediately or suffer the inevitable consequences.

At the Acqua Santa road block, the troops had been on the alert all night, with orders to stop and shoot if necessary, at any German vehicle trying to go through, but so far they had been very lucky. No one had tried.

At five o'clock that morning, papa' had to report to the depot for work, but he decided not to go.

"This is going to be one of those days, when the safest thing to do, is to stick around the house and mind our own business, and that goes for you too." He said looking at me. "We have enough problems as it is, we don't have to go out to look for any more. Understand?"

At one o'clock, for the first time, we heard some positive news about the fight that broke out the night before. Two regiments of our light armored division "Ariete" had contacted the German forces at the Cecchignola, and were pushing them back toward Ostia and the sea. Another reassuring and very important factor, the announcer said, was the presence in and around Rome of four more divisions of Italian troops that were ready to be used if needed.

In fact, shortly after two o'clock, some fresh regiments arrived at the Acqua Santa to reinforce the road block. The highway was really well guarded now, and we thought that it would have been very foolish for the Germans to try anything.

With more pieces of artillery over the Tombe Latine, and more mortars and machine guns placed all along the crest of the other lower hill on the opposite side, that started right across from Mr. Oliva's pub and continued almost as far as the old Fort, our troops were in a very advantageous position, and had absolute control of the Appia Highway for miles.

It was nice to see them here eager to defend the city, but at the same time, we sincerely hoped that nothing would happen, for their sake and ours as well. Due to our location, we would be standing exactly a few hundred feet ahead of the Italian front line, therefore we would be left out, and right in the middle of the shooting. The idea didn't appeal to papa' at all, and beside worrying about my brother Carmine, who had not called us yet, we started worrying about ourselves.

"I wish we had never moved out here," complained papa'. "If they ever start anything, they will make meat balls out of us."

Just then, Nino, passing by, stopped to chat with papa' and came up with a reassuring answer to our mutual problems, by saying: "Sebastiano, what are you worrying about? If anything develops, we will all go down to the grotto. There is lots of water, lots of mushrooms and a mountain of straw to keep us warm. All we need is a few frying pans," he said walking away and laughing. "And don't forget to bring a few decks of cards so we can kill the time ......" Good old Nino. He has been very helpful and kind to us.

After five o'clock, we shared a meal with the army. Once the soldiers had their rations distributed, there was so much food left over, that the cooks didn't know what to do with. Really, it was hardly worth mentioning that they would not throw it away, knowing how very little we civilians had to eat.

All the families around got their share, so did we, as Mario and I came back with a big pot of macaroni soup and several loaves of fresh bread, and big fat chunks of meat. Wow. We hadn't seen such a quantity of food on the table, since we left Ceprano, and we all showed signs of it. I was on my third bowl of soup, when to our surprise, Carmine turned around the corner. With his greasy pants rolled up over his ankle, a dirty yellowish tee shirt and a paper hat over his head, looking more like someone just coming from work than a soldier of the Italian army.

"What happened to your uniform? And how come you are here at this hour?" Asked papa' with a sudden coolness in his voice. " What is the matter, have you deserted?"

"Well. You can call it whatever you want papa'. But I wasn't going to remain there and get killed like a mouse in a trap." Carmine answered very calmly trying to hide his rage. "I haven't touched food since five o'clock last night," and pulling out a chair and flopping on it heavily, he added: "I am exhausted, thirsty and hungry. And I don't feel like arguing papa'. So let's eat."

"Sure, leave him alone," said mamma walking to the kitchen and coming out with a clean plate which she filled with a couple of ladles of hot soup, and placing it in front of Carmine: "Here son, eat, eat slow."

Between mouthfuls, Carmine explained the situation to papa', who with a very preoccupied look on his face, listened carefully. "This is the end for us papa', nothing will save us now. Our generals have betrayed us, they have sold Italy to the Germans once again, like they did in 1917 at Caporetto. The grenadiers and the soldiers of the division "Ariete" since this morning had the Germans on the run. They were doing a swell job, and it would have been all over by now if our dear generals had let them. It was around three o'clock this afternoon, when the order to cease firing and surrender at once to the Germans came from Rome. At first, no one could believe it, because it seemed Impossible. Slowly chaos and indecision began reigning among the officers, no one knew exactly what to do, as orders and counter orders were given to the different regiments. Scared and unable to make a decision, more than majority of the officers, in a hurry to be free of their responsibility, gave the order to surrender, and that was the end of it. The soldiers, some of them willing, but many more not willing, followed their leaders example and threw away their weapons, then like the sheep without the guide of the shepherd, quietly began dispersing. That moment of uncertainty on our side, was enough for the Germans, who quickly reassembled and with the full weight of their forces, attacked and destroyed the few battalions of our soldiers that under the resolute orders of courageous officers were trying to hold them back. From then on, everyone looked after himself, so did I.

At Porta San Paolo, the civilians have armed themselves and have joined a company of grenadier that have placed themselves on the old Roman walls with machine guns, with the intention to stop the Germans from entering the city, but it is sure suicide. Now it will be only a matter of time, because nothing, nothing will stop them, unless a miracle happens.

I was scared all the way," Carmine went on, "and I couldn't believe my eyes when at the road block I saw all our soldiers standing calmly at their usual post, talking and joking around. In fact, for a second, the thought of telling them what I knew, entered my mind, but I was afraid that they might recognize me and stop me even though I had thrown away shirt and coat and made myself this paper hat."

"This is ridiculous," shouted papa'. "I don't believe a single word you are saying. It sounds too much like a fairy tale. Why don't you come out in the open instead and tell us the whole truth? Did you get scared and run? Do you know," yelled papa' stretching his body across the table trying to get hold of my brother: "What a deserter gets if he is caught? Do you? Do you know?"

"Listen papa'. Don't jump to conclusion so fast. Calm down. I told you the truth, I swear it on the Holy Cross," Carmine said quickly getting up.

"You better have, for your own sake. Do you know what they do to deserters? They shoot them in the back." Then pointing at me with his finger: "Come with me. Let's go down to the road block, one way or another I am going to find out the truth."

To my great disappointment, when we got there, we found that nothing had changed, the soldiers on duty were placidly walking back and forth behind the barbed wire and wooden horses, the guns were trained on the same spot as before, while their attendants, leaning on them or sitting nearby, were reading magazines.

The same young lieutenant that was on duty the day before, was now talking and laughing with one of the attendants of the seventy five millimeter guns, when suddenly, coming from the Statuario, two Germans on a motorcycle with sidecar, appeared on the highway as they were making the turn around the bend in front of the Golf Course, speeding toward our direction, and firing at us with a machine gun mounted on the sidecar.

"Get down. Get down" The young lieutenant yelled at us, then turning to his men he ordered " Fire. Fire."

"The third shell hit the motorcycle head on, sending the vehicle and its occupants flying up in the air in a million pieces, but the young lieutenant was not there anymore to see it. A German bullet, caught him exactly between the eyes, killing him instantly."

"His mother will never know how he died," murmured papa' as his body was being carried away. Poor lieutenant, he was so young.

For a while we didn't move from where we were, but when nothing else developed, we got up and walked away.

What had happened, occurred so fast, that it seemed like a dream. Here now, gone next, and somehow it didn't seem real.

The lieutenant's death, seemed to have demoralized the soldiers around him completely, they were lost. All the one's we approached were talking about him, and everyone of them had something good to say about him. They referred to the lieutenant, not as their officer, but as Alfredo, their friend, their companion, their brother. Apparently, he was very popular among them, and many of them were crying, but their tears wouldn't bring him back. A group of young recruits standing around him, were listening attentively to their old sergeant, who was very bitter about the whole thing. "There goes another one," he was saying, referring to the lieutenant. He thought he was going home soon, instead he will be buried six feet underground, and over his grave, they will put a wooden cross with an inscription saying, "Died valorously for his country" After that, he will be forgotten and left there to feed the worms. Damn it. Damn it." The sergeant continued bitterly shaking his head.

"In this last three years of war, I have lost more friends than all the hairs on my head, and, strangely enough, while they were dying, none of them resembled the heroes that we usually see at the movies, or the way they are described by the newspapers, or by the poets. No sir. And would you like to know why? There are no heroes, there is no glory, but there is death, yes dear old just plain horrible death. When all my friends died, and death did not arrive instantly or quickly as you have just witnesses, I heard them cry out loud like babies, imploring for help and for their mothers. I have seen so many of those cases, that now the words, hero, bravery, courage, human sacrifice, do not exist in my dictionary any more. They are a lot of nonsense, horse shit. Those are the words often mentioned on bulletins or communiqué to praise their memory, but they mean nothing to whoever is not there anymore and a lot less to me. Sometimes after their death, as to make fun of them and their memory, preceded by a big parade and a bigger ceremony, their names were called out loud, and ironically someone among the crowd answered "Present".

Medals of all kinds were awarded to their memory, usually posthumously, gold medals, silver medals, the cross of this and the cross of that, but none of those decoration brought any of them back to life yet. No, because they are gone forever, just like our lieutenant."

Can any of you tell me why and what they lost their lives for?" He asked looking around.

"No. because nobody really and truly knows. We are fighting and dying for our beloved country. Ha. Ha. Ha. What a terrible joke. I am disgusted and sick to my stomach every time I hear this big lie. Our beloved country it is we, you, me, and our families, our homes, our fields. I am positive that none of us wanted to kill or to get killed. We were too happy to get along with the guy next door, because he is like us without malice and wickedness in his heart. Our dear king Vittorio, his family, and the rest of his noble blood suckers, generals and ministers, are the ones that brought the so called beloved country of ours to disaster, and now that everything is gone to pot, they have left us holding the bag and hoping for the best."

"If the war that they prepared and declared is supposed to be over for them, why it is not over for us? After all, our skins are worth as much as any of those blue-blooded coward, in fact more, because we have always been useful to society, because we always earned our daily bread with the sweat of our foreheads, not like them parasites, which I doubt if they ever worked a single day of their lifetime."

He stopped talking, pulled out a cigarette, lit it, and said: "Sorry boys for giving you this disappointing lecture, but I thought you should all know the truth. I wasted my best years under this uniform, but you don't have to. You are all so young, full of energy, better educated than myself, and have a whole life ahead of you. Don't let somebody else ruin it for you like they have done with mine."

The sergeant stopped, looked again around, then with a sad smile on his face, "I know what a lot of you are thinking of me at this moment, I have a big mouth and I know it. Someday it will get me into serious trouble, but don't let that worry your little heads, because I don't care anymore. Come on, break it up now, back to your posts..... Corporal?"

"The sergeant is right, and it is too bad that we are not thinking like he does," a young recruit said to his companion.

"Maybe he is right," his friend answered. "Maybe things would be different, but how many among us would have the courage to speak up and say what is in our minds?"

"I bet very few would. Even him, he talks like that only when he has had a few extra glasses of wine."

"Surely, I heartily agree with you," said the first recruit. "But don't forget that," Vino veritas".

As we moved along and into the pub, we found out that the German soldiers and officers who had been kept prisoners all night in the big ball, had been transferred somewhere else in the downtown area, and the place was again, what it had always been. A drinking saloon. The air was heavy and filled with smoke that we could hardly see who was at the other end of the room. Mr. Oliva, was as usual busy behind the counter, while his daughter, the beautiful Santina, ran from table to table, laughing and joking with the soldiers, unloading trays full of glasses, bottles of wine and going back for some more.

Only half an hour ago, when we heard the rattling of the machine gun and the roaring of the cannon, for a moment we thought that the world had come to an end. Now, look at it. Soldiers and civilians were leisurely enjoying their drinks, playing their game of cards and chatting nonchalantly, happy to be together again, as pleasure and relaxation had replaced fear and hate once more, and life went on following the same old routine. Everything was forgotten, even the lieutenant's death, exactly as the sergeant had said a few minutes ago.

Papa' and I came here to find out what the score was among the troops stationed on this very important intersection, and everywhere we turned and looked, all seemed to be normal. Soldiers and officers were at their places following a well ordered and disciplined schedule.

As we came out of the pub, papa' began talking loudly to himself and shaking his head kept repeating: "It is impossible. It is impossible. Never mind the soldiers because they are always the last ones to know and to be told, but is it ever possible that not even the officers are aware of what is happening at the Cecchignola and at Porta San Paolo? I doubt it. And again, could it be possible that amid all the chaos these troops have been completely forgotten by the high command? There is only one answer to this mystery," he said looking at me. "Either your brother has lied to me, which I doubt very much or," he added, shaking his head once again, "something is wrong somewhere, and if I say that it is wrong, it is very, very wrong, which it wouldn't surprise me in the least, because I know those bastards too well from way back. In fact, nothing would surprise me anymore, and Armando, mark my words, history it's repeating itself. This people have been forgotten the same way they forgot us in 1917 and before the night is over we will know the truth."

How strange. It didn't take much for my father's prophecy to materialize.

The daylight was gradually being replaced by the darkness, as we silently walked the few hundred feet of highway. We were just entering the dirt road leading to the grotto and our house, when suddenly from the road block; we heard some shouting voices, immediately followed by rifles shots. Instinctively we ducked, thinking that the soldiers had mistaken us for Germans, but we soon found out that it was only some trigger happy fool celebrating.

As we walked back, we were told that an army major had just arrived from general headquarters in Rome, bringing with him the bad news. The order of our troops was to destroy their weapons and disband.

While there was a great mixture of reaction among the soldiers and civilians, we noticed how very little concern there was about the significance and gravity of the whole situation in general. Personally we thought that the moment was more than tragic, not just for us, but for the entire nation.

With a deep sadness in our heart, we walked back to the house, concluding that the only bright spot of the day, was the fact that Carmine had not lied to us, everything he had said was true.

Through the evening until late at night, it looked like a procession. Soldiers and officers alike, came to our place and our neighbor's houses begging for help, asking for civilian clothes of any form and shape, as long as they were not green. Surprisingly enough, everyone got something, pants, shirts, coats, hats, and when at last there was nothing left to give, Nino opened the grotto's doors and permitted as many that came to spend the night in it.

Because of the continued knocking at our door, nobody had a chance to sleep during the night. Soldiers were pouring in steadily from all over the city, mostly southerners trying to get a good early start for their homes. By morning, there were so many of them that the grotto looked more like a recruiting center than a place to grow mushrooms. They all looked tired and worried, and they all had different stories to tell, everyone had his own version, but they all coincided at the same point. If the Italian generals had not betrayed, if they had not been so eager to capitulate, the situation now would have been a completely different one. With five divisions to defend Rome, she would have never fallen under the Germans, no instead, thanks to them, they all had to run and hide like hunted criminals.

Around six thirty on my way down to the store to buy our daily ration of bread, passing through the Tombe Latine, wherever I rested my eyes on, I saw hundreds of rifles, most of them broken in two, machine guns, cannons, mortars, those too were damaged or the obturator or other parts were missing. Boxes and boxes of all kinds of ammunition, carts, tents, complete field kitchens mounted on wagons, pans and pots, canteens, and many, many army sacks scattered in every direction. The sacks like everything else, had already been searched and emptied of their contents by the early scavengers, who were still prowling around like hungry hyenas.

Believe me, it was a very pitiful looking sight. The weapons lying on the ground like the men who once carried them, were defeated, lifeless and armless forever, thus putting a catastrophic and dishonorable end to a war which should have never been started.

When I got to the store, I could hardly believe my ears, and to make sure I did not misunderstand, I asked the same question over and over to the baker, who always had the same answer: "There won't be any bread today, nobody worked last night. Try tomorrow"

Dirty bastard! I wondered right away were all the flour went if they did not use it. To the black market for sure. Luckily we still had plenty of soup and bread left from the night before, given to us by the army cooks, otherwise we would have had to pull in our belts. As a matter of fact, we were supposed to have soup for lunch, but twelve o'clock seemed too far away, and our empty stomachs couldn't wait that long, so we helped ourselves prematurely.

In the meantime, while I was gone, some new soldiers had arrived and taken refuge in the grotto. About twenty five air force soldiers from the Ciampino Airport, the majority of them half dressed and bare footed, that walking through farms and fields, had missed being captured by the Germans.

Like everywhere else, everybody, soldiers and officers alike, were completely in the dark. For some reason or another, the order to surrender hadn't got there, and in the middle of the night, they were caught in bed sound asleep. It seemed that not more than a couple dozen of German pilots and soldiers, that had been stationed at the airport for quite a long time, taking advantage of the fact that our soldiers were still on friendly relations with them, free to walk around the camp unmolested and working separately or in groups of two or three men, they had approached our sentries and disarmed them one by one, then at gunpoint, they had forced more than hundred and fifty men out of their beds and locked them up in an empty storage room.

What a shame. This was one of the many cases, where needlessly, our soldiers had been humiliated and abused by the Germans, which it could have all been avoided if there had been a greater sense of responsibility in our Generals and their officers but, like rats on a sinking ship, they had thought only of themselves, the hell with the rest.

The night before I hadn't paid too much attention or gave much importance to what the sergeant had said about our country's leaders, but now I was beginning to think that maybe he was more than right.

The eight of September, started with the American bombing of Frascati, where eight thousand people lost their lives. In the afternoon the announcement of the armistice, in the evening the fighting broke out between the Germans and Italians.

It will be remembered as one of the darkest days in our country's history, in fact, that day, marked the end of one era, and the beginning of another one, the German occupation.

Sometimes it is very easy to criticize on my part, but looking at it in a different perspective, was it really a big mistake or a good move by the Italian command to surrender to the Germans? Yes there were five divisions defending Rome, but were actually our Infantry and light armored forces a good match for the German Panzer Division with over two hundred and fifty "Tiger" tanks that were rushing toward our city from Monterotondo? Without any doubts, the honor of our army would have been saved, but it would have been a complete massacre, maybe even the city itself would have suffered great damages, without mentioning the losses of lives among the population and to the old art and antique treasures that could have never been replaced.

Chapter 11

Three days later, the soldiers that extended their presence down at the grotto had all gone. Everyone for his own destiny, very few headed north, the rest headed south even though they all knew that there were no means of transportation of any kind available to them because the life of the whole nation had been paralyzed, without mentioning the great danger of being picked up by their angry ex allies, waiting at every corner with revenge in their hearts, they left behind them, the safety of the grotto, for the uncertainty of a very long and treacherous journey to their hometown, that many of them might reach, and many might not.

We knew for sure that the Germans were still desperately fighting down south, but we were not so sure if the Americans had landed in Salerno or not, a small city on the Tyrrhenian Sea, about seventy five miles from Naples. Like I said, we had no confirmation or any details of this operation, because the German propaganda machine was already at work, and the newspapers and radio controlled by the surging Fascist Party followers, were not divulging any military news. They were keeping the people completely in the dark.

At night, German columns made up of hundreds of our buses and trucks, spread out all over Italy, loaded with troops, ammunitions and supplies, kept rolling steadily on the main highways toward Naples and the front line. At the rate they were going, soon there wouldn't be a bus or truck left in the whole city, as they were taking almost everything that was on two or four wheels. Food and dry goods warehouses were invaded by the arrogant teutons and emptied to the bare walls, factories were dismantled, the machinery taken apart, and with many thousands of other items, including trolley buses, street cars, were all loaded in box cars and flat cars and shipped to the north and Germany.

They were everywhere and with the fascist's help, they kept a real close check on everything. A few old street cars overlooked by them, were running again, the flour mills were once more operating but unsteadily, as the wheat, corn and other dry legumes, were already beginning to fail to reach the warehouses. The stores had reopened their doors for business, but they did not have much to sell to the public

To make our life more miserable we got a cut on our daily rations of bread and macaroni, oil, lard, salt, meat of any kind, potatoes, charcoal, and any kind of essential as milk, butter, sugar, had become a rare item.

Papa' was back to work, but I was not, I had lost my job. Without even going back to the Statuario, I found out from some friends that the place had been shutdown, the reason was a shortage of material as we had feared, but also for another good reason. Down at the grotto, the foreman Nino, had been informed from the main office to discontinue the operations; to keep only Ruggiero and Ferrari on the payroll and to lay off the rest of the men working under him, until he received further orders personally from Mr. Spinelli.

Nobody could tell for sure what was behind such a drastic measure, but when Nino, who seemed to know quite a bit about Mr. Spinelli's past, had a couple of glasses of wine, he became quite a talker, and that night was one of those times the truth came out.

It seemed that Mr. Spinelli used to be an ardent fascist follower and a very good friend of Mussolini's son in-law, Ettore Ciano, who was one of the prominent figures of the Fascist Party. Their friendship, started in Africa during the Abyssinian war, which was exactly the same time that the fortune of Mr. Spinelli began.

For a long time, it was murmured that Ciano was the real owner of the land at the Statuario, where the housing project was being built, as well as all the farms around here, the grotto and the Golf Course. But being Ciano was first the Minister of the Exterior and after the Ambassador to the Vatican State, he not only had no time to look after this huge estate, but wanting to keep it a secret from the indiscreet eyes of the people and friends, gave carte blanc to Mr. Spinelli who became the administrator of this huge wealth.

When the Fascist Government was overthrown on the twenty fifth of July, many of their leaders with Ciano and Mussolini included, Mr. Spinelli claimed that the estate was his own, and got away from having all the properties confiscated. How he did, it remained a mystery, but at the time of the investigation, nobody was able to pin him down, no one could prove that he was not the rightful owner, and things remained as they had been up till then.

After the eight of September though, Mussolini was liberated by the Germans from Campo Imperatore, a mountain near Rome, where he was kept prisoner since the day of his fall, and helped him to reform a new Fascist Government.

As the fascists were coming back to power, bringing with them hate, revenge and a lot of trouble, many people trembled. Even Mr. Spinelli who once was one of them, and seemingly with a dirty conscience, knowing what their return meant to him, before it would be too late, was taking all precautionary measures to insure his wealth and immunity of his properties, as well as his own life, by disappearing from the scene until. . . . .who knows. Only time would tell.

As I said, the fascists were coming back and how. Many old timers who up till then had been silently and patiently avoiding to appear in public for fear of being recognized by their old victims, were now popping out form their hiding places, and once again, like they did in the early twenties, they were taking the initiative of reforming the brigades of black shirts. Even the Italian African police, was reorganized, so were the Guardie di Finanza (Frontier Guards) but the Carabinieri did not respond to the new government's call to join as easy as the others did. The carabinieri knew better. Being our fugitive king's most loyal troops, and the same ones that arrested Mussolini on the twenty fifth of July, knew that sooner or later, one way or another, he would make them pay for the mistake made by their monarch.

As for the Army, Navy and Air Force soldiers, in spite of the continued appeal from the government to join again, they refused to present themselves. Thousands of them had just got home, in fact lots of them hadn't got there yet, but they would rather starve and hide, than wear the uniform and collaborate with them or the Germans.

Since the Armistice, we had been waiting and wishing for the return of our dear Peppe, but so far, nothing. The last time we heard from him, was on September the sixth. The letter said that his ship a tow-boat was anchored in the Leghorn harbor for a checkup at the engines.

Every morning at dawn, since my younger brother Mario had come back from Ceprano, he had been going to the old house in Via Marmocchi, to bring food and clean clothes to nonno Edoardo, who lived there all by himself. After the eight of September though he went twice a day, morning and night. Papa' wanted to be sure that if Peppe came home, someone of the family besides nonno was there to welcome him and show him the way to our new place of residence.

Whenever we answered his letters, we always gave him the old address, so he would not worry about us, as a matter of fact, Peppe didn't know yet that our house had been bombed, because we never told him.

One day though, instead of good news, Mario came back with a red card, sent by the Chief of Police to my brother Carmine, ordering him to report immediately to Police Headquarters for questioning.

Many young men had already received those cards, and we knew what they were sent for. The fascists needed fresh blood to fill the ranks of their unpopular brigades, but they were not succeeding too well, and they were using every method they could to get it. Naturally the invitation was ignored, but Carmine on papa's orders, ended up by spending most of the days and nights, hiding in an abandoned smaller grotto, we found behind the house.

Naturally Carmine didn't like the idea at all, but it couldn't be helped.

Nonno Edoardo was instructed that whoever asked him about Carmine, he was to say that he was up north, Mario instead of going directly to the house, for the time being, was to meet nonno in different places.

After papa' inquired from some friend of his at the Police Headquarter, what was the procedure for cases like Carmine's, they told him, that the first two weeks after they sent the card, it was the most dangerous time because they usually sent someone to check, but after a couple of times that they couldn't find out nothing, they closed the file, and unless someone brought it up again, they forgot about it.

There was one more place where they could find out where we lived, and that was the depot where papa' worked. He had three weeks' vacation coming to him, and he thought that this was the best time to take them.

Of all the friends, relatives or people that we knew, no one had ever come to visit us, and apart from our present neighbors, no one else knew exactly where we lived, really, unless it was somebody that knew the place real well, it was almost impossible to find us, as the house was located right on the middle of a small valley surrounded by farce land, hidden from the highway and without a street name or a rural number.

Carmine's new quarters had its entrance right in the middle of a ravine, about two hundred feet behind our house, and well hidden from every indiscreet eye. Right from the beginning, this little grotto, was a real mystery to us, because we couldn't understand why whoever dug it went so far, then stopped. Surely Nino and the others must have known of its existence, but they never bothered with it because they had no use for it.

First of all, it was not more than five hundred feet long, but much narrower and not so high as the main grotto, but an ordinary man could comfortably stand up. Secondly, it was not on the same level as the other one, which seemed to go deeper into the bowels of the earth. Thirdly, about fifty feet before the end of the tunnel exactly where it crossed on top of the main grotto, there was a certain spot where you could distinctly hear everything that was said underneath.

Carmine discovered it one day during one of his many inspection of the tunnel. In fact, as he was moving along, when he heard some noise, he moved closer to where it was coming from, and by dusting off a fine layer of dirt, he found four pieces of very thick and wide construction planks resting flat on a couple of two by sixes.

With a feverish curiosity, he moved one of the planks, and what did he see through the cracks? A big ray of light coming through a ventilating shaft about ten feet long connecting the two grottos, from which besides hearing everything Nino and Ferrari were saying, being the hole right in the center of a huge room, he could see almost everything from corner to corner.

At supper time that night, he told us about his discovery, and papa' told him not to mention it to anyone, most of all to Nino, and when Carmine asked why, he answered by asking another question by saying: "Have you guys noticed how many times he has taken us right down into the heart of the grotto? Never. We don't know how much valuable stuff he has down there, maybe nothing at all, but being as jealous of his domain as he is, I wouldn't bet against it, and I am almost positive that if something was ever missing, he would blame it on us right away. Also I do sincerely hope that you don't have to ever to use it, but if you say that the shaft is wide enough for a person to go through, it wouldn't hurt to have a good rope handy. I have been worried by the thought, that if someone ever came looking for you, you would have been trapped like a rat. At least now you have a way of escape, and put my mind at ease."

"Now," he concluded, "once more I recommend that you stay in hiding as much as possible, because those guys out there are not fooling. They are picking up young men by the hundreds. Understand?"

Papa' was very concerned about Carmine, and he was taking all the precautions, but as we all knew, they were never enough. In the eyes of the new government, by not reporting to the authorities, my brother was a fugitive, a deserter, and if they ever caught him, he would be treated as such. Shot to death to make an example for the others, or sent to a German labor camp, and the thought of either one was not too appealing.

To make matters worse, Mr. Oliva's son had joined the Italian African Police, and Mr. Fano's son, four days later, had enrolled with the Fascist Brigades. The two pub owners never liked each other too well, from what we had heard, they had always been like cats and dogs, and we presumed that they must have forced their sons to join and put themselves on the safe side.

Since the day Mr. Fano forbade my brother to talk to his daughter, we never went back to his pub. And that didn't help any to better our relations. On many occasions he openly showed his hostility toward papa', but my father never paid any attention to him. He was not worth it, he said.

Three days after his son had enrolled with the Fascist Brigades, he came home that afternoon all dressed up in a shiny uniform, armed with an automatic rifle and hand grenades, parading around as though he owned the earth.

Later that same evening, to prove to some friends of his that the weapons he had were the real thing, he threw a hand grenade in the back yard, scaring the wits out of Ruggiero and his family who were seated outside having their supper.

When Mario and I got there to see what was happening, while the stupid punk, thinking that what he just done was funny, was bragging and laughing his head off, Ruggiero was furious. Usually calm and friendly with anyone, he did not look like himself at all. Shouting and shaking his head with rage, the veins which stood out in his thick red neck and face, normally of olive complexion, were then swollen and drawn under his skin, ready to burst any second. Luckily for Mr. Fano's son that Nino and some other men were on hand to keep them apart, until Mr. Fano and his wife warned by their daughter, came running out of the cellar as fast as their fat bellies would permit them, and angrily pulled their son away from the scene, just in time to avoid a clash between the two.

How much we could believe of what our neighbors said about Mr. Fano, was impossible to measure, because we were newcomers here, therefore, we had to go by what little bits and pieces of information we could gather by just listening to them talk, but the general opinion seemed to be that he was quite a character not to be trusted. He was the type of guy that would strike in the dark in his own way and at the right moment, when no one could see him.

Maybe the incident of that evening would have no ill consequences, but if the son was half as bad and vindictive as his father was, soon we would hear from him and somebody would suffer.

September went by without any other incident worth mentioning. Paolo and all the men working under the grotto, had left for their homes right after they were laid off and the dwelling they occupied was closed. Since then, we had been living all alone, and finally at the beginning of October, the new tenants for the next door apartment arrived, and we were very pleased. The component's family were three, Piero, tall and handsome a former soldier that lost one arm in Africa, his wife Rosa, not too beautiful but very sympathetic, and their only two year old son Leo. Immediately we became friends, mamma and Rosa seemed to like each other very much on sight. At last mamma had found companionship, they got along real well and we were glad, so had papa' in Piero. Together they spent hours talking about the old times and the localities were Piero came from, where papa' had spent his soldiers years in 1917-18. Piero used to work under the grotto before he was drafted into the Army, and knew the surroundings and the farmers quite well. Through him, we were able to buy a little lamb, which was the nicest thing that happened to us for the longest time, believe me, if we had received a gift of a million lire, it would not have been appreciated more.

My little sister Maria was delighted, so was Leo. We never owned one before and soon the little animal became a household pet. It was with consternation in our hearts, when we thought of the time he would become the main course of our meal, but for the time being, we couldn't deprive Maria of amusing herself with her constant companion. She tied a bow and a little bell on the rope around his neck and wherever she went the poor lamb had to follow.

She spent all day long picking up fresh and tender grass for "Pasqualino" combing him and dressing him like as if he was a little doll. At night she held him in her delicate little arms until they both fell asleep, and only then with her eyes half shut, did she let it be taken away from her.

The weather got worse as October came rolling along, raining almost and very unusually every day, and we were confined to our homes more and more with nothing to do. Time was long, and the evening endless. News dribbled in very secretively that the Neapolitans had been harassing the Germans for days, and at last actually broke out in full armed revolt before the advancing American troops finally arrived to liberate them and Naples.

To our surprise, it seemed that every morning Piero our next door neighbor, was always well Informed on the latest events, and one day after a few pointed questions he finally confided that he had been listening to the radio and a special program called: "Radio Londra" (The Voice of London).

This went on every night at Nino's office, with Ruggiero, Ferrari and other close friends attending.

Piero begged us to keep it a secret, and promised to take us too if we cared to go, but when papa' and I went down for the first time, we were discouraged by the cold reception we got. That same night, many more people had the same idea, and for fear of being discovered, Nino called the evening off, and we never tried again.

As time went on, our supply of meat increased as our little lamb had become almost a medium size lamb, and by mid November, we were tempted to stop his growth, but at the mere mention of killing him, Maria threw a fit. We were faced with the problem of how the feat would be accomplished when the proper time came.

Food was getting harder and harder to obtain, as the food stores were completely out of any type of food supplies. They were going on day by day, at least that is what they claimed, but if you were in the know, some essential articles as flour, bread, macaroni, oil and salt or sugar, could be bought if you had the money to meet their prices. The Borsa hera (Black Market) was booming, and money among their operators was floating easily. With luck, some of these people were managing to accumulate tremendous fortunes.

While the first Fascist Government were in power, and during the duration of the war under them, they never did much good for the people. But not even they would tolerate these black market dealings. If they were found, they were shot to death without much ceremony. Now instead, amid this chaos they were working freely, and in many cases, they were getting their supplies directly from the Germans, the fascists and from the Vatican.

In fact, riding under the immunity and protection of the white and yellow flag of the Vatican City, the huge fleet of trucks and trailers, were free to travel anywhere in Italy and abroad without being molested or controlled by neither the Germans or the fascists. It was a lucrative business chain that involved hundreds of persons, from the big guys with money to the small profiteers, who taking advantage of the great need of the people and with ready access to most of the above mentioned items, were charging fabulous prices for their merchandise.

Monday morning, the whole family was up bright and early. We got wind that at the nearest store, had arrived a whole truck load of charcoal, so while we left mamma and Mario in line to get some, papa' and I proceeded for Piazza Vittorio and Alibrandi's, the well renowned butcher shop, where they had just received some hogs.

Maybe the word hadn't been out yet, because when we got there, there was only a short line of customers, and surprisingly, in a matter of half hour, we were in and out each one of us with half kilo of beautiful pork sausages.

Laughing and joking, we were happily walking along under the arcades of Piazza Vittorio, when papa had to spoil by saying: "You know what? While we are here, we might as well pay a visit to our old friend Signor Spizzichino. Maybe we can find a winter coat for your sister. She sure needs one. What do you think?"

"Papa', you know how much I hate that place. Why don't you go ahead alone, in the meantime I could go back to Alibrandi's. With a little bit of luck, I might be able to get more sausages."

"Don't make me laugh will you? Do you think the policeman at the door is stupid? That guy has eagle eyes, he will recognize you right away, besides, and I doubt it if there was much meat left. Come on. Come on. Signor Spizzichino will be glad to see you after all this time."

"Sure. Sure. He will welcome me with the red carpet. That cheap son of a bitch." But I hadn't finished saying it when I had already regretted it. Papa' put on the brakes so suddenly, that instinctively I jumped to one side, just in time to avoid his big blow that whistled by missing me by a hair.

"Don't you ever use that kind of language in front of me or anybody else," he said, his face turning as red as a hot pepper. "Mascalzone. Come on."

Like a beaten dog, I put my tail between my legs and at a safe distance I tried to follow him, amid the traffic that as the city was awakening, was getting heavier and heavier.

Piazza Vittorio is a real huge square from every sense of the word. At the end of the building there are arcades, we crossed the street and as we entered the other arcade, someone going in the other direction, very quickly drew my attention.

A red headed tall guy was walking very fast ahead of us. There was nothing being red headed, but in Rome especially, you don't see too many of them at any time. The majority of our men usually are dark haired, that's the reason why it caught my eyes right away, and I don't know why, it immediately made me think of Sandy. I had always seen him dressed in shorts and Khaki shirts, with his hair cut very high and short, this guy instead was wearing light brown pants, a heavy brown winter coat with his collar turned up, and his hair in the back were square and low and thick like we all had. From behind, his wide shoulders, and the way he was walking, leaning very lightly first to one side, then the other, resembled a lot like Sandy. Now suppose it was Sandy, what in hell was he doing here in Piazza Vittorio at nine thirty in the morning? I wished papa' moved a little faster so I could catch up with him, and for a moment I almost told him about my doubts, after all he knew Sandy, by name of course, because I had mentioned his name quite often, but in the mood he was in, I didn't dare. Besides, as we passed a hardware store, he stopped to look for a paraffin lamp and almost bought it, but when the owner told him that he had no kerosene, he left it there.

When we got to Signor Spizzichino, he gave us the biggest and warmest welcome, as though we were his own relatives, but after that, the crying began, complaining that he was a victim of the war. Knowing that he was a Jew, many old fascists, came daily to his store, bought what he called the cream of the crop, but very seldom paid what he asked for it. He called them, "a bunch of rascals and parasites." I doubt very much if he would have talked like that to someone else, but he knew that my father was on his side and could trust him, so the poor man let some of the steam out. He talked and talked, and we patiently listened to him, then: "But why am I crying on your shoulders, when I know that you must have your own problems. Let me see, what can I do for you today?"

"I need a winter coat for my little girl Maria," answered papa'.

"Yes. Yes. Maria. She must have grown quite a bit since the last time I saw her. How old is she now?"

"Almost nine. She is about this high," said papa' bringing his hand just below the belt, "and very tiny."

"Any special color you have in mind?"

"Not especially. As long as it is nice and warm, and even if it is a little bigger, it doesn't matter, she will grow into it."

He stopped to think for a second or two, then: "Come with me in the back of the store, I think I've got exactly what you are looking for."

As they both disappeared behind the double doors, I had just set my eyes on a beautiful white shirt, when from inside the bathroom, located right behind the counter of the cash register, I heard someone pulling the toilet chain, then the door swung wide open, and who came out of it? The red headed guy that I had seen fifteen minutes ago walking under the arcade, but this time I had no doubt about his identity and from the deep of my lungs I called: "Sandy!"

"Armando!"

Spontaneously we threw ourselves into each other's arms, and when we let go, I was the first to break the silence.

"I always thought that by this time you would have been safe and sound behind the allied lines, instead, here you are in Rome. Did you come in to buy something?"

"No. No. No." He started out laughing. "I work here for Signor Spizzichino."

I could hardly believe my ears, and for a moment I remained speechless and somewhat undecided as to what to say next, because not only had he spoken to me in Italian, but in perfect Roman dialect. His words had bewildered me, but they had also hurt me, deep, deep inside. I had always doubted that he understood our language, but between a doubt and a certainty there is a big difference. The sole fact that he understood and spoke it very clearly, in itself, was not very important, what really bothered me, was the fact that all the time that we had spent together, while I had trusted him in any sense of the word, he had mocked me, he had betrayed my naivety, my friendship. Why. Why did he do it? What was the reason? There must have been a very important one for him to hide it from me, but that did not help me in any way. I was so upset and so indignant, that he must have read it on my face, because he put his hand over my shoulder and started to say something when, Signor Spizzichino and my father came back, and the surprise of the surprises, was given to me, when Sandy walked toward my father saying: "Buongiorno Signor Viselli. Come sta'?"

"Good morning. Look, look who is here!" My father exclaimed, stretching his hand to shake Sandy's. "It has been such a long time since the last I saw you. You are a man now. "

In the meantime having regained my composure from the sudden shock, I tried to butt in saying: "Papa' this is Sandy my polish friend." But it was like talking to a stone wall, as he kept repeating.

"I know him, you don't have to tell me. I have almost seen him grow up in this store." Then turning again to Sandy: "By the way, how is your schooling? Did you finally graduate?"

"Well. Not precisely," answered Sandy. "Many, many things have happened since the last time we met."

"Papa' he was in the concentration camp behind Cinecitta', and he is the same guy that was working with me at the Statuario. You remember I spoke of him more than once to you and mamma. You remember?"

This time it was my father's turn to be shocked.

"Him a war prisoner? Are you crazy?"

"Yes. Armando is right. I have been in the camp since nineteen forty one." "Well. This is really news to me, and kind of disappointing," turning to his old pal: "How come you never mention it to me?"

"Forgive me Mr. Viselli. But it is such a sad long story, and I thought that you wouldn't have been interested to hear. By the way, someone told me that you lost your house and that you had to move," said Signor Spizzichino changing purposely the unpleasant subject. "Where are you exactly staying right now?"

"I rented a house at the Acquasanta."

"At the Acquasanta? Isn't that where you played golf?" He turned inquiringly to Sandy.

"Yes. Yes uncle. You are right." And looking at us: "Then you must be living in one of the houses above the grotto where they grow mushrooms," he added showing more

Interest. "I know that place so well, in fact I loved that area so much, beautiful open country, peaceful, quiet. That is where I used to go horse riding after every game of golf."

"Then, you must come and see us sometimes, we don't have much to offer, but there is still a fairly good glass of wine at Mr. Oliva's," said my father.

"Oh good old Mr. Oliva's, is his lovely young daughter Santina married yet?"

"No, she is not, but she is as beautiful as ever."

"If that is the case, I must come to see you one of these fine days," said Sandy with a gleam in his eyes.

As an old couple walked into the store, Sandy looked at them and took off through the back doors. Papa' was ready to resume the dealing, because he had already pulled out some money from his wallet, but this time there was no need, as signor Spizzichino rolled the beautiful lamb coat in a heavy sheet of paper, and shoving it under my father's arm, he said: "This is my Christmas present for Maria. Go now go!!"

Papa' tried to argue with him but to no avail, and as he pushed us toward the exit, before we walked out in a low voice he said: "Mr. Viselli, mi raccomando. Not a word to anyone eh. Arrivederci."

Everything had happened so fast, that I was still astonished, yet, my mind was not rested, trying to put all the pieces together, when as though talking to himself aloud, thinking the same thing that I must have been thinking, suddenly my father exclaimed: "That explains why he disappeared so suddenly."

"Yes papa'. He was studying in England, and that is where he enlisted in the British army."

"Ho capito. I understand, now everything is clear to me."

Maybe it was clear for him, not for me, and since the puzzle was still quite complicated, I asked if Sandy called Signor Spizzichino uncle, does it means that he is related to him somehow?

"Certainly his mother is Signor Spizzichino's sister. After the death of his two sons in an automobile accident, realizing that he was getting up in years, and that at his death he would have no one to leave his business to, he asked his sister if she would have liked to send him the youngest of her sons. She agreed, and I am not too sure of when he got here, but if I am not mistaken, it was either during or after the Spanish war. He was a frightened little boy then and couldn't speak a single word of Italian. Listen to him now, he sounds like a Roman."

"I know. And this particular fact, really drives me up a wall. Why did he keep it a secret from me and the rest of the gang that worked with him?"

"You fool. Have you ever realized the advantages he had over his captors by remaining incognito? I don't know how good his English is, but that boy, speaks fluently in polish, German and Italian. Besides, he is a Jew, and his real name is not Sandy, but Samuele. Do you know that the Jews are being persecuted everywhere? Do you know that they are dying by the thousands? And I presume, that the less the people knew about him the better it was. The heart doesn't hurt if the eye cannot see, capisci?"

With the sun shining up there, it was a beautiful fall day, instead of going around the piazza, we decided to cut through the park.

It felt good to get away from the cement sidewalks, the street, the noise and the people. The trees still had all their leaves, the grass was a rich green bottle, and the air was clean and fresh, but the benches along the path were empty, with a solitary old man here and there, and all around us, silence, dead silence.

There was no signs of children playing under their mothers watchful eyes, the kiosk where the puppet theater with all the marionettes that entertained not only kids, but people of all ages, was now shut, and the row of sitting benches in front of it, vacant and cold. There was no water running from the drinking fountain, nor was there any water in the little pond. The canal feeding the pond was dry and full of rubbish, and the little hillock of granite from where the water was rushing down forming fall after fall, was now covered with a thick mould of greenish color that looked like velvet. This was supposed to be the cat's sanctuary for hundreds of them.

I don't remember how many times I stopped there to watch them. It was a real past time, and a very interesting sight especially at feeding time, when the former owners came to take care of their pets. They were all hungry and they were all waiting, yet, when the old familiar voice called, only one, the one that belonged, came near meowing. He ate enough to satisfy its need, and then and only then, when he was satiated, he would share his food with his less fortunate companions.

When I didn't see any around, for a moment I thought that they were on the other side of the hillock warming themselves up in the sun, but even there, there was nothing but bare granite. I asked my father where they all went and he burst out laughing.

"The Romans should know where they all went. After all if a cat is well cooked, it tastes as good as any rabbit, and only his head will tell the difference, especially if they show it to you after you had just finished eating it."

Chapter 12

One evening in the last week of November, while we were all seated in our bedroom around the fire pot, we were startled by a cautious knock at the door. Taking a chance on spending this cold and rainy night with us, Carmine, that was startled just as much as we were, quickly darted under the huge bed of our parents

"This type of weather is only good for ducks. Who could that be?" Asked papa' looking, inquisitively at us, then getting up and reaching for the hatchet teaming against the wall behind the bedroom door, looking directly at me he ordered: "See who it is."

We had heard so many unpleasant things happening in the last couple of months, that we couldn't trust anybody anymore. Since we moved out here, papa' always had his revolvers hidden in both night table drawers, but after the Germans enforced the law to turn in all firearms, his old Mauser, and the newer Beretta, ended up under the shingles of the roof. After that, he relied entirely on a brand new hatchet.

"It is not as fast as a gun, but it is silent, and just as deadly," he said the day that he brought it home. "Let's hope that we never have to use it."

Opening the door, in the dim blue light, I could not recognize the tall figure standing there all bundled up in a black trench coat with the hood pulled over his head until cheerfully he called me by name. Recognizing his voice instantly, I yelled: "It is Mr. Nino. It is Mr. Nino papa'."

"Well. Let him in," he answered from behind me, putting the hatched back in its usual place.

Shaking himself like a shaggy dog, Nino stepped inside the house, and we shut out the night once more.

"You don't give us the honor of your presence too often," Papa' said coming forward. "To what do we have to attribute your pleasant visit? Please, come and sit down near the fire pot."

"No. No. Thank you Sr. Sebastiano. I am sorry to inconvenience you at this hour, but it is something very important that brought me here. . . .And if it is not asking too much, I would like to talk to you in private."

"Well," answered papa' with a deep chuckle in his belly, "you know this apartment if not better, as well as I do, there are only two rooms all together, so take your pick."

Naturally they chose the kitchen, and everybody moved back into the bedroom, closing the door behind me. After a good half hour, papa' invited me to join them in the conversation, and briefly, Nino instructed me in what he wanted me to do for him, and with a shaking of hands he saluted and left.

Next morning at the farm house, which was about a kilometer from where we lived, Mr. Tortore, a farmer that I had previously met, was expecting me with several parcels of food, and a bundle of clothing, which I had to pick up and deliver to someone waiting for me at an appointed place near the Central Station Terminal. A few minutes before ten o'clock, time of the rendezvous, I set the package down to rest my tired arms and looked around for a familiar face. Nino would not mention any names the night before, but told me that it was someone I knew, and that someone, whoever he was, knew me.

Curiosity was getting the better of me, as I recalled the secretive way all this came about, and I was wondering, where those packages would finally find a resting place. Could these parcels be intended for someone hiding from the police? The mystery was real intriguing me, and I would soon find out who this mysterious person was, but looking around, I saw no one, and impatiently I decided to roll a cigarette. Between puffs, as people went by in every direction, I tried to visualize which of them could be the one, could be this one, could be that one, but so far I had been wrong every time, and after several minutes, I started wondering if I had come to the right place.

I was positive, there was no mistake, I was in Via Marsala, and this was the building with the bar right at the corner. I had noticed a man wearing a black coat and a black hat, pacing up and down the sidewalk on the opposite side of the street, but I doubted very much if he was the person concerned, because if he was, why had he not come to see me by now?

After what seemed a long while, I inquired about the time. Twenty past ten. Wow, I had already been here more than twenty minutes and with the wind blowing from a north direction, I was getting colder and colder. Pushing my hands further down in my coat pockets, I promised myself that I was going to wait another ten minutes, and if no one showed up I was going home.

The man in the black coat must have sensed my thoughts, or noticed my impatience, because he quickly crossed the street, approached me and without stopping he ordered me to follow him. He went by me so fast that I couldn't see his face, but there was something in his commanding voice that couldn't be mistaken.

It was Mr. Spinelli himself, the "Commendatore" my former employer, our landlord, the owner of the farms, the grotto and the Statuario housing project. Suddenly everything was clear to me, and that explained why there was so much secrecy about the whole affair.

We boarded the next tramway Number Nine and sat one opposite the other. As he kept looking outside the window, I had a close look at him, and strangely enough, had pity for him. The old hat was pulled over his eyes, the collar of his greasy coat lifted covering his neck, a sickish look on his unshaven face for at least three or four days, he resembled more a convalescent patient just coming out of the hospital and not the old elegantly dressed Mr. Spinelli, a man that only a few months ago, everybody respected and feared.

At the Parioli, a residential district, one of the newer sections of the city, we got off and he led the way to a luxurious apartment building. In the lobby we stopped, and for the first time since we had met, with his usual imperative voice, he broke the ice asking: "Do you remember who I am?"

"Certainly! You are Mr. Spin. . ."

"Never mind that!" Abruptly cutting me short before I could fully pronounce his name. "From now on, whatever you hear or see is none of your business. Don't you ever mention my name or this address to anyone and everything will work out fine between you and me. Is it clear? No one."

Waiting for a second or two to get an answer from me, as I was only able to nod my head, he proceeded.

"Now, listen carefully. Go upstairs to the third floor, knock at apartment seven and ask for Miss Cora. She is expecting you and knows what to do, but pay attention now, if the person answering the door is not a young lady, forget it, excuse yourself and rush back. Hai capito? But I am almost sure she is in. She has red hair and probably wearing maternity clothes. You know what I mean? She is expecting a baby, you can't miss her. In case there is no answer, here is the key," pulling it out of his pant pocket. "Go in, look in every room and make sure that there is no one and come right back. And don't forget the bathroom. Go now and hurry."

I have always found stories of intrigue and mystery very interesting, but I never expected to take part in a real one, and at that very moment my heart was beating a lot faster than usual with excitement. What would I find up there?

Climbing the stairs two steps at the time, I reached the third floor, stopped for a few seconds to regain my breath, then slowly I walked to the door marked with a shining number seven and gently knocked several times. I heard some steps approaching and almost instantly the door opened partly, showing a tall slender young lady with a beautiful face and thick long copper red hair falling loosely over her shoulders and wearing a light silk robe.

"What is it?" She asked with anxiety in her voice.

Immediately I noticed that she was not wearing any maternity clothes, but a quick glance at her slightly protruding belly, was enough to assure me that I had the right person and place and just to double check, I asked: "Are you Miss Cora?"

"Yes. Yes. At last, I was waiting for you." Taking the chain off the catch and opening the door wide, she pulled me gently inside saying: "Come in. Come in. I will be right back." Running along the corridor and rushing downstairs.

A minute later, puffing and panting, they both reappeared, closed the door and while he gave a dirty look as he passed me, they proceeded toward the kitchen where they unloaded all the parcels on the kitchen table.

After the heavy necking was over, he finally freed himself from her embrace, then while he was busy in the bathroom shaving and taking a bath I helped Miss Cora to clean the vegetables. When he came out, looking like a human being again, acting as though I was not even there, they started all over again.

Miss Cora couldn't have been more than twenty seven, twenty eight years old, and compared to him she looked like his daughter, but by their behavior, they gave me the impression of being everything but father and daughter. Naturally, remembering what he had said to me earlier downstairs, I shut my ears and closed my eyes, trying to keep busy, washing over and over the fresh lettuce. In spite of her youth, Miss Cora seemed to be an experienced cook, and between a kiss and a sip of vermouth, another kiss and another sip of vermouth, around one o'clock, dinner was ready to be served. The table was loaded with so much food that I could hardly believe my eyes. I hadn't seen such a rich assortment for ages. Chicken noodle soup, breaded veal cutlets, fried potatoes, tossed green salad in olive oil and vinegar, chunk of cheese, homemade bread, black grapes and apples, all fresh food from Mr. Tortore's farm.

Wow. I could almost taste everything in my mouth, but when it came time to eat, I felt as though my movements were frozen, and I couldn't explain what it was. I never felt at ease in front of Mr. Spinelli, his presence alone made me very uncomfortable, his rude manners, his dictatorial ways, the cool look in his eyes had always given me a sensation of fear and distrust, and now, damn him, more than ever. Everything looked so delicious and inviting, but just the thought of sitting at the table with him, watching me eating, spoiled my appetite, and when finally the meal was over, even though my stomach was still empty, I felt a lot better and relaxed.

Right after the dishes were done, the boss handed over to me a list of all the things he wanted me to pick up at the farm the following morning, a sealed letter for Nino, and with a warning to keep my mouth shut once more, he sent me away saying: "For today, take the afternoon off, but be here by nine thirty tomorrow morning and don't forget, I like punctuality."

From there on, day after day, with very little change in the schedule, I followed the same routine, every morning I gave Mr. Tortore the order for the following day, he handed me the two shopping bags full of groceries, meats, fruits, and fresh vegetables, and from there I was on my way to the apartment.

Right from the beginning, even though I ate there, it seemed to me that we were consuming a lot a food. Even if I shared one meal a day with them, they were only two people, and I am sure it was more than they actually needed, while at the house my family had less than the bare essentials.

One morning I decided to do something about it. Instead of going straight out to board the street car, I made a short stop at the house. Mamma was surprised to see me back so soon, and when I confided to her my intentions, she was terrified and tried to stop me, but I went ahead with my plans just the same. One by one, I opened all the packages and took out part of their contents, then carefully wrapped then up again. I didn't dare take out too much, Miss Cora might notice it, but a little bit here, a little bit there, was enough to fill my little sister and younger brother's bellies, at least for a fair meal anyway.

I knew exactly what I was doing, it was plain stealing, but I also knew that God would forgive me, after all, He himself said, "help yourself and I will help you," and that was exactly what I was doing.

The operation was repeated morning after morning as regular as clock work, and to make sure not to arouse any suspicions in the lady of the house, I unwrapped everything as soon as I got to the apartment and placed it in the containers or into the ice box.

In spite of my dislike for Mr. Spinelli, I enjoyed my new job. It was clean and easy, I was decently dressed all the time, the hours were reasonable and the salary was very good. As far as Miss Cora's character was concerned, hers was the opposite of his. She was very sympathetic and very kind. Courtesy was her motto, and thanks to her wonderful sense of humor and companionship, my time flew by.

Her gay young voice was like a ray of sunshine in the house, and at times, I wondered how a nice looking girl like her, ever got mixed up with a man like Mr. Spinelli, who to me, was nothing but a great big bear always in bad humor.

Talking about bad humor, one evening in December, papa' was furious.. When he was in that mood, I knew by experience that the best thing was to stay away from him. To find out what was the cause of his unusual behavior, I signaled to Mario to come outside, and this was the story he gave me.

Late in the afternoon, a group of young fascists with Mr. Fano's son leading the pack, after spending several hours drinking and playing cards at his father's pub, went first to Nino's and Ferrari's houses, then came to our place and Piero's looking for an unknown cache of arms, holding everybody at gunpoint while searching through the apartments. Carmine, who had been spending a good deal of time with us lately, had just left to go back to his hiding place and was missed by them by minutes. Naturally, when papa' came home from work and found out what had happened, ignoring mamma and Piero who were begging him to forget the incident, sputtering and purple with rage, rushed to Mr. Fano's pub, but since his son was not there, grabbed him by the neck and shaking him vigorously, warned the old pot full of worms that if anything happened to our family, him and that son of a bitch of his son, would have to deal with him.

Mr. Fano with a yellow streak in him, a mile long and a yard wide, shivering with fear was trying to free himself from papa's iron grip, at the same time mumbling and stuttering that he did not know what papa' was talking about, yelled for help. His wife ran to the door, but only to find that everybody was coming, but not to help, especially Ruggiero who hadn't forgotten the grenade incident of a month or so ago. Taking papa's side, reminded Mr. Fano that it was about time that someone told him off adding that we didn't like to be pushed around not by him and less yet by his son and son's friends. "Because they wear that black shirt doesn't mean that they have the right to terrorize our families," he had said angrily. "If they do not stop acting foolishly I will report them to the "Capo Sezione" and if that is not enough, by Jesus, if it is trouble that you people want, just say so, we will try to accommodate you."

That same evening, papa' still in his towering rage and unable to calm down, blew his top at poor mamma for not keeping my brother Carmine away from the house, at the same time, turning his angry eyes at me he said: "What is this I have been hearing about you? Are my sons going to turn thieves too? Is this the way you are repaying Mr. Spinelli for giving you a job?"

"But papa' I thought that…"

"Never mind what you thought," cutting me sharply. "That kind of help I do not need, and we will have no more of that," pointing his finger threateningly at me, and in a thundering voice: "Understand? No more. We will manage with what food we are able to buy like everybody else."

For the next couple of days, we expected to have some retaliations from Mr. Fano and his son, but there was no sign of either one. I had seen papa' take down his revolvers from under the roof and clean it under mama's despairing eyes, in fact she begged him to put them back, but he told her not to interfere.

"It is my business," he said sharply, and since then, no one knew where he kept them. Those last two days had been like two long years, everybody was nervous, and at night nobody slept. The littlest sound and everyone in the family was up, and finally the third day when we received news that Mr. Fano's son had been transferred somewhere in Northern Italy, we all felt relieved.

"Good, good for him," papa' commented that evening with a cold look in his eyes. "I swear that if he ever came around to molest us, he was going to get his share of lead in his belly, but I guess it is better this way. I hope the partisans will take care of him up there."

While this was going on, at work I was badly worried and even mentioned to Miss Cora who had already noticed the signs of preoccupation on my face, and as if the matter interested her personally, anxiously inquired every morning. When I told her that everything was back to normal, she was very pleased. Dear Miss Cora, she was so sweet.

As for Mr. Spinelli, as far as I knew, he had never left the apartment since the day he moved in. He was reading all the time, lately he had confined himself to the bedroom, and other than meal time, I saw very little of him. He was getting more irritable than ever, but I was also beginning to understand him and his moods much better now, and as long as he didn't take it out on me personally, I didn't pay too much attention to what he said. His growling was a part of him and his unfriendly personality.

I hadn't stopped at the house any more since papa' had told me that night, and that morning, as usual I picked up the supplies and started for the apartment, but when I got there, to my big surprise, Miss Cora and Mr. Spinelli were already up and busy packing some clothes in a suitcase. Apparently one of them was leaving, and immediately wondered whether that was going to be the end of my job, at which thought, feeling a sudden depression, I walked straight to the kitchen and started putting away the groceries. I found out later that it was the boss that was leaving, and his departure was not affecting me and my job in any way, in fact the orders were still the same, except that now Miss Cora was under my care until he came back, and instead of leaving the apartment at three o'clock as I had been doing for the last months, I had to remain until five o'clock.

The added responsibility made me feel very important, and at the same time a little more self conscious. In fact, when the time came for me to leave, a worrying thought assailed me because of her precarious conditions. It was women's business, and I didn't understand much about it, but listening to them talk, I gathered she must have had another four months to go at least before her baby would arrive.

What would happen if she was all alone during the night and suddenly she should need a doctor or something? As far as I knew, she had no relatives or friends close by, and the only means of communications with the outside, was the telephone that half of the time was not working or the line was busy.

Lately it had become a habit with me, In fact at the last moment, just before I stepped outside, I would ask her, "will you be all right until I come back tomorrow?"

"Ha ha ha. Sure," she would reply smiling. "Cora is a big girl now, she can take care of herself. Stop worrying and go home, before you get caught on the street by the patrols. You only have two hours left before curfew time. Go now. Go." Then she would open the door and gently push me outside saying: "See you tomorrow. Good night"

Every day, when she went out to do her shopping, I accompanied her, and on those little trips consulted me about her various purchases, which bolstered my ego a great deal. She could see that I knew very little or nothing at all about ladies clothes, but it didn't matter, she took the trouble to show me things, and it pleased her to hear my approval or disapproval. Walking beside her, made me feel like a man because she treated me like one, and naturally I was very grateful to her. She counted and confided in me as much as I did in her, and slowly a warm friendship developed between us.

It had become almost a habit for her, that if we didn't go out shopping, after lunch as soon as the dishes were done, she would go to bed for an hour or so, while I read or relaxed on the living room couch. The bedroom region had always been out of bounds for me, nor had I ever attempted to go in, but this afternoon I heard her cough first and then I had the impression that she was crying. I could have been mistaken, but to make sure I called out: "Are you feeling well Miss Cora?"

"Yes. I am fine." She answered in a very weak voice. Then a little louder, "Will you please bring me a glass of water?"

I went to the kitchen and as I passed by the sink, I opened the cold water tap to let it run for a while, then I got a glass from the kitchen cupboard, filled it and hurriedly walked toward the bedroom, in my haste, spilling almost half on the rug, knocked at the door and when she ordered me to enter, I walked in the room.

She was laying on the bed, propped up on two pillows with a light cover over her. She reached for the glass, but in doing so, the movement caused her robe to fall aside, exposing a full well rounded breast with a pink nipple like a delicate flower bud. Instantly feeling my face catching fire. I turned my head away full of embarrassment. She noticed right away, then with a surprised look in her eyes, with a gentle smile she asked: "What is the matter Armando? You have never seen a woman's body before?"

Shocked by her words, I turned and looked at the beautiful face that I had worshipped as a goddess since I had known her, but unable to speak I lowered my eyes and remained silent.

Laughing at my embarrassment, she caught my shirt and gently pulled me toward her. I tried to say something, but I only heard myself stutter, which made me feel more and more like an idiot, then, while still smiling, she took my hands and slowly laid them on her gleaming flesh. Confused and surprised I kept trying but I couldn't speak as a warm tingling sensation crept up my arms and surged through my whole body, with a throbbing pulse pounding in my ears.

Quickly I pulled my hands away as though I had just received an electric shock and rushed away from the room, mortified and a little ashamed of myself. I thrust my hands deep in my pants pocket and pacing the kitchen floor up and down, I began wondering what I should do next. I felt I could never face her again, and yet, I wanted to go back there and touch her soft body again, hold her in my arms and tell her that I loved her. But to do those things, a person needs lots of courage, and at that very moment I am afraid to say that I did not have it.

Go back, go back, something kept repeating inside me, don't be a coward, but I did not dare, I was frozen to the pavement, my legs wouldn't move. Standing there in the middle of the kitchen, trying to collect my jumbled thoughts, I noticed the bedroom door opened, and slowly she came up to me saying: "I am sorry if I have embarrassed you. Come on. Let's make a good cup of coffee and forget the whole thing. We are still good friends, aren't we?"

We finished the day as though nothing had happened, but at home the same night I couldn't sleep. Visions of her loveliness kept appearing before my closed eyes, making me toss and turn till finally Mario my younger brother who shared the bed with me again, woke up and yelled: "Are you going to stop? It is the fourth time that you have pulled the blankets off me."

"Shut up," I said angered.

"And you stay quiet. This is a bed, not a dancing hall"

The noise woke up papa' and immediately we both changed tune, as I hissed a very long "Shhhhhhh" to Mario and threw all the blankets over to cover him, after which I laid there wide awake and tormented until the early light of dawn came through the window. It must have been papa's day off because I didn't hear him get up to go to work, so as quietly as possible, so as not to awake anybody. I slid slowly from the bed, dressed and tip toeing, went to the kitchen. There I washed my face and combed my hair, then walking in the brisk cold of the December morning I rushed to get our daily ration of bread and by the time I got back, it was time to go to the farm, where I picked up my usual two bags of groceries and with an empty feeling in my stomach, I hurried toward the apartment and Miss Cora.

Chapter 13

Winter was in the air with the Christmas Season approaching. The little lamb had been growing by leaps and bounds, and without any doubt he would provide us with an ample meat supply for quite a while. There was still plenty of time to prepare Maria for the upcoming painful separation, and knowing how much she loved her Pasqualino, I began to wonder if she would accept a new playmate when the lamb would be finally butchered. In the meantime, I had to find something to replace her precious lamb, and once I did, I decided that I would bring it home one evening when coming back from work.

In talking to Miss Cora about it, she sympathetically suggested to look for a little puppy, the best suited candidate to replace the beloved lamb, and that afternoon, we both went out, making a trip to Piazza Vittorio, especially for that reason, but when we got there, there was none.

"Nowadays, a dog is a luxury, not a pet anymore," a pet owner told us. "Who can afford to keep a dog, when there is not enough food for our children?"

It sounded unbelievable, but it was the holy truth. We could say nothing but agree with him, and in leaving the premises, I felt very depressed, but not for long, as Miss Cora was there to cheer me up, in fact: "Never mind the pets, come with me," she said. "We will find something."

At a toy shop, after looking around, she selected the largest doll available, with spontaneous generosity she paid for it, and handing it over to me she said: "There. We are all set now. You will see Maria will be happy with it."

She did everything so casually, that her noble gesture caught me completely by surprise, and deeply touched, I remained lost for words.

For the first time in public, she tucked her arm under my elbow and guided me out of the store. Spontaneously, as though it were the most natural thing to do, I put my hand over hers, and timidly looking at her, with a sudden joy in my heart, I felt like saying to her many things, such as: "I love you Cora. You are beautiful, you are wonderful, and again, I love you, I love you."

Instead the courage failed me again, and something like, "thank you Miss Cora," was all I was able to whisper, almost not even loud enough for her to hear me. Poor me. I had always been under the impression that nothing could scare me, that nothing would stop me from saying or doing anything I felt like doing or saying, but I had not included or thought that I would be afraid of a woman. This was not only a completely and unexpected different matter, but seemed to be the most delicate one and the hardest to handle of them all.

"Now that we have solved one problem, let's see if we can take care of my little baby," Miss Cora said, waking me up from my daydream. "I know I have at least another three months to go, but I better start preparing for his arrival.

Armando tell me, what do you think, it is going to be a boy or a girl?"

We were just crossing the street in front of a stopped street car of the line Number Twelve that was unloading passengers, when the "ding, ding, ding" of its bell made us look up. There was papa' smiling and waving, then he stuck his head outside the door calling loudly: "Come on up for a ride."

"That is my father Miss Cora. Come and meet him." Then, without waiting for her approval or disapproval, pushing her from behind, helped her to get aboard.

After I had introduced them, I thought she would have liked to get off again, but since she gave no indication of being annoyed, and kept enjoying talking to my father, he pulled the driving handle and away we went. It was only two blocks to the end of the line anyway and in less than ten minutes we would be back, but when we did, the place was not exactly the same as when we had left it.

On the opposite side of the street, closer to the arcades, at each entrance of the same, and from the middle of the road parallel to the tram line, every hundred feet or so, they had placed a guard line of fascist and German soldiers with Tommy guns in their hands.

For a moment, we thought they were mopping up young men, but when we saw four trucks parked right inside the arcade, with soldiers laughing and joking, carrying in their arms all kinds of merchandises, we knew right away what was happening.

The toy store, the big shoe store, the fabric and clothing store of Signor Spizzichino, the jewelry shop, the book and records store, the pawnbroker shop, were being ransacked by the fascists and Germans, right under the astonished eyes of their owners, that were being rounded up one by one, and at gunpoint, forced to climb on the back of an open truck standing about hundred feet away from us.

It was right in the middle of the afternoon, the street car was almost vacant, in fact there was only two passengers beside Miss Cora and myself, to have a better look at what was happening, papa' brought the trolley down to almost a crawling pace. Miss Cora and I were standing right behind him, when we heard him exclaim: "Mascalzoni! Look what they are doing to that poor old man." And abruptly bringing the convoy to a sudden stop, he opened the inside window and looked outside at the same instant that Signor Spizzichino was pushed on the platform of the truck by a German soldier.

Their eyes must have met, or he must have recognized my father, because a horrified cry came out from the throat of Signor Spizzichino: "Mister Viselli aiutami. Help me. Please help. Don't let them take me away. Please. Please. Aiutami."

While the piercing shriek of the old man kept shredding our heart to pieces, completely stunned by the unbelievable cruelty inflicted on him by his abductors we couldn't remove our eyes from the scene of the crime. Enraged and heartbroken, but unable to even lift up a finger to help his old friend, tears started running down my father's cheeks as he kept saying: "Cowards. Cowards. Only heartless bastards like them are capable of such a scurvy trick."

Without stopping with froth arms and open hands stretched out up in the air, Signor Spizzichino hysterically kept imploring my father to help him, when with the intention of silencing him, two soldiers climbed in the back of the truck and with the butt of their rifles started to hit him.

Like a lightning, someone jumped right behind them, and with the fury of a demon from behind, he grabbed the two Germans by their wide leather belt holding the cartridge boxes, and with unexpected brutal force, actually tossed right off the truck both, sending them flying right in the air and landing heavily on the hard, cobblestones, then, with the agility of a feline he jumped off the side of the truck, and started running toward our direction.

"Papa' it is Sandy," I shouted as I recognized him, then at the top of my voice I started yelling: "Sandy. Sandy. Over here"

I have never seen my father move so fast. First he opened the gate wide open, then he regained his position at the control and just as Sandy grabbed the two brass handle bars and set foot on the running board, he pulled the driving handle so fast that the tramway took off with a sudden jerk making us loose our balance and throwing us backwards a couple steps.

Right then, a violent burst of bullets from the Tommy gun of one of the German soldiers hit the pavement but it was too late. Luckily for Sandy and I suppose for all of us too, at the exact moment that Sandy had stepped inside the tram, another convoy coming slowly from the other direction, saved our day. In fact by the time the other convoy must have got out of the way for the German soldier to resume his shooting, it was too late, we had already left the piazza and at full speed we were sailing along, ding, ding, dinging our way thru Via Principe Eugenio without stopping, across Viale Manzoni almost causing an accident with another Tranve dei Castelli and flying along Via di Porta Maggiore.

In the meantime, while I was checking if there was any vehicle following us, papa' was giving Instructions to the trembling Sandy.

"Have you got any money?"

"No. They took everything away from me, money, wallet, watch."

"Very well then. First of all, stop shaking; you are making me nervous too. Here is some money," he said, pulling out ten lire from his wallet. "You remember where we live?"

"Yes. I do, at the Acquasanta"

"Good. Then at Porta Maggiore, grab the first circolare and get lost. We will see you at the house tonight. You think you can make it?"

Sandy nodded and put the money in his pant pocket, moved closer to the exit door and while waiting, with fear in his eyes kept looking behind.

Among all this excitement, I had completely forgotten about Miss Cora, I turned toward her and looked. There she was in a corner, as white as a sheet, watching silently and holding in her hands the beautiful doll.

At the busy intersection we all got out and in a hurry we took off in different direction. At a bar, I called Nino and told him to inform my mother that she was going to have a visitor that afternoon, then knowing that Sandy was going to be taken care of, for the first time, I turned my full attentions to Miss Cora and on the long way back to the apartment, I found the time to excuse myself for having caused her all the inconveniences, but she had already regained her usual self, in fact with an unusual and unsuspected presence of mind, jokingly she said: "At least we cannot say that my baby has never seen any action."

It really surprised me to see that among all the tragic events, she still hadn't lost her good sense of humor. Once I knew that she was going to be all right, my main concern then turned to my father, because he still had to go back to the same place and maybe they were waiting for him. Maybe he had been followed, maybe someone had taken the number of his tramway and reported him, and maybe they had already arrested him. In the past he had plenty of troubles with the fascists, and now it wouldn't take them much of an excuse to beat him up or jail him, so until I would get home that night, and seen that everybody was safe and sound, I couldn't relax or stop worrying.

The next four hours, seemed endless, but like everything else in this world that does come to an end, so did they, slow, but they passed, and when I finally got home, thank God, I found out that I had been preoccupied for nothing.

Forty five minutes after we had left him, with his heart in his hand, papa' went back to Piazza Vittorio, while trucks and soldiers were all gone, a general pandemonium was reigning all around the stores with their doors left wide open purposely by the Germans, to give a chance to the looters to finish the job they had started, and in the end, blame them for it.

On his last ride, the people were all gone, but all the stores on Signor Spizzichino's block, were completely vacant, fixture and all were gone, even the doors had been uprooted from their hinges, and of their owners, no one knew their fate.

While papa' was relating the whole story to us, Sandy never said a word, but at the end, silently started to cry.

A week before Christmas was the date set for the killing of Pasqualino. Such operation was supposed to be a very simple one, instead it turned out to be a very complicated affair, in fact, when I got home the same night of the big day, to my surprise, there was the lamb as large as life. . .

"How come you are still walking around? You are supposed to be hanging by your heels. don't you know that?" I asked him scratching behind his ears.

"Sure. Sure. Your father didn't have the courage to kill him, and unless you do the job, we are going to be without meat for Christmas," mamma said disgustedly.

"What kill him? No mama no, not me. The very thought of it puts butterflies in my stomach, besides, I don't mind being without meat, mamma, I am getting used to being without it."

"Liar. Liar. You know very well that you eat it almost every day, and don't tell me otherwise," she answered angrily. "Carmine won't do it either, so I am afraid Maria is going to keep her lamb, and one of these fine days, the Germans or the fascists will see him and good bye lamb. That will be the end of him."

The very thought of the fascist getting it, seemed to galvanize Mario into action, and suddenly he jumped up from where he was sitting, then with his young chin sticking out, determined, he said: "I will do it mamma. Give me the knife."

I am positively certain that the job was as distasteful to him as it was to us, maybe more, but the situation seemed to call for desperate measures. Believing he wouldn't have the courage, in fun, mamma handed him the big butcher knife, but he was not fooling. Without any further hesitation, he called the lamb as he had done so many times before, that not knowing what was going to happen to it, innocently came to him. Very seriously and complete in command of the situation, Mario grabbed him by the snout, and lifting his head quickly, he coldly pulled the knife's blade across his throat, cutting deeply through the jugular veins,

The poor lamb let out one pitiful bleat and fell to the floor in a pool of blood that immediately began forming under his head. Not paying any attention to what had been said, as soon as she saw the blood come out of the lamb's throat, as though she had been stabbed herself, with an anguished cry, screaming wildly and kicking her feet, my sister Maria became hysteric, while mama, without paying too much attention to her rushed inside to get a pan to catch the precious blood that would be used later for blood pudding or sausage.

Awoken by all the fuss made by Maria, with the belt in his hand ready to use it on one of us, papa' came out to see what was going on, but when he saw the reason for all the commotion, turned pale, as white as a sheet and walked back into the house. As for myself, I couldn't move or talk, as I felt every muscle in my body tightening up.

After he had done what no one else wanted to do, with a shocked expression on his young face, Mario looked at his hands covered with fresh blood, then dropped the knife on the floor, and sobbing as though his heart was breaking, quickly ran back inside.

Once the impact of the first shock was past, papa' rolled up his shirt sleeves and got busy helping mama to finish the job. There was a lot to do, the carcass had to be skinned, quartered and hung to cure, and while they did that, I tried and hurriedly succeeded in calming Maria.

I intended to give her the beautiful doll that Miss Cora had bought for her on the eve of the Sixth Day of January, when San Nicola comes down thru the chimney, but I couldn't wait that long. This is the right moment to give it to her I told myself, and following my thoughts, I went inside, reached for it hidden behind a dresser, and lifting it up in the air, rushed outside yelling:

"Here Maria! Look, look what I have for you."

But neither my action, nor my words, had the expected result, she would not even look at it. Again I tried my best to attract her attention, but it was no use. At this moment, nothing could replace her Pasqualino and nothing could console her broken heart. Only time would cure her pain, but believe me, it didn't take long.

When bed time came, Maria was not completely reconciled to the fact, but her sobs had lessened considerably, and her attention was all for the doll, that was sitting on one corner of her bed, with her pretty little dress spread out over the blankets.

Since the addition of Sandy to our household, the little grotto where Carmine had spent on and off the last three months, lately had become very useful. It had no electric light and no running water, but in return it was very safe and very dry. Carmine and I had made a decent door out of a piece of corrugated sheet of iron, and we had covered the floor with a couple of big army canvases, two army cots, with relatively good mattresses, plenty of army blankets, all part of the loot gathered by us after the eight of September. Two homemade stools and table, plus an oil lamp that half of the time wasn't burning because there was no oil available, plus one or two decks of cards, lots magazines, books, puzzles and crosswords, was the whole furniture around, yet, in spite of its primitive look, it was almost inviting.

After the close call of Piazza Vittorlo, Sandy was so badly shaken that in the daytime he very seldom put his nose out of the grotto, which he had been sharing with Carmine, with whom, right from the first day of his arrival among us, had become very good chums, but he couldn't stay there forever, and neither could we hide his identity forever. Nino and company, plus the guys working in the fields, had already seen the both of them a couple of times coming to the house together, so, to whoever asked who was the newcomer, we said that he was an ex sailor from Sardinia, good friend of our brother Peppe, that like many others, was waiting for the war to be over so he could go back to the island and his family.

Having no problem whatsoever with the language, in a very short period, he became one of us, in fact, under papa's suggestion, Mr. Tortore offered him and Carmine a temporary job. Both started to work in the farm with a bunch of ex airmen from Cianipino, all Sicilians that couldn't make it home. All parties concerned, seemed to be quite content, particularly mamma that was getting a fresh supply of vegetables mostly cauliflowers, spinach, pumpkins and turnips, making it a little easier for her to prepare the daily meals, which, as the ingredients were getting scarcer and scarcer, it had become quite a chore, especially after she had acquired a new mouth to feed in Sandy.

I don't know how much truth there is to it, but an old proverb claims that a guest is like a fish, the first day it gives a great pleasure to have him around the house, the second day he begins to annoy, but the third day if he doesn't leave, he starts to stink.

Sandy's case was not entirely the same. He was not a guest, he was no relation to us, he was merely an occasional friend, and if we wanted to get right down to it, he was a complete stranger. By helping him, we had nothing to gain, on the contrary, quite a lot to lose, yet, to us he meant much more, he was a symbol, he represented freedom, and by accepting the challenge, my father was partially revenging all the vexations he had to endure in the past and present. He was defying the authorities, the law, the fascist, the Germans, the whole government apparatus. By sheltering Sandy and by hiding him from them, he was reversing the cruelty and injustices committed on his old and dear friend Signor Spizzichino, by allowing Sandy to stay with us, he was not just offering a helping hand to a friend, he was assisting and trying to save a human being completely lost in the sad trail of the war, one of the many among millions of unfortunate derelicts, homeless people scattered all over the world.

Personally I regarded the new addition to the household a real Christmas and Christian act of charity, but many times I couldn't help asking myself the same question over and over. "Was it right to do what we were doing?"

I know that papa's mind was made up, he was set and completely convinced that he was doing the right thing, and no one could make him change it, but actually what right did he have to impose Sandy's presence on the whole family?

If the fascists or the Germans ever found out that we were helping and sheltering not just a Jew, but an English prisoner of war, surely we would have been in deep, deep trouble. Why, why did we have to take such a big risk?

One thing was to help him escape, an act actually executed in the spirit of the moment, and that could have very well turned into a great disaster, one thing was as I did in the past to bring him tomatoes, fresh fruits, the odd sandwich and the odd bottle of wine, but to see him sitting at our table, eating our food, sharing the little we had, for me, it was a little bit too much. Yes, it did bother me, but since I was stuffing my belly at Mr. Spinelli's expenses, I didn't resent it as much as my brother Mario, who almost daily, quietly made a big issue of it until one Sunday afternoon Papa', Carmine, and Sandy, were outside cutting a long street light pole for fire wood, mamma had finished preparing some fried cauliflower sandwiches and had just put them on the table, they were not much of a sandwich to start with a couple of mouthful of each and they were gone. When Mario had finished devouring his, he picked up another one and asked mama if he could have it.

"No. You cannot." She replied firmly. "One is for your father, one for Carmine and the other one is for Sandy".

"Sandy. Sandy all the time." Argued Mario really upset. "Why do we have to share our food with him, when we don't even have enough for ourselves?"

"Shame on you, you selfish little rascal," answered mamma angrily.

"Mamma. I am not selfish, I am just hungry. Do you understand?"

"I am hungry too," she shouted back. "I haven't touched a piece of bread in two months, and yet do you see me starve? But this is not the point, and don't you ever bring up Sandy's name again. He is with us and with us to stay. Capito? Besides, at this very moment, maybe some poor family like us could be doing for your brother Peppe, exactly what we are doing for Sandy. Have you ever looked at it that way?"

Needless to say that that was the end of the discussion and from that moment on, the question of Sandy was never raised again.

Poor Sandy, he was so nice, so friendly, always ready to give a helping hand, always so courteous and understanding, but above all so taciturn and sad, and nothing we could do about it.

Christmas eve morning, as usual papa' left early for work, and when it was time for me to go, mamma and Mario came with me, while Maria which had already transferred all her attentions to the doll and took her wherever she went, stayed home with our next door neighbor Rosa, until mamma came back.

At Piazza Vittorio we separated, mamma and Mario were going to do the big Christmas shopping, which I believed it would be considerably meager this year, and I headed toward the apartment and Miss Cora.

I hadn't seen or heard about Mr. Spinelli since he had left, but I never missed him, I didn't know where he was and

I never inquired if he was coming back, in fact deep in my heart, I was hoping he would never come back.

With Miss Cora, every day was the same, quiet and peaceful. It had been like that since the famous afternoon when I had seen and touched her body, yet, I tried my best to hide my feelings, but I have to confess that I couldn't get her off my mind, in fact, just the sole thought of seeing her again the same way I had seen her that day, would start my heart pounding.

With Christmas at the door, I wished I would have been able to buy her a present. but all my earnings were turned over to papa, which he in return, gave me enough for car fare and sometimes for my rations of cigarettes, which I had to share with both my brother Carmine and Sandy. Damned. I wished we weren't so poor if I had money, but I don't know, maybe it was better that way.

What could I buy for a beautiful woman like her who already had everything? With this kind of thought in my mind, I wandered along till I reached my destination and slowly climbed the stairs, with the key she had given me, I opened the apartment door and quietly walked to the kitchen and began unpacking the bag's contents.

I expected to see her smiling face appear through the archway any second, but there was not a sound in the house, and I gathered she was still in bed. With as little noise as possible I put the coffee pot on, and while waiting for it to boil I prepared breakfast. She ate so little in the morning that even a child could prepare it for her.

When the coffee was ready, which was not exactly real coffee, but toasted barley water, I set it on a tray with a few homemade cookies, a couple teaspoons of homemade marmalade, then balancing it on one hand, gently knocked at her bedroom door.

"Is it you Armando?"

"Yes. I have your breakfast ready. Would you like to have it?"

"All right. Come on in."

She hid deep down in the bed and I could only see her coppery hair spread out on the white pillow. One arm, then the other came sneaking out from under the covers then she stretched and yawned loudly, reminding me of a little kitten.

"Good morning dear." She said, stretching herself once more. I am being lazy this morning. Oh. How sweet of you, you didn't have to bother. What have you got here?" She asked raising her head.

"Very little, coffee, cookies and jam."

"Good. Bring it over here, will you please?"

I walked around the bed to lay the tray on the night table, but. . . .

"No, no, no. Here on my lap," she ordered, raising herself on the pillow.

"Thank you. Now go get yourself a cup of coffee and join me. Will you?"

Wearing the sheerest of night gowns which did very little to conceal her, but that seemed instead to enhance the glow of her natural color, she looked lovely.

I didn't need to be told twice, but in my haste to get back, I spilled half of the coffee, and the cup was almost empty when I got there.

"Sit over here," she said patting the side of the bed, and gingerly I complied with her wishes, happy to be close to her in this intimate way.

"Now, tell me. What will we do today?" She asked casually and delicately, while balancing the cup and saucer in her graceful hands.

"I don't know," I said shrugging my shoulders. "Do you have any shopping to do?"

"Oh no, not today, I don't feel like going out. I am too lazy."

Nervously gulping my coffee and causing the cup to rattle against the saucer, I realized that I was shaking and hastily rested it on the night table. I felt she was watching me with a secretive little smile, as though she was enjoying my discomfort, and to cover my embarrassment, I reached for the tray and asked: "Are you finished with your coffee?"

"What is your hurry? We are not going anywhere, relax." She said smiling at me suggestively, then suddenly giving a little twitch as though in pain, she caught my hand and put it on her stomach, then in an awed whisper she added: "Feel. Do you feel that?"

I let my hand rest on her, and sure enough, there was a little movement.

"Did you feel the baby move?"

This time I put both hands on her belly and I could actually feel a lump move from one side to the other. Talking in low whispers, as though afraid to disturb the baby, innocently and with curiosity, I asked: "How old is he? And How are you going to get him out?" But I am afraid I must have asked the wrong question, because she burst out laughing making me feel very foolish, then, suddenly sobering up in an incredulous voice: "Armando? Don't you know about babies? Where they come from and how they are conceived?"

Feeling very stupid and ignorant on the subject, but at the same time hurt for her thinking of me as a child I replied: "Sure I know, my mother had six babies and every time she went to the hospital she came back with one of us. I can't remember all that, but I know for sure that when Maria was born, I don't know exactly what, but they did something to my mother because before she entered the hospital she looked like a balloon, and when she came out, she was as thin as a rail, again she burst out laughing, then she drew me down, and cupping my face in her hands kissed me tenderly. "My poor little innocent lamb," she exclaimed. "What a lot of things you have to learn, and how would I like to be your teacher."

"Have you ever had a girl friend? Have you ever kissed a girl like this?"

Circling her arms around my neck and pressing me close to her warm soft breast, she reached for my mouth with her fleshy moist lips in a passionate embrace.

For a breathless moment, waves after waves of ecstasy washed over me, making me feel as though I was drowning, but it felt so sweet, yes so very sweet. What a wonderful way this would be to die. I heard bells ringing and angel's wings fluttering over my head. It must be like this in heaven, I said to myself. At last, even though she had released me, with my eyes half shut, I could still feel the wonderful thrill of her nearness, as in a daze I seemed to hear her murmuring in a low voice: "Are you sure you never kissed a girl?"

She was still laughing at me, she was still mocking me I thought miserably bringing me back to reality with a start, then with a sudden rage, without answering, took her passionately in my arms and furiously kissed her again and again.

I didn't know what I had done, but judging by the way she responded to my kisses it did not seem like a farce anymore. With her hands rubbing the back of my neck, my hair, my back, she began pressing her body against mine, putting fire into my veins. She was breathing heavily now, I was too, in fact I was having difficulties with my breathing, as my lips sought her lips, her eyes, the soft spot on her throat and her pretty little pink ears, which when I breathed into them, made her squirm deliciously in my arms, driving me nearly mad with desire.

Somehow I discovered my shirt had come off, only my trousers and shoes remained to be removed and I didn't waste any time in doing that, leaving me as bare as she was, then, laying down beside her and the warmth of her body, her legs and thighs against mine, with our two bodies forming not quite a perfect body because her belly was in the way, there was nothing left to do, but to let nature take its course.

But it wasn't as easy as I thought it would be. Although I could feel her warm and lively body against mine, laying on the side, especially in the conditions she was in, was not the best position for making love, it seemed that we were too far apart, her protruding belly was not allowing me to get closer.

My body was as tense and vibrating as much as the cord of a guitar well tuned, and while my hands and limbs kept furiously digging, I was getting nowhere. So close and yet so far, I was going crazy, with the animal instinct of losing the prey, with brutal strength I rolled her over with me on top of her, but with the sudden jolt she let go a little scream, saying: "Take it easy Armando. You want to kill me?"

Automatically I said I was sorry, but I didn't mean it, in fact, finding myself lifted over her protruding belly as though I was on a roller coaster, realizing that instead of getting closer to my yearned aim, I was getting further away, the frustration increased my impatience and anger.

She read my mind and began to laugh. "Now, now my young bull, this is not the way to go to paradise, get off me and lay flat on your back," she said reproachfully. "There is more than one way to go to heaven, and your little Cora will show you one of them."

We didn't take long to switch position, and this time she was on top, finally we were on the right track and away to the races and boy o boy, did she ever show me. Only once I had previously made love to a woman, and to be honest, besides losing my virginity, I had been somewhat disappointed. To assert that I did not enjoy it would be lying, but it was not the same experience as the one I just had with the lovely Miss Cora. True, neither the woman, nor the place or the circumstances were the same, maybe if we had more time on hand it would have made a big difference, that I wouldn't know, I only remember that when that young woman was finished with me, in spite of the fact that I had enjoyed an orgasm, I still had a hard on, and to satisfy my unsatisfied manly needs, I had to go to the bathroom and finish the job by myself.

Good gracious. What a difference between the two performers, no comparison at all. Without any doubt, Miss Cora was a great teacher and I must have been either a bad or a very slow learner because, not once, not twice, we had to try three times before I could fully understand the lesson. Yet, even though we were tired, exhausted, we were not completely satiated.

To my dismay, the clock on the night table showed almost four o'clock. We must have fallen asleep. Slightly turning my head, I noticed Miss Cora was still with the angels, her face flushed and still showing signs of unspent passion. I tried to get up from the bed without disturbing her, but at my first movement she drowsily murmured my name as though she were dreaming.

"Armando, don't go away, stay with me," she said pleadingly clinging to my arms.

Now she is mine! I thought exultantly. All mine. Adoringly I looked at her and dressed at the same time. I was starving, and while I prepared something to eat for the two of us, many thoughts began coursing through my mind.

What will happen when Mr. Spinelli comes back? Surely if he ever finds out, he will kill me. But how? Who is going to tell him? Not me for sure, and I am positively certain that Miss Cora won't either because she feels the same way I feel about her, we love each other. Besides he is not her husband and she doesn't love him, she is staying with him only for his money, I am sure of that. So the hell with him. And pushing away all the worries, I picked up a tray full of sandwiches, two glasses and a bottle of wine, and as I was walking toward the bedroom, kept repeating to myself:

"The hell with Mr. Spinelli. She is mine now, no one else's."

My, how the time flew. It was six o'clock when we both realized with surprise that it was time for me to go, the thought of having to separate broke my heart, but I had no choice, I had to go and leave her alone and yet I could not amend myself that easy, and hoping that she would go for it, I said: "I have an Idea. Since you are going to be all by yourself tonight, why not come with me and spend Christmas Eve with my family? We would love to have you, in fact, mamma is always asking about you."

"Oh. No thanks. I really appreciate your invitation," she said as she caught my face between her delicate hands and kissed me gently. "Thank you my love, but I had enough excitement for one day, and I am afraid it would tire me out. You go home and enjoy yourself, I might read for a while and then go to sleep."

At the door, we clung to each other and with a lump in my throat and a big effort after kissing her soft lips, I gently freed myself from her and managed to say: "Merry Christmas love, I will see you tomorrow," and before she could see the tears running down my cheeks, I shut the door behind me.

We didn't go to church for the traditional midnight mass, as we were forced by the curfew to break this millennial ceremony. We didn't eat the same succulent dishes that year after year mamma had always prepared for us with a special pride. Undoubtedly, many more families were in the same predicament, which in reality, was very small consolation, but the thought that perhaps next year would be different, kept our morale up. We enjoyed what we were able to get, and that was very little. If we hadn't had the poor lamb, we would have had no meat at all of any kind, because mamma could not find any at the market of Piazza Vittorio.

Matter of fact, they found nothing of nothing. They stood in line for two solid hours to get some apples, and when they finally got there, there were no more apples. Thank God we lived right in the middle of these vegetable farms, and we had plenty of them.

Personally I was too happy, wrapped up with my secret love to care one way or another, which, it was not at all right, because I was just being plain selfish, and, Christmas comes only once a year.

Mario and Maria were the real victim of these unfortunate circumstances, and they were not very happy. They missed everything, but mostly the little "Creche" that Carmine prepared for them, year after year, in a little room with the infant Jesus, the Blessed Virgin, Saint Joseph, the cow, the donkey, plus the countless statuettes of shepherds, soldiers, flocks of sheep, and the different scenes of the background with the stars, the white snow, the dim lights of the houses scattered all around the country side, to form a realistic of the original legendary story of the stable where Jesus was born.

Those things were not there this year, because everything that had been carefully packed and stored by Carmine, did not escape the bombing of that unfortunate "Black Monday" the 19th of July. and were still hidden under the rubble of our house.

What was also missing this year, was the Christmas spirit, the air of joy that hung under our roof, and the hundreds of neighbors that used to knock at our door to see Carmine's work of art. The happy groups of friends, gathering for the occasion to spend the entire night playing cards and Tombola (Bingo) were just memories of past Christmases. Then, twelve o'clock found the festivities just beginning, this year everything was quiet, dead quiet, no friends came calling at our door, neither did we visit any.

Mama and papa' were the quietest, and had a sad look on their faces all evening, they were preoccupied about my older brother Peppe, whom, as far as we knew, disappeared before the eight of September and had been silent since.

Gosh. What a Christmas. The hours dragged by, and when finally the fire on the pot died out, we gladly went to bed, but damn it, even there things were not the same. Nonno Edoardo was here to spend the holiday with us and consequently he shared the bed with me, while Mario moved in with Carmine that had temporarily lost his companion.

In fact, for the first time since he had moved in with us, and taking a big chance wearing a borrowed uniform of street car conductor, Sandy had left early this morning with papa', to spend the holidays with some old friends near the Vatican, and would be back after New Year. His departure, was also part of a long planning between him and papa'.

It seemed that his friends, very rich and influential, were the same ones that had already helped him to get those false identification papers that he had lost the day of the German raid to the Jewish stores of Piazza Vittorio.

In the meantime, while he was staying with them, they were going to procure him with a new identity card, which to be valid, needed a recent picture of him.

Besides the new documents, another big reason to be there in person, was a very important one. It was nothing definitive, but if I understood correctly, there was some serious talking of the possibility of Sandy leaving us permanently. His friend was trying to get him out of Rome, behind the allied lines.

As I said, I had to share the bed with nonno, but he was a lot bigger than Mario, and the single bed was way too small for the two of us to be comfortable, therefore, to simplify the situation and before we started an argument which I was certainly going to lose, I picked up a few blankets and slept the rest of the night on the floor. Damn it. What a way to have spent a Christmas Eve.

At dawn, when we had to get up and get dressed to go out for the Christmas mass, outside it was still dark, my eyes were having a hard time staying open, my bones were aching, and even though the floor was not too inviting, I wished that I could have remained between the warm blankets and sleep some more.

The day was dull and foggy which didn't do much to lift my spirits, the cold wind went right through my clothes making me shiver, and by the time we arrived at the church, I was almost half frozen.

Inside the church where it was nice and warm, while we were waiting for the priest to come out, I must have fallen asleep, because when the mass was over, I didn't remember neither the ceremony nor a single word the priest had said.

Once home again, for breakfast, we dunked homemade doughnuts in warm wine, and by the time we were finished, the clock showed eight o'clock and it was time for me to leave. Mamma had already prepared a big package, and handing it over to me she said: "I doubt that you will be able to come back home for dinner, so I thought you had better take it with you. There are enough potatoes and roasted lamb for you and the Signora. All you have to do is warm it up, tell her that I am very sorry, but it is all we have, and don't forget to convey our good wishes to her."

The wine went right to my head, which didn't make me too steady on the legs, but the cold air in no time took care of that. At the farm house, Mr. Tortore had forgotten all about my coming, but it did not take long for his wife to gather up what was needed, and in a hurry she filled up the two shopping bags with so much food that with the one parcel that mama had given me previously, made my task quite hard to handle.

For a change I found the street car empty, so I sat down near the window, and while enjoying the ride, my thoughts were full of Miss Cora.

It took me a while to realize that the streets of Rome were completely deserted, Christmas was here, but the happy things that usually came with it, were not visible. Besides the very few people going to and from the churches there was not much activity anywhere. The wounds of the war were still very fresh, the echoes of the German soldier's boots and vehicles were still echoing up and down the deleted streets, even though they were nowhere to be seen.

The youth of Rome, the proud Romans, all dressed up and showing off, were not in evidence on this great day when families make every effort to be together.

Hearts were heavy with grief written all over the faces of the men, women and children. It was a sad Christmas, a Christmas without the peace on earth that this day was supposed to bring, and everyone was aware of it.

Proceeding toward my destination, even though I could see and feel these things all around me, I didn't seem to care too much, because my mind was filled with another thought, a thought strong with passion and sweet with love for Miss Cora.

When I got there, she was already up, which really surprised me, more beautiful than ever, dressed in her maternity clothes that concealed her condition very well. Opening my arms in an attempt to get hold of her and kiss her I shouted: "Merry Christmas Miss Cora!"

"Shhhhh," she whispered, putting one hand over my mouth and with the other one pointing at the bedroom. "He is here."

"Who? Mr. Spinelli?"

"Yes you damn fool. Who else did you think would come?" She answered angrily.

Feeling as though someone had just thrown a pail of water over me, I stood there helpless and wordless till finally I found enough strength to open my mouth again: "When did he come back?"

"Last night, and try to be quiet will you, he is still asleep."

How, I will never know, but I had forgotten him completely, and suddenly realizing that after all, this was his house, that she still was his mistress, I followed her on tip toe to the kitchen.

As I began unpacking, I could not get over the shock of him being back. Damn him. Did he have to come so soon? Couldn't he have remained where he was for a few more days?

"Where was he?" I asked Miss Cora who seemed to be very, very upset.

"Don't ask me," she answered coldly. "Wherever it was, it must have been very far because he told me that he hadn't slept for four days. Believe me, he must have been very tired, dead tired, because he didn't even have enough strength to take his clothes off. In fact, if I hadn't helped him to get undressed, and get into the bed. . ." She kept talking, but I wasn't paying any attention.

The thought of them in such intimacy had sent a stab of jealousy through my heart, the vision of them together in the same room, into the same bed where only yesterday we had spent the happiest hours, loving each other, caressing, kissing and whispering endearments to each other, was unbearable, agonizing, cruel. Just the thought of her touching him shocked me, it made me feel dirty, and suddenly my tongue was tied, a sense of shame, embarrassment and a complete abandon of strength invaded my mind and all the muscles on my whole body began feeling weak and limp as an overcooked strand of homemade noodles.

She continued talking, but her voice, that same voice that I loved so much to hear, now seemed to be coming from a distance, then as if waking from a bad dream, she got through the numbness and somehow, for the first time, I started I to see things in a different light.

Her attitude was cold and almost indignant. The words I was hearing, were not coining from the same Miss Cora I had in my arms only yesterday, but from a Miss Cora that I had never really known, not even like the Miss Cora I knew at the beginning when I started to work here, because at least, then she was firm and polite.

Yesterday didn't mean a thing to her anymore, the tender caresses, and all the passionate words she had whispered in my ears, were just a bunch of lies. They were part of an act, part one the beginning, and part two the end.

Why had she let me make love to her? Was it only to satisfy a whim? Maybe to her it was just a caprice, but not to me, because I loved her, yes I loved her. The fear of losing her, which had bothered me all through the night, was finally coming true, and much sooner than I expected, the fact was too ugly to face and I didn't want to admit it even to myself.

Lowering her eyes to the floor as though embarrassed, she said: "There was no need for you to come this morning, I didn't expect you anyway, and I should have told you yesterday to take the day off."

This must have been the last part of her act the finale, a sudden rage almost tempted to answer back, but was it worth it? Besides, what good would it have done? I had lost and the best thing to do was to retreat, quietly and politely, which I did, and before I realized it, I found myself walking, on the street. As I was walking and talking to myself on the deserted road, suddenly an empty feeling entered me, as my whole body began aching, while a steady pounding at my temples, kept growing and growing, which almost drove me crazy. All of a sudden I couldn't breathe, I was choking. My clothes seemed too tight around me and I had to stop to unbutton my coat, my tie and my shirt, but it didn't help. What is the matter with me? Could this be the effect of the wine I had drank earlier? No. It is impossible. Wine bothered me before but not this way. Could it be what a lot of people call lovesick or heartbreak? Bah... I don't know. But if it is, it is terrible, and I would not wish it on my worst enemy.

At home, they were very surprised to see me so soon. . . . dinner was almost ready to be served, and mamma quickly added another plate for me, but I was not hungry.

I told everybody that I wasn't feeling too well, and to hide my sorrow, I went to bed and spent the rest of the day there.

Chapter 14

Time went by as did New Years and Epiphany, but my feelings were still hurt, and my constant contact with Miss Cora, didn't help the situation. It was like slow torture. Day after day when Mr. Spinelli slept or read in the bedroom, I tried to talk to her and even tried to make her smile, but she wouldn't even look at me I knew that what had happened between us was a moment of weakness on her part, caused by being alone for too long, I also knew that she would never be mine ever again. This much I had realized and accepted, but what I couldn't understand and accept, was the fact that she was so distant and so cold with me.

I didn't expect any particular favor, all I wanted was the same old respect, friendship and companionship as before, but I was not permitted even that. She denied me everything and avoided me at every opportunity. Only at meal time when we were all seated around the table, she was different and talkative. Knowing how I felt about her, she took a great pleasure in mocking and tormenting me.

"Armando?" She would say. "You are not hungry lately, what is the matter, you don't feel well?" Or, "you don't seem to be in good humor, has something happened to you?" Or again "Did you have a fight with your girl friend? Come on, cheer up, don't let that bother you," she would go on and on, time after time, with her angelic voice, doing everything so casually, so nonchalantly, that even Mr. Spinelli found her remarks so amusing that at times he even smiled, which for the old bear was quite unusual.

She was being sarcastic and cruel, and sometimes, I wondered if she was enjoying herself in hurting me. The thought of her laughing at my expense, was very humiliating and made me quite angry, and sometimes, even though I knew that I would have regretted it for the rest of my life, I felt like slapping her face, instead, I kept calm and swallowed it as best as I could.

Working with her, and being so close to her for at least six hours a day, seven days a week, was becoming un unbearable torture, and often I wished I didn't have to comeback anymore, and so far, what kept me from quitting was our financial need, unless I went to work for the Germans, it would have been impossible to find a job somewhere else, because first of all, we were in the middle of winter, secondly, because everything was either locked up for shortage of material or it had been bombed and destroyed, therefore, in spite of my feelings, the sense of duty and responsibility toward my family had priority over and above everything else. All of nonno Edoardo's and papa's savings had been spent, we were broke.

With the rent for the house that took a big chunk out of papa's salary, plus the medicine for nonno Edoardo who had been in bed with a bad case of bronchitis since right after Christmas, there wasn't much left for everything else. Money was not worth much, but without it we couldn't survive.

Flour, oil and salt, the most essential items were precious as gold, and prices on the black market were rising daily and sky high, because even for them food was scarce, as a matter of fact, scarcer than ever.

The New Year 1944 didn't seem to be too favorable for some fascist black shirts. The Germans were not too pleased at the way things had been going, and Mussolini was ordered to do something about it. It seemed that "Operation Purge" had been just concluded with the arrest of many old time fascist leaders.

What they had been doing all over the country, was "dog eat dog" even Rome had new rulers, new personalities with different names, different faces, but they were just as bad as the ones we had before and maybe even worse.

Apparently the people that had been after Mr. Spinelli, headed by a certain unprejudiced, Pelandrini, had all been imprisoned and he seemed to be very pleased of the changes, but did not dare show his face in public, not yet. He was waiting for something more important happening up north, and usually as always, patience paid off. On the eleven of January, with big headlines, the newspapers announced the end of the trial of nineteen leaders of the fascist party that one way or another, had betrayed our country and the fascist cause. Once the tribunal found them guilty, they were sentenced and shot to death in the back like traitors.

Among the executed there was Ciano, Mussolini's son in law. The bulletin said that at the order to shoot, Ciano tried to turn his face toward the firing squad to plead his innocence once more, he was not killed instantly, and had to be finished off with the pistol of the officer in charge.

I believe that the death of Ciano, must have been the big news that Mr. Spinelli was so patiently waiting for, now that there was no one else to claim the huge wealth accumulated by him for Ciano, being the sole registered owner of such wealth, and not being afraid of retaliation any longer by Pelandrini and company, he decided to come out in the open.

"From now on, a maid will take care of Miss Cora and the apartment, therefore I don't need your services around here anymore," he announced to me in his commanding manner one morning. For a moment, the dreadful thought that he had discovered my earlier indiscretion, caused me some alarm, but when he went on to say that he had something more important lined up for me in the future, I was instantly relieved. He sounded more like a promotion instead of a demotion, and immediately deep inside me, I felt a surge of gratitude, tinged with shame for my behavior, as I stood in front of him shame faced with confused emotions, already wondering what he had in store for me.

I wanted to get out of the apartment and everything and everybody that lived in it but now that my wish was becoming a fact, I was afraid, I was not as happy as I thought I was going to be, because Miss Cora was still in my mind. I thought I hated her, but it was not true, in spite of what she had done to me, there was still a soft spot in my heart for her. I was going to miss her a lot, but not seeing her any more perhaps would help me to forget her.

During his solitary confinement in the bedroom, he must have spent endless hours planning for the future, because that same afternoon, as if he intended to recover the tedious hours wasted doing nothing, Mr. Spinelli launched into action with an extraordinary vigor, his prepared detailed plans he wanted set into operation immediately.

He must have had an iron memory to remember everything after such a long time of inactivity, and really surprised me, when seated closer together around the table, explained detail for detail exactly what he wanted done."Well? What do you think, can you handle it?" He asked me at last.

To be honest, he had told me so many things, that I was kind of confused, but I wasn't going to let him know, and timidly nodding my head, I promised that I would do my best.

"Good. I know you can do it. We start tomorrow then, and remember I am counting on you, the less people we involve in this job the better it is, so let's keep it as secret as possible," getting up and leaving the room right after.

During all this time, Miss Cora was sitting on an armchair busily knitting a little sweater for the baby to come, leisurely looking in our direction, watching and listening to our conversation.

Later, when I was ready to go, while he was resting in his room, with a sardonic smile written on her face, she came close to me and whispered: "Good bye Armando. Are you going to miss me?"

Damn her. Even now she had to mock me. Disgusted, I picked up my coat, striding to the door with the intention of leaving, but at the last moment stopped and looked back, waved at her for the last time, and with an uncontrollable rage, silently in my mind I said: "Good bye devil and thanks for the lesson."

The housing project at the Statuario, consisted of forty five units, most of them were luxurious villini, with about ten already completed, some even to the furnishing, while the others were still in various stages of completion.

After the eight of September, the construction was halted, the place was closed up, and only four men that were actually living with their families in the four furnished villini, were left in charge to see that nothing was stolen.

There were millions of lire worth of construction and otherwise material scattered around this huge property and the fact that it had never been molested was a mystery to everybody, and no one had a real particular reason for explaining such phenomenon. As I just said, so far he had been very lucky that no one had ever attempted to touch anything, but how long this luck would last in the present chaos, with the Germans and fascist friends always on the lookout for an easy way to make a buck, and with so many people out of work and starving?

To keep it there any longer, it would be foolish, so now for fear that the worst would come, and before it was too late, Mr. Spinelli had wisely decided to remove everything that could be put in storage. All the bulk and heavy material would be carried down to an unused part of the grotto, where Nino would be responsible for the receiving and unloading part, the small and more valuable merchandise was to be delivered to the downtown main office, where Mr. Spinelli himself, would direct the operations. My job was to supervise and make sure that nothing was left behind or stolen while the operation was in progress. The two drivers and the four watchmen would obey my orders, and if I were in any doubt or needed anything in a hurry, Nino would be there to help and advise me.

That morning bright and early, down by the grotto entrance, two carts were ready. Nino gave me some final instruction and away we went, Ruggiero and me on the first cart, and Ferrari following behind with the other.

In January the days are very short, and if it happens to be one of those lousy days rainy or foggy, it seems like if there is not too much difference between daylight and nighttime, because it is always dark. Fortunately that day the weather was assisting us, in fact, in spite of the early hour and the heavy dew on the ground, the air was kind of chilly, but with the sun shining on us all the way we felt warm and comfortable and enjoyed the outing and the fresh air.

The horses were not very young any more, but like us, seemed to enjoy just as much the ride on this brisk morning air, and trotting along the almost deserted Appia Highway, we made good time, and when we got to the Statuario, we headed directly to the main warehouse, where the four watchmen were already there waiting for us.

There were six large rooms with all kinds of merchandise in them, sinks, bath tubs, toilet bowls, metal cabinets and mirrors, electric fixtures, lamps of all sizes and shapes, piles and piles of ceramic tiles, hundreds of boxes of window glasses of different sizes and many mope items that systematically had to be removed. Would I be able to handle it? I asked myself, realizing how big the job was. Would the men resent my youth and my orders? I had always received orders, and now that I had to give them, especially to men who were as old as my father, I felt embarrassed.

I didn't know how to begin or how to go about it without hurting their feelings, but they were all pros, and as though they could have read my thoughts, without my saying a single word, and without any delay, they got organized and ready to roll.

After the first moment of uncertainty was over, and reassured by their cooperation I got at it with more faith in myself, and as the men started carrying out the different articles, I checked their condition and made a list of them, then once the two carts were well loaded, I locked up the place and while the watchmen went back to their homes, we headed back for the highway and the grotto.

In the morning, before we left, I reminded Nino that if he needed any help for the unloading, my brother Carmine and Sandy would be available, and sure enough, when we arrived, they were on hand itching to get going.

Right from the beginning of our move to this area, the grotto had always aroused my curiosity, but never, not even once, had I the opportunity to visit the inside, I mean not just around the entrance, but way, way in. As a matter of fact, the furthest I had gone, was a few yards past the main doors to take cover during the air raids, now at last, my curiosity would be satisfied, and I followed the two carts slowly entering the darkened interior, leaving behind us the daylight, and entering the pitch darkness reigning in the grotto.

The sudden change almost blinded me but not for long, as my eyes gradually accustomed themselves to the dim light coming from the small bulbs placed almost every hundred feet apart, and hanging on a single line up high on the wall.

The tunnel was approximately twenty feet wide and ten feet high, with a small ditch and the water main on one side, and the electric line on the other, running all the way down to supply the several short tunnels opening on both sides, where only a few months ago, more than a couple dozen men earned their daily living growing mushrooms, now, only Ferrari grew them just for himself, and some other people like Nino, Mr. Spinelli and a few more chosen favorite. Always making sure that no one was watching us, more than once, on the manure pile, we dug out the stem and pieces that were thrown away, after the mushrooms had been sorted out, and we always got a good feed out of it for the whole family.

As we descended, every time we passed a square from which other tunnel branched off, Carmine, Sandy and myself looked very attentively in the ceiling trying to locate the ventilating shaft going up to the smaller grotto where Carmine and Sandy slept, but it was not where we expected it to be. In fact, Sandy was lucky to spot it, because it was located at the center of a dead end fifty by forty rectangular room branching off the main artery and completely vacant.

Proceeding further down, we lost both, hydro and water, and we had to make use of lanterns to lighten our way, and the further we went, the more interesting it became. Wow, it was amazing what man can do. It must have taken them years and years to dig it with pick and shovel. The layout was almost the exact duplicate of any small city, with its main street and little squares, its intersections, and its numerous side roads branching out in every direction for miles and miles. Really unbelievable. With its twisting and turnings, it would have been very easy for anyone to get lost in this mammoth underground labyrinth, and believe me, Ruggiero told me that to date, no one was ever able to explore it fully or know how far it extended and where. The general opinion was that the grotto reached the Coll Albani, but it was just a guess, because no one had ever proved it.

A couple of years ago, before I quit school, our juristic geography professor, took us on a tour of the ancient Catacombs, which we read so much about in the roman history, and where the early Christians, gathered, prayed, hid and buried their dead, and until that very moment, I thought that the grotto was an abandoned part of them, but I was badly mistaken, because the Catacombs I saw, with their narrow lanes and low ceilings, were midget compared to this one.

Definitely the grotto was not part of them, but was believed to have been built by the Christians to provide a place to live and also furnish a means of entering and leaving the city of Rome without being noticed by the Praetorian Guards that were constantly patrolling the old Appian Highway looking for them.

With Nino leading the pack and Carmine and Sandy bringing up the rear, following the main artery for a good fifteen minutes, we finally turned to a side road where at its end, we turned again and stopped in a dead end tunnel with a peculiar triangularly shaped room, very narrow at the entrance, in fact it was so narrow that it was just wide enough for the carts to go through, but once inside, it was ten times as wide at the back and at least one hundred and fifty feet long. Apparently, we had reached our destination, because "this is it," hollered Nino his voice echoing and reverberating in an eerie way, lifting up his lantern and hanging it on an iron bar sticking out on the wall, followed by Ruggiero and Ferrari that did the same with their own lanterns.

Beginning from the back and at one corner of the room, piece by piece, everything was carefully unloaded and placed on the ground by the four men, while Nino and I, counted the items together to make sure that it checked with my list.

The room was so big, that once we had finished unloading the two carts, we could hardly notice any difference in it. It looked like a grain of sand in a glass of water. Believe me, it would take more than a trip or two, before the place would be filled, and I thought that Mr. Spinelli could not have chosen a better spot to hide his merchandise.

Down there, it was quiet and peaceful, although, the least noise sounded ten times louder than it would outside, it was also nice and warm, but the air was heavy and stuffy, and we were very glad to see the daylight again.

Time went fast. In the afternoon we repeated the same operation of the morning, and when finally both carts were unloaded, satisfied of a day well spent and for a job well done, we slowly headed back for the grotto exit, then, as Ruggiero and Ferrari leading the horses to the barn, disappeared in the dark of the evening arms in arms, Carmine, Sandy and I headed home.

We were all tired but we didn't seem to mind it, we had loved working part of the day together and enjoyed loosening up our soft muscles, especially me that for the last couple of months did nothing but babysitting. Now walking side by side, freely once more, it felt good to go home together as we used to do often in the past. For us, this was a happy day, because at least we had achieved something, and we reminisced about gay times when we worked steadily helping papa' earn our living, but unfortunately those beautiful days were just memories, which seemed to be so far in the past to have been gone forever. Since the dreadful nineteenth of July when all our troubles started, we had been running, hiding and suffering, as a matter of fact, besides the short vacation spent at my grandparent's place, I couldn't recall a cheerful event since then, only misery and plenty of it. That evening we were happy and proud of ourselves, which showed in the way we were walking and talking, even Sandy for a change was loose and relaxed. It all showed in the way we unconsciously held our heads up, the way we expressed our feelings, and discussed our hopes for the future.

Not even once, could I remember the two of us singing together as we used to do with our friends, but that evening after supper, because we were thinking the same thing, spontaneously, Carmine and I began singing, first joined by nonno who feeling much better now, began to harmonize with us, then mamma, then papa' very soon, Piero knocked at outdoor with his wife and little Leo, then Nino just passing by with Ferrari and Ruggiero, stopped and couldn't resist temptation.

While the singing was gaining crescendo and momentum, wine was brought out, which warmed up the hearts and the spirits and cleared the throats of all the members of the choir, that were encouraged by the sudden arrival of a group of ex airmen from the farm that had come down bringing a guitar, accordion and mandolin with them.

By then we were packed like sardines and very wisely, Nino decided to open the apartment where the working men used to sleep in and had been vacant since their departure, very soon the entire neighborhood joined in the festivities and the party was really underway, with drinking, singing and dancing.

How strange it was to see that it didn't take much to reunite people and how little it took to make them happy, and no matter who they were or where they came from, they all loved singing. Yes, it seemed so strange that singing came so easy, so natural to us, maybe because singing is so warm, so full of life, so full of love and expressive of inner happiness.

While the songs we were singing came from the bottom of our hearts, our voices loudly and clearly, were saying to the world how good it was to live contentedly, but like a human cry, a cry of hope, they were reminding the world that we were young, in love with freedom and peace, the same freedom that we lost at the same time that we lost the peace that Christ preached.

It was not normal to live in constant fear, it was not normal to be afraid of everything and everyone, to be confined to our homes without work, without friends, and without the necessary things that were normal in our everyday life.

The sun would shine again, love on earth would once more prevail, that day would surely come again and could not be too far off, because God is there, and sooner or later our prayers would be heard, I felt sure of it.

It seemed that this type of gathering and singing, was something completely knew to Sandy, and that evening, he enjoyed himself immensely. He confessed that as a child, he had always spent his time between school and the clothing store of Signor Spizzichino. His uncle and wife were not very talkative, and very seldom took him anywhere. They were lonesome and moderate people, church, store and house. The only extravagance they permitted him was to watch the puppet show in the park of Piazza Vittorlo every Sunday afternoon, and that, because it was free.

Our singing, reminded him of home and his parents, which reopened a fresh wound in his heart, in fact, through his friends, he had learned that his whole family couldn't be found anywhere, and it was feared the worst, but not to lose hope completely. Soon he had to go to visit them again, and then they would let him know for sure

It was very late when everybody decided to call it quits, and before going to bed that night, Miss Cora entered my mind, but to my own surprise, for the first time in weeks, I felt light, free. Finally I got her out of my system, and I was glad, because from now on, I would be able to sleep without being tormented with her in my dreams, and confident in the future, I walked to the bedroom, undressed and stepping on the mattress laying on the floor, I got comfortable under the cold blankets and after my prayers, with a clear conscience closed my eyes and fell asleep.

It seemed that Mr. Spinelli was not too pleased with the way we were doing things

"You guys are going to slow," he had said to Nino. "This way it is going to take us all winter, so let's speed it up, get the farmers out and put them to work," and that is where he had been the night before, to talk with them, in fact, next morning, when I arrived at the rendezvous, beside Ruggiero and Ferrari, there was Mr. Tortore and another farmer waiting for me, each with their respective cart.

In order to avoid any suspicions, allowing a good fifteen minutes in between, we started off one cart at the time.

The weather was holding, and from that moment on, it meant going steady from dawn till late in the evenings, for the whole crew, as for me, I had no time to spare, I was working steady, always busy, and since it was impossible for me to accompany each driver, I gave them the list of their load and Nino checked at the other end.

Making eight trips a day, two for each cart, at the end of the fourth day, we had removed everything that was stocked in the warehouse.

Next in line, were all the big fixtures, frames and doors, the tons of roof tiles plus all the tools and various pieces of equipment scattered around, plus the entire blacksmith shop, where the machinery had to be taken apart, we had to dismantle the whole kitchen with all its appliances, and this required time. We couldn't work anymore as fast as before, because the handling of the heavy pieces, required patience, experience, a lot of time and more manpower.

Once again, Mr. Spinelli became impatient, in fact, the same evening, after Nino had given him the daily report and explained what we had accomplished; I heard his thundering voice explode on the phone: "Damn it. At the rate we are going we will never see the end of it, and I haven't got that much time. We have been very fortunate so far, but let's not press our luck, it could happen any minute now, so I don't care how you do it, but do it. If you need more help, hire it, and let's get cracking. Is that clear? And bear this in mind Nino. If you are not capable of handling the job any more, just say so. I will get somebody that will. Understand?" And without giving him a chance even to utter a single word in defense, suddenly closed the line, leaving poor Nino as white as a sheet. Poor Nino. What could he do with such an arrogant bastard.

I felt so sorry for him. After all, he was only a man and doing his best. I bet that if things were normal he wouldn't take any of this guff from him, but they were far from being normal, and a job these days meant survival.

Taking a big chance of being caught on the highway, either by the Germans or the fascists that were much worse, four ex airmen left the safety of the farm's sanctuary and came to the Statuario with us. On one trip, even Carmine and Sandy adventured themselves on the Appia highway, but when papa' knew it, hell broke loose and they never went back.

With four more guys, things really got moving and in four more days, we cleaned up the whole place. With the last piece of machinery delivered under the grotto, there was not one inch of space left available, and the huge triangular room was completely packed to capacity with a fortune worth millions of lire. No one would ever come down to the grotto this far, but just in case, a brick wall was erected from end to end, closing and sealing the entrance to the room forever. After that, we unloaded about ten loads of dirt right in front of it, planting on it a big sign with great big letters saying: "Danger. Cave in."

Once the two big doors at the grotto were closed and the place as usual forbidden to any intruders, a part of Mr. Spinelli 's treasure was buried within its walls and the secret with it. Only few of us knew about it, and he counted on our discretion.

Our next job, should have been the removal of all the expensive furniture and other various assets from the villini, which was supposed to go downtown to the main office, at first, he gave the order to go ahead, but at the last minute, when we were all set to go, there was a change in his plans.

"Forget the furniture, it is not that important. Start on the lumber immediately" He ordered Nino, then "let me speak to Armando will you?"

"Listen to me carefully," he said when I came to the phone, "if you remove all the lumber in less than a week, there is five thousand lire to be split among all of you. What do you think?"

He knew that it was almost impossible for us to do such a big job in so short a time, so did I and the rest of the guys, but the word bonus acted like magic to our ears, and we accepted the challenge.

"Behind the carpenter shop, there were about forty piles of all kinds of expensive lumber, mostly all two by six, eight and ten, walnut planks, averaging between twelve, to ten and eight feet long, neatly stocked in piles of twelve to fourteen feet high, which had to be brought and stored under the big shed where they used to keep the manure for the mushrooms, and right across from the house where we lived in, and exactly opposite the vacant apartment.

Starting earlier than usual in the morning, and quitting late at night, going at it like little beavers, at the end of the second day, almost half of the lumber and been moved. All Ruggiero's kids, my brother Mario and even nonno Edoardo who was in no physical condition to work, was helping us. Our spirits were high and we were almost certain to reach our goal which meant a whole fifteen hundred lire plus our regular pay for Carmine, Sandy and myself if we succeeded, when feeling as though the money was already in our pockets, our dream was brought to an abrupt end, when in the middle of our sleep, we were thrown out of bed by a continuous and infernal blast.

"What in hell is that?" Cried out loudly papa' getting up in a hurry, and holding up his pants he rushed for the outside door, but forgetting that Sandy was sleeping on the kitchen floor, he stumbled and surely must have hurt himself because right away, we heard him invoking graciously the lord, our lady and all the saints put together.

It was not a regular habit for papa' to use profane language or swear, but when it did happen, he sure made up for it, which lately was quite often, especially when he was deprived of his regular sleep.

Its regular ten hours at work, were spent riding a street car usually packed like anchovies, and dealing with some of the most ignorant, arrogant and impatient people, better known as the Romans, me included, which all by itself, it was a real chore. If it wasn't enough for one day, when he came home he had to listen and possibly solve our many problems, and when he finally went to bed, being the whole family relegated to one single big room, it was almost impossible to pretend absolute quiet, therefore, if it wasn't Maria, it was nonno or someone else and he could never get a full night of sleep.

No wonder he was always nervous and crabby lately, he badly needed his rest and if he didn't get it, he made sure to let everybody know about it.

He was still unstringing the rosary, trying to find and add new saints to his personal list, when scared to death and half naked, we all ran outside to find the cause of the tremendous explosions and where they came from. The earth under our feet was shaking, the glasses on the windows were rattling, but there was nothing in sight. We explored the sky searching and carefully listening for a distant humming of airplanes, but we saw nothing, while in the distance the blasting grew in strength and noise.

"Those are not airplane bombs falling" Exclaimed papa "Those are cannons shells and big ones too. I think they are big cannons all shooting at the same time. Listen. Listen!" Bringing his hands up to his ears. "Can't you notice the different sound in the explosions as the shells hit the ground? Anyway, whatever and wherever they are, they can't do us any harm as they are too far away. Come on, com on let's get back into the house before we catch pneumonia."

The tiresome music went on and on all night long and when finally dawn came and we had to get up and get ready to go to work, no one felt very ambitious, it really showed on our tired faces that none of us had his regular rest.

It was still dark outside when we walked down the dirt road to meet the rest of the gang, which as usual were waiting for us in the little office discussing the night's events. As we entered the room, dancing with excitement and unable to hide his feelings, Nino shouted at us: "Ragazzi. The Americans have landed in Anzio. They have landed. Do you understand?" He kept repeating to us with tears in his eyes. "Oh my God, what a dream, can you believe it? Soon we will be free."

"It is true, isn't it? You are not kidding me are you?" Asked Sandy repeatedly, his voice trembling with excitement.

"Sure it is true. I heard it on the radio one hour ago with my own ears. It said that the American troops have landed along the beaches of Anzio, finding on their way very little resistance or none at all from the Germans. They are advancing rapidly toward Rome and if all goes well, they should be here any moment."

"If that is the case, the hell with the work them. Let's all stay home and wait for them," Carmine shouted excitedly, always ready to take advantage of every little situation or any excuse to dodge work.

"Yes. It is a very good idea. Let's all do that," said Nino turning to the rest of us. "I wouldn't venture on the highway not today. There might be some shooting before this is all over, and Mr. Spinelli's lumber is not worth that much to risk our lives' for it. As a matter of fact," he added, "I think it would be safer to have our families standing by the grotto, and the sooner the better, because it won't be long now."

Following Nino's advise, we all hurried to our homes and in no time we were back at the grotto entrance with women and children, where with anxiety in our hearts, hoping and praying, we waited for papa' to come home and for the Americans to arrive. Long hours passed by, it was almost dark again when finally papa' came home, but of the Americans, no sign at all.

"Christ!" Swore Ferrari. "Even if they were walking they should be here by now. What is holding them up?"

"I bet the Americans must have stopped to sample the golden wines of the Colli Albani, and now they hate to leave it behind them," Ruggiero retorted jokingly.

"Something must have gone wrong somewhere, something was holding them up, but what? Who?" Were the questions running from mouth to mouth. Not the Germans for sure. We hadn't seen a single car, truck or tank on the Appia highway not just for hours, but for days, in fact we wondered if they even knew about the landing. Besides, even if they had known, they certainly couldn't have done much about it, because their main forces were well engaged and fighting hard at Cassino.

So, even though we were not expert on warfare, it was quite clear that with this unexpected landing operation, the Americans had caught the German command by surprise, but for some unknown reason to us as much as to the rest of the world they had not been able to take full advantage of the situation.

When on the night of the twenty fourth of January, exactly forty eight hours after the American landing at Anzio, the first contingent of fresh German troops and armored tanks appeared on the Appia Highway speeding south to meet and fight them, our hopes of being liberated were lost, vanished in the air, and frustrated and disappointed we returned to our homes.

It would have been nice to be free again, too nice, but even though our dream was once more abruptly interrupted by the Germans, our hopes were now fading, as a matter of fact, they were growing, because now we knew for sure that the big day was not too far away. Sooner or later, the Tetons would be defeated, and silently we began praying and looking forward to that day.

Now the big guns were firing constantly day and night, in fact they hadn't stopped since the night of the twenty first of January. Apparently the Germans had launched a counter offensive trying to push the American troops back into the sea, but they had failed completely, and after suffering heavy losses in men and material, the battle of Anzio came to a standstill.

With the front line less then forty miles from us, it only meant one thing, more troubles and more hardship.

The German troops that came rushing south to hold back the American threat, brought with them lots of armaments and ammunition, but very little food, and now Rome had to feed them, they also needed more manpower to do their dirty work and the city offered a good grounding prospect for their mass deportation. In cooperation with the fascist, Guardie di Finanza and the Italian African Police, thousands of men from the age of eighteen to sixty five, were seized on the streets, cafes, theaters, in their own homes, pulled out of bed in front of the terrorized eyes of their dear ones and taken away, loaded like animals in sealed freight cars and shipped north to Germany, where they would be put to work in their factories, or if unable to perform, shot or put to die slowly in concentration camps, but the majority were brought directly to the Anzio battleground, where under the incessant shelling of the American guns, were forced by their trigger happy captors to dig trenches and graves.

Terror and fear reigned all over the city and surrounding villages, no place was safe anymore, as the desperate yelling and cry of the people, "I tedeschi, I tedeschi"(The Germans, the Germans) resounded at any hour and anywhere.

Now orders were more strict during curfew hours, no one was permitted to walk on the streets, only the utility people, street car personnel, hospital staff and doctors, and other indispensable service workers, had special passes released by the authorities, and even though they were carrying those passes, time after time, many of these people had been harassed and ill treated.

Papa' had one too, but we all wished that he hadn't. The special tram that made the first run to pick up all the street car personnel and brought them to the depot, did not come to the Appia Highway any more as it did before, instead, he was picked up at the Arco di Primavera on the Tuscolana Highway, and papa' had to leave the house around four o'clock and walk a good mile through a completely dark road full of holes and mud to get there.

At that early hour, the place was completely deserted, not a soul in sight, just the posted guards, who would sneak from behind their hiding places and scare the wits out of him.

Every blessed morning he had been going through the same routine. He had to show them his pass, which it was just another piece of paper and didn't mean a damn thing to them; in fact, they respected more the uniform he was wearing than his papers. Papa' was terribly scared, so were we, therefore, every morning until we received his phone call, we were on pins and needles.

The Jewish community, already well under fire in the past, had now become the centre of a continuous and ferocious onslaught of the German reprisal. Men, women and children alike, were hunted from house to house, from store to store, in the allies, in the attics and on the roofs like rats. Entire families were wiped out overnight, robbed of their most personal belongings, barbarically beaten and dragged unconscious to waiting trucks and deported to only God knows where. Their stores and properties were savagely ransacked and emptied to the bare walls by the Germans, whom at the end of their looting, now it had become a habit with them, purposely left all the doors wide open, so the Roman population could be blamed and punished for a crime that they had never committed.

The Police Station of Via Tasso, only a few hundred feet from Piazza Vittorio, was controlled by fascists and Germans together, here, political and non political prisoners alike, were interrogated and tortured to death, with methods that not even the ancient torturers dreamed of. Only at the mere mention of that obscure place, people were terrified. It was so bad, that everyone living in the same street or neighborhood, were afraid to talk about it, so it was only whispered that during the night, the inhuman cries of the victims, could be heard for blocks.

Chapter 15

My grandparents from Ceprano and the two youngest sons of my aunt Giovannina had just arrived. On any other occasion, we would have been thrilled to see them, but when we saw them, we knew right away that their being here, meant only one thing: Another tragedy, and unfortunately we were not wrong.

Ceprano is only thirty miles from the German stronghold of Cassino on the Casilina Highway, and even though, the battle for this old city had been going on for months, the numerous German troops stationed behind the front lines, had never trespassed or molested nonno Agostino's property, not until two weeks ago. One morning two German officers came to his farm, looked around, inspected his and the neighbors houses on the hill, asked where water could be found and quietly went away. A few hours later, they came back with two trucks full of soldiers and many antiaircraft guns. They placed the guns all over the hill, took over the houses, the barns, all the buildings around, and ordered the farmers to evacuate, without even giving them the time to pick up their personal belongings All the people on the hill tried to argue, but in vain, they begged and tried to remain in the houses, but they were thrown out. In the barn, nonno tried to get the cow and the donkey loose, but when they found out what he was trying to do, they kicked and beat him until he lost consciousness.

They went halfway downhill and not very far from his own house, to live with another uncle of my mother, but the moment the American planes spotted the position of the German guns, the whole place became an inferno.

Six days later, during an air raid, two uncles, my aunt Giovannina and two of her four kids, were buried under the rubble of their home, killed by the American bombs. Nonno turned to the Germans for help, but they too were having their hands full of troubles, with plenty of damages and casualties. "Go away from here. Go away," they told him.

Lost, frightened and homeless, with nonna and the two kids, they went down to the valley to seek assistance from their nephew Paolo, our old friend, who used to work under the grotto. After dressing, lodging and feeding the four of them, for a whole week, having himself a large family to take care of, he suggested that nonno and nonna with the two kids go to Rome, gave them our address, a little bit of food, a few hundred lire and his blessings. Now, here they were more frightened than ever, but thank God, safe and sound, and here to stay.

Without any hesitation, papa' called Mr. Spinelli and for the same amount we were paying for our, he rented the vacant apartment next to us, where in the golden days, when the mushroom business was booming, a bunch of workers use to sleep in. The place was still loaded with single beds, and with a generous hand from our neighbors, we finished furnishing it, making it as cozy and as attractive as possible for them. Now we were a great big family again, and since there was more room to spare, nonno Edoardo, and myself moved in with them.

Now it was our turn to play host, to provide them with food, to take care of them, to lift their morale, and, most of all, to make them feel wanted, especially our two young cousins who were still grieving for their parents' and their two older brothers' deaths. They were completely demoralized and lost.

I was just getting acquainted with my new sleeping arrangements, and I didn't know yet if I had gained or lost in the exchange. Before it had to be too quiet, I couldn't talk or move for fear of waking papa', now it was the complete contrary set up. The noise, heavy snoring and farting of my two grandfathers, plus the frequently crying of the younger cousin who was having nightmares, kept me awake half of the night. About my two grandfathers, since the two drunkards had gotten together again, reminiscing about their younger days and better times, somehow, to make up for the lack of food, they always managed to find enough wine to get quite tipsy before they went to bed.

Although broken hearted over the loss of her sister, mamma accepted the fact with an air of resignation. At the beginning, we had thought that she would have a nervous breakdown, but it was all over now. Life had taken on a new meaning for her, and she came out of this lethargy period, stronger than ever.

Now her ingenuity was put to a more severe test than ever, when it was time to set the table. She performed miracles. Every day, she and nonna Teresa spent hours digging out of the almost frozen earth, bags and bags of dandelions, Swiss chard, turnips and carrots. Quite often, they paid a visit to the farmers and without fail they never came back empty handed, one time they even brought back some potatoes. Anyway, no matter what they prepared, boiled, fried, breaded, stewed or just with vinegar and oil, it tasted delicious.

Aldo and Angelina, my two orphan cousins, found in my younger brother and sister, new companions and playmates, but it seemed that a full day couldn't go by, unless they had a little quarrel among themselves, that undoubtedly, was completely forgotten minutes later, till something else came up.

The newcomers were starting to feel at home once more and it pleased us. They had lost their homes and four member of the family, something which is not easy to forget. Under those terrible circumstances, we wanted them to be as happy as possible, and in the overall picture, our efforts were paying off.

As far as our daily routine was concerned, papa' hadn't missed a day at work, but us, like the rest of our friends, we hadn't done anything or gone anywhere since the Anzio landing. We had been spending most of the time near the grotto entrance, the best place to hide in case we had to run, or by Nino's little office, listening to the lies of Radio Roma.

One day, Ruggiero and I ventured toward the Statuarfo to find out how things were out there and if we could resume work, but we rushed right back. The place was in a hell of a mess. The Germans had invaded the Statuario and requisitioned four of the almost finished villini, the warehouse, the blacksmith shop, and the carpenter shop. In the carpenter shop, the Germans were busy something like twenty four hours a day making coffins. The funny part of it was, that to build them, they were using Mr. Spinelli's precious lumber.

No wonder he was in such a hurry to get it out. I bet he knew what was cooking in the old pot and was trying his darnedest to win the race, but the Germans beat him to it.

Knowing him as well as I did, I am sure he must have been very upset, but actually there was very little he could do, but keep his mouth shut and be grateful for what he got out of the whole deal, which was worth a lot more than just the lumber.

By the way, although we couldn't go back and finish the job we had so willingly started, for two long days, we had all worked our little butt off, but he had paid us only regular hours, the bonus was not even mentioned, not even a simple, "thank you guys" instead, and no one knew why, day after day, he had been hollering at Nino, threatening to fire him, calling him incompetent, good for nothing, and blaming him for everything happening under the sun. Poor Nino, every time he came out of the little office after he had spoken to the beast, that is the way he called him, he was as red as a poppy.

One afternoon, there was only the two of us, the phone rang and he went in the office to answer it, after a while, when he came out I could see tears in his eyes, and I really felt sorry for him.

"What is the matter with him? Why is he picking on you all the time?" I asked.

"Oh, it is an old story my boy. No matter what I do for him he will always treat me like a rag. It has always been that way, since I came back from Abyssinia, he has never been the same. Money went to his head, and he thought that money could buy everything, but he was wrong. I told him many times, but he never listened to me. That man has never had a moment of happiness in his life and he never will. He bullied his way through and accumulated everything he owns, by cheating or by force, and now it is starting to backfire on him.

You see, seven or eight months ago, his downfall began, and it has been going from bad to worse. First he almost lost his life when the fascist were looking for him, then he had to stay in hiding for no one knew which way the wind was going to blow, then the Germans took over the Statuario, and now he has lost the most precious thing he ever wanted, a son of his own. But he forgot that there was a God up there. He wanted a son from his mistress, he wanted it very badly, but he did not want to marry her, and God has punished him. You remember Miss Cora, don't you?"

Just the mentioning of her name, suddenly reopened the old wound, and sent a sharp pain in my heart.

"Who?" I retorted as if I didn't know who he was talking about.

"The young woman that lived with him in the apartment. Don't tell me that you have already forgotten."

"Oh yes, yes. I remember"

"Well," Nino went on, "she fell from a chair and had to be rushed to the hospital. Her time was not up yet, the baby was just a little over seven months old, and when the doctor operated on her, in order to save her life, he had to forget about the baby."

"Oh my God. She lost the baby. When was that?"

"A week or so ago, she is much better now, but he is not. He is in a bestial mood, and it seems that everything and everybody irritates him lately. I hope he doesn't take revenge on her because now that he doesn't need her any more, he might just throw her out in the street, and believe me, he is the type that would do such a thing. I have known him long enough, that nothing he does surprise me anymore."

Poor Miss Cora, the thought of her being mistreated, really bothered me, and left me with a hollow feeling in my stomach all day long. That same night before falling asleep, I prayed for her.

At dawn, a heavy pounding at the inside wall startled us and got us all out of bed in a hurry. The signal meant trouble, in fact at the door, all dressed and ready to go to work, papa' was all excited.

"What is it," I asked with my eyes still half shut.

"The Germans are here, they are moving in on a full scale"

"What do you mean, are they raiding the place?"

"No. No. I don't think so, they are not the S.S. I hope not, but it looks like they are looking for a place to hide and rest for the day."

We rushed to the pump house and from up there in the dim light of this early February morning, we saw them parked on the dirt road and lined up all the way back along the Appia Highway, with trucks, carts, horses and men.

The rest of our family, Piero and his wife Rosa, had joined us, when suddenly coming up slowly around the bend and hidden from our view, a truck made its appearance between the steep canyon walls. Caught by surprise, we quickly turned and as nonchalantly as possible, headed back for the house, but not fast enough.

After a moment of indecision, the vehicle stopped, then proceeded, then stopped again, and this time, right along the shed where the several piles of lumber belonging to Mr. Spinelli were kept.

Two soldiers got off and almost immediately began yelling: "Comrade. Comrade. Come here."

Frightened we stopped. "The rest of you go home" Ordered papa' in a very commanding voice. "I am going to see what they want," turning and walking toward them, with Piero at his heels.

By that time, the whole community was up, with everybody standing and watching. I was shivering in my boots, but stubbornly, ignoring papa's order, followed right behind them. This was the first time we ever had a direct contact with the Germans, and I wanted to see for myself what kind of people they were.

One of them, seemingly the leader, speaking in almost perfect Italian to papa' in a friendly way asked: "We didn't mean to scare any of you people. Do you all live around here?"

"Yes we do," answered papa.

"Good. Good. Do you know if anybody uses this shed during the day?"

"No. Not that I know of," answered papa' indecisively, raising his hands and shoulders at the same time.

Scratching his head, after a moment of silence, the man asked again: "Is there any water available?"

"Certainly. We have nothing else, but water we have lots of it."

"By the way, on the way up I have noticed two big garage doors. Is that a mechanic shop?"

"No it is not," said papa' dryly.

"Well. What are they for then?" Asked with a sudden interest the man.

This time papa' couldn't avoid giving a straight answer.

"They are for the grotto "

"Grotto?" The German repeated questioningly. "What is that?"

After papa' painstakingly had explained to him what was meant by the grotto, now smiling amiably, the man politely asked to show it to him by leading the way.

Suddenly realizing that unwittingly we could have provided them with an ideal shelter, where they could hide all their equipment animals and men, hoping the German would change his mind, quickly papa' said: "If you want I will take you there, but I don't think the place would be of any interest to you, down there it is damp and cold, besides it has been closed for many months."

"Oh. A little dampness doesn't bother us, we are used to sleeping outside." Taking a gentle hold of papa's arm, and asking again firmly this time, "shall we go and see it?"

I saw that papa' was quite upset, but the damage was done now, and reluctantly we let ourselves be led down the road.

Near the little office, we found Nino looking very confused and bewildered, surrounded by a group of soldiers and the rest of the neighbors, whom had gathered here to investigate the commotion and the sudden activity in our quiet community.

"This is the foreman," said papa', introducing the man to Nino.

"Sergeant Hans?" A tall well built man in a German officer's uniform, head and shoulders towering above the rest of the men around him, called brusquely. "What have you found?"

"Over here sir," answered the man that had been talking to papa', "I have something very important to show you sir."

Casting glances toward our direction, the two spoke for a minute or two, then moving briskly, the officer stopped in front of us, clicking his heels together, saluted smartly and introduced himself: "Lieutenant Schmidt," he said in a guttural voice, offering his hand in a traditional gesture of friendship.

Stunned and surprised, papa' quickly returned the shake, introduced himself and once again Nino. I could be wrong, but I was almost positive, that the German was mistaking papa' for a police officer, in fact, with his black street car conductor uniform, he looked a lot like a city policeman, so

I turned my face and with a big effort, I restrained myself from laughing, for fear of incurring his anger.

From then on, being Nino the foreman in charge of the grotto, he became the center of attention. Confronted with no choice at all, he had to make the best out of this disagreeable situation, the doors were opened, and the unwilling landlord showing very little enthusiasm, led the way down to the grotto to allow his undesirable visitors to examine the place.

In a short while they were back, and seemingly they approved of it, because a satisfied smile showed on the two German's faces, and while Nino as white as a sheet, was helplessly standing and watching them, the order to move was immediately given, and slowly, as we all stood by silently we witnessed that whole column being swallowed in the vast reaches of the underground caverns. When the last man and cart had disappeared from our sight, if it wasn't for all the trucks parked under the long shed, we could have sworn that they had never arrived. The thought that it was going to be just for the day, had entered our minds, but when we didn't see them come out at night, we knew that they were here to stay, and how, and the grotto was going to be their quarters.

We were uneasy and worried, and now that all the community was sharing a common foe, it was decided that we would stay out of their way as much as possible, but at the same time, keep a close watch on them and their movements.

As the days passed, in spite of our fears, regardless of their presence, life went on pretty much as usual. Papa's orders to us, was not to fraternize with them, and although we tried our best to avoid them, at times it was almost impossible. Actually we saw very little of them, but when we did, we couldn't turn our backs to them all the time, because it would have been too obvious. The children were attracted to them like a magnet. As the soldiers would bring out the horses or mules to be brushed and cleaned, the kids would swarm around them like flies. Occasionally, while they exercised their beasts, they placed a child or two, even as many as three at a time on the animal's back, and let then ride around, while they screamed and shouted in delight. If they let them, they would never stop, they just loved it.

Sometimes and when they thought they were quite alone, while sitting under the sun, from our vantage points, we saw them picking the lice from their bodies and crushing them under their thumb nails, affording us much amusement at their discomfort. They were not all Germans as we had previously assumed, as a matter of fact, there was only a handful of real Germans. The rest of them, were composed of mostly young men between the ages of nineteen and twenty two years old, of Yugoslavian birth, Polish, Hungarians and Romanians. Watching them playing with the children, we came to realize more and more, that they were friendly souls just as we ourselves were. No doubt they were missing their own families, and in spite of the many warnings from our parents, we found ourselves making friends with them. As time passed, our fears were gradually subsiding, and we learned more and more about them and why they were encamped here.

It seemed that they were a utility group, left behind to service the main body that had continued to the front lines at Anzio. Every day after dark, three big trucks loaded with provisions and huge kettles of hot food, travelled all the way to the lines, where they unloaded the whole thing, and came back with the empty containers, just before daylight.

At times the drivers brought back all kinds of loot, picked up in the abandoned farm houses scattered on the country side, and tried to sell it to us, or exchange it for little favors, such as laundering their clothes, mending them and other insignificant little things.

Since their arrival, even if involuntarily, they had been helping our food scarcity. When they got here, many of the' animals were sick and exhausted, and the Germans, found it necessary to dispose of them, and once or twice a week, the same operation was reenacted.

The animal, was taken to an open area behind our house and shot through the head, then, they took the best of the meat for themselves and left the rest of the carcass to rot. It didn't remain there too long though, because we watched like hawks, and as soon as they were gone, like vultures, with axes, knives and saws, we descended on it, and when we were finished with it, all that remained to be buried, was the intestines, hooves, head and tail.

Mind you, the meat was hard, but our teeth were just as tough. Because boiling, roasting or frying it made no difference, and the only way we knew how to tenderize it, was to start chewing and keep on chewing. Out of it, we made meat balls, sausages, stew, and when we couldn't do anything else with it, we made horse meat broth, which required plenty of boiling, and this is where Mr. Spinelli's lumber came in very handy.

From the beginning, the Germans had been carrying it down to the grotto using it as fire wood, naturally when we saw that, it didn't take us long to follow their example. In the end they would be blamed for it, so while everybody else was doing exactly the same thing and no one was complaining, not even Nino, piles of good lumber kept reducing daily.

When the weather was good, the air raids were more frequent and more intensive than we had been having, but they were not as ferocious and as long as the ones we had the summer before. During the day, they were mostly small formations of three, six or nine lighter planes that kept patrolling the highways, and now and then attacked and destroyed vehicles, bridges or other strategic points.

Without any warning signals to let us know of their coming, most of the time the raid was already over even before we had a chance to take cover, they came down so fast, that there was no time to run.

Since their arrival, the Germans had placed a sentry post right at the grotto's entrance, and since we had nowhere else to go, as the grotto had been our only shelter, we were forced to find another place to hide and protect our family.

Only a few hundred feet from the house, on the cliff formed by the sudden drop of the terrain, there seemed to be an archway with its design distinctly marked on the earth wall. One day, Carmine, Sandy and I, decided to find out what was behind it and after a couple hours of digging, we discovered a smaller version of what existed of the old catacombs, a tunnel about seven feet high and no more than three feet wide, extending all the way back toward the cemetery of the Tombe Latine.

At the beginning, nobody cared too much to use it, but as the air raids became more and more frequent, and being so close to the house, we all found it very handy.

At night, in addition to the distant artillery firing that kept us awake, the Anglo-Americans supplied us with a beautiful fireworks display. They were guarding the sky and the highways by dropping flares that illuminated the ground making it seem like day. If the flares revealed movements or traffic of any sort, inevitably the plane nicknamed by us as "The Moscone" (The big Fly) circled around a couple times, then dropped one or several of his eggs and unmolested continued on his way.

By the way, we all noticed something very peculiar about the grotto tenants and couldn't figure out why they were behaving so strangely. Besides coming out daily with their animals, which was a necessity, none of us had ever seen any of them to wander the country side, nor around our place. Maybe they had been ordered not to, because they did not want to be discovered from the air, which was a very good reason why they spent most of their time inside. On different occasions, we found out that they were absolutely terrified of the American airplanes.

As papa' had predicted, the hole of the ventilating shaft in Carmine's grotto one day might come in handy, in fact even if no one had yet used it as an escape route, lately, it had become our main sources of information on the Germans.

Lieutenant Schmidt, seemingly the officer in charge of the detachment, had chosen the big rectangular room as sleeping quarter for his orderly, the two sergeants and for himself, and by adding a desk, and a telephone, he had made it his permanent headquarter.

We couldn't have asked for much better, and with Sandy that understood German, we had no problem in getting all kinds of useful little pieces of information concerning our community and what was happening at the front line.

The activities of the grotto's occupants very seldom changed though, they followed the same routine day in and day out, in fact they became so boring to watch, and that we stopped spying on them all together.

To be sincere, right from the first day of their arrival we feared and anticipated plenty of trouble, instead it turned out be to our advantage, because not only we didn't hear or see them that much, but with their presence, neither the Germans nor the fascists came nosing around like they used to, in fact just because of them, it seemed that we enjoyed more freedom than ever.

Only Sandy was never relaxed, he was always jittery, he avoided as much as possible to have any contact with them, but when he did, he never spoke German, or polish. It had become a habit for him to wear papa's uniform every time that he wanted to go downtown. Besides the fact that he didn't have to pay for the tram fare, made it very easy for him, to get into some places, where he could have never got even near them without the uniform.

It was time for him to pay his final visit to his influential friends, to find out what progress they had made toward the fate of his parents, and about the possibility of leaving Rome. Months had gone by since the last time I had been in the heart of the downtown area, and when Sandy asked me to go along for the ride, I accepted, knowing that the outing would do me good.

During the whole journey, Sandy was unusually smiling happily and full of hopes. We got off near Saint Peter's Basilica and started walking. It didn't take me long to realize that he knew the city a lot better than I did, because once we left the main road, we went through side streets and lanes as if he had lived here all his life. When we reached our destination, a grey old building, at the side door an elderly gentleman let us into a hall with a crucifix on the wall and a couple of benches. The whole room was so unfriendly and cold, yet it looked so familiar to me, it resembled the convent parlatory where I used to meet my parents every time they came to visit me.

Sandy asked for someone, and not long after another man, much younger and very soberly dressed, which looked to be a prelate to me, invited Sandy to follow him into the other room.

Ten minutes went by, then a half an hour, then an hour, the place was so quiet, so dead still, you could actually hear a mosquito fly. I got so tired of looking at the white bare walls, that I started to pace the floor and count all the tiles on it. At one point I got so restless that I almost got tempted to knock at the door and inquire, when finally a disgusted

Sandy appeared through the archway, with a face as long as, if not more than the suitcase he was holding in his hands.

Right away I could see that he was very, very upset, and once we were outside and alone, I asked him what was bothering him.

"Nothing, nothing," he answered, at the same time walking so fast that I had a real hard time keeping pace with him.

"What do you mean by saying nothing? If there is nothing wrong, why then are you so ready to blast off?"

Suddenly he stopped, and with big tears running down his face, he said, "my parents are dead. There is no trace of them whatsoever. The last time they were seen, it was entering a concentration camp in Poland, after that nobody seems to know where they have disappeared to. The same thing has happened to my brothers and sisters, they are all missing."

"I am very, very sorry Sandy. I know that my words cannot relieve your pain, but do not despair, have faith in God." I encircled my arms around him and hugged as him as hard as I could.

"It looks like you are my only family left," he said jokingly patting me on the shoulder and forcing a sad smile, we started walking again.

Not a word was spoken for quite a while, until breaking the heavy silence hanging around and over our heads, trying to sway his thoughts somewhere else, I asked: "By the way have they said anything about you leaving the country?"

"Yes. The bishop wanted to but the other guy said that he needs me here and..." Suddenly, as if he had said something that he was not supposed to, stopped. "They said that since I am in no immediate danger, to stay exactly where I am at, which is much safer than any other place inside the city. But I don't care to go anymore anyway there are more important things to do right here, and from where we are, I can be very, very useful to them. I will be able to operate as freely as I want and with minimum risk. I make sure that those damned bastards pay for their crimes."

He was talking, but by the expression of deep sadness on his face and voice, I could see that his mind and thoughts were somewhere else, the pain was actually choking him, and in his heart, nothing else could be lodged, but a great hate and an immense desire of revenge.

After a couple of unsuccessful attempts to draw his attention, I forbeared from asking any more questions and only when we were standing on the very back of the street car, noticing him putting down between his legs the small suitcase, I opened my mouth again: "What have you got in there Sandy?"

"What does it look like to you?" He answered, smiling for the first time.

"A typewriter"

"It is exactly what it is."

"Maybe sometime you will let me use it. I know how to type you know. I took a night course on Via Piave."

"Good for you," he said dryly. "But this one has got some special keys on it. When we get home I will show it to you," he added sarcastically.

Wow, it sure had some special keys, it was none more than a radio transmitter/receiver set to communicate with allied command. And he had already been instructed on his first assignment.

It was past the middle of March and all the time the rumble of the artillery fire had never stopped, as it could be heard in the distance night and day. But lately something different had disrupted the lethargy of a stagnant war.

Sandy's mission was to find out and let the allied command know the exact position of the big gun, a new instrument that the Germans had added to their music, which with its nightly bombarding, was causing very heavy damages and many losses of life behind the American lines in Anzio.

Fortunately for them and for us too, this mammoth cannon, was not used every night, otherwise we could never have slept. When it belched forth its fire of destruction, even when we were at a good distance, the earth under our feet trembled, and all the doors and windows rattled.

Four days before, on the twenty third of March, an unforgettable incident happened, which created a terrible tragedy, to be remembered for many years to come. It seems that a German platoon of S.S. soldiers, made up of mounted sentries, had a change of guard at various locations around the centre of the city, and everyday like clockwork, around eleven in the morning, singing and marching briskly, they would go down through Via Rasella, which is a very narrow side street thickly populated.

Anyone watching the German's actions for a few days could tell precisely where they would be at any given moment during that hour, and the story goes that someone did exactly that, because a time bomb was prepared and placed in a street cleaner's cart to explode at the exact time the German platoon would pass at that point. When the bomb exploded, it killed thirty two German soldiers and wounded several others.

The great big hero who was a so called partisan, responsible for the stupid carnage, was well aware of the consequences and cost of lives for such an act. Namely, that for every German soldier killed, ten Italian civilians would die in retaliation.

Without any delay, both ends of the streets were blocked and methodically, as a precision machine, every male occupant dwelling in the block area of Via Rasella were uncerimoniously dragged from their homes with their loved ones down to the street. They were herded together like cattle and marched amid kicks and curses, pistol whipping and anything else the Germans could think of to abuse them without killing them outright.

After they were assembled and counted, there was only about a hundred and twenty all together, which wasn't enough, and to make up the difference, the S.S. men emptied the political prison of Via Tasso, and when the still didn't have enough, they went to the male prison of Regina Coeli, where, no one knows for sure how many were collected there.

It was a known fact that later they were all taken out of the city in trucks to a section of the catacombs of Cecilia Metella and there, they were gunned to death. To finish the job and make sure that no one came out of it alive, they sealed off their atrocities by blowing the whole section up.

This unbelievable German act of reprisal, was nothing unusual or new to us. We knew they were capable of such cruelty, but they could hardly be blamed for it entirely that time. They had warned the population not to interfere with their soldiers, and the barbarical slaughter they committed, was only to protect themselves and discourage anymore attempts to their lives.

The party that planned and plotted the bombing, are the real ones responsible for the massacre of so many of our innocent people, because they knew of the tragic consequences that would follow, but they went along with their foolish plan, regardless of the cost, just the same.

I hope with all my heart that someday, God will punish them, because, if they were so brave and eager to fight the Germans, they should have joined the armies of partisans operating out in the open, away from the city and the population.

Then, and only then, they would be recognized, respected and honored as real patriots, fighting the enemy, and risking their own lives, not as they did at the expenses of some harmless and innocent people.

When papa' was told of Sandy's assignment, he almost had a fit.

"Now, listen to me son," he said when he finally regained control of himself.

"I don't mind your being with us, on the contrary, I am honored with your presence, but you know how vulnerable your position among us is. If they catch you, it is not just yours, but the end of all of us put together. Have you ever thought of that? Maybe I am being selfish, but I am old enough to have seen so much, that nothing it is worth risking your life for, besides, you have already done your duty, you have already repaid your country or whoever, with the best three years of your existence in captivity. Don't you think you paid enough?

It is very easy for those yellow sons of bitches sitting nice and cozy and hiding behind a desk to give orders, when they damn well know that it is your life that is on the line, not theirs. My advice to you, it is to forget about the whole affair, because, and mark my words, no matter how much you do for them, once this war will be over, it doesn't matter if you come out of it dead or alive, no one will remember your name, no one will even remember that you existed. You have done your share, it is enough. I have lost already one son six months ago, now I don't want to lose another one. Do you understand?"

Sandy had a great respect for my father, while he was talking, he never interrupted or raised his head, and when he was finished, he had tears in his eyes

"Mr. Viselli, thank you for your concern," Sandy said with a trembling voice. "There is nothing but truth in what you said, but no one is forcing me to do anything, I want to do it, because it is the only way I can have peace with myself. The bloodshed of my whole family has to be vindicated, and until I can make the responsible people pay for their cowardly crimes, my father and my uncle will never stop appearing in my dreams. An eye for an eye, that is what they ask and that is what I will have to give to them. As far as to jeopardize the existence of the whole family, do not fear, I am moving out as soon as I find another place to stay."

"What? Don't be childish now. Nobody is asking you to leave. I was merely warning you of the danger, and maybe succeed in making you change your mind, but now that I know the real reason behind your stubbornness, let's forget everything I said. After all, you are not the only one, I have also more than just one bone to pick with those villainous. As far as moving out, you are going nowhere, we are all together in this crazy adventure, besides, where could you find a better hiding and operating place? Maybe I was exaggerating when I said that we are all risking our lives, but it wouldn't hurt to be very, very careful from now on, because we are sitting on top of a dormant volcano. Have I made myself clear? Now. Che iddio ce la mandi buona. What is our first move?"

Sandy put his heart and soul into his new occupation, while Carmine and I did our best to help him. By asking here and there, but without making it look so obvious, we were able to pinpoint more or less the location where the big gun was shooting from, I said more or less, because no one could give the exact position, and only by spending every blessed night for a whole week in the open we came to some accurate conclusions.

First of all, it was not just an ordinary gun, but a real monster. It was a huge long cannon, mounted on an armor plated train, proceeded and followed by two flat cars, with the whole convoy, pulled by a small steam engine, that during the day, was kept hidden in a long tunnel at Colonna on the Casina highway, about twenty miles south of Rome.

At night, especially in foggy and rainy weather, the Germans moved it just below the hills of Albano, and from there they bombarded the American lines at Anzio. It never came out at the same hour, and it never stopped at the same place, it was only used at intervals of fifteen minutes each time after which, they moved the whole convoy to another not too far location and started the same music once again. Absolutely no civilians were allowed more than half mile near the heavily guarded tunnel, and a direct bombardment from the air, would have been a useless waste of time, material and energy because of the mountain right above.

Do to their system of switching so often time and location, it would have been almost impossible to catch it right in the open, therefore, the only way to slow down its operation, and make him inoffensive, was to block off both entrances of the tunnel and destroy the railway tracks along the line they were using.

After we had gathered all this data, one evening, while Carmine remained on guard outside the pump house, Sandy and I pulled up the radio from the well where it was hidden, and at eleven o'clock on the nose, Sandy sent his first message.

We were so thrilled and yet so scared, that later on, it took a whole fiasco of wine to reestablish the calm and confidence in our heart and soul. I was so excited, that I must have asked Sandy the same question over and over again, because at one point, I must have become so petulant, that finally Carmine had to tell me to shut up.

From that night on, we contracted a new feeling, something we had never experienced before, we were doing something important, something worthwhile. The sole thought that we were needed, made us feel great, for a change our life once again meant something, it was smiling at us once more.

Spying, lying, cheating, intrigue, suspense, subterfuge, new expedients, were all part of a game completely new to us, a game that we enjoyed playing, yet a very dangerous and deadly one, and only the future would tell how deadly it could be.

Chapter 16

Spring was here, the days were longer and much warmer.

Early in the morning of the first Sunday of April, a German soldier came to the house to let us know that earlier in the day, the German lieutenant in charge of the men under the grotto, was giving a party held at Nino's apartment and everybody was invited.

We got there at about four o'clock in the afternoon, and the party was already well under way. Right away we noticed a bunch of ill reputed girls brought in by truck from the city, that were already imposing their presence on everybody by shouting and laughing vulgarly.

Even though the sky was completely covered, the air was sweet and balmy, the doors and windows of Ferrari and Nino's houses were wide open and you could have heard the notes of an argentino tango a mile away. The music supplied by records played on an old gramophone was really inviting, and different couples took turn to dance, looking around as they swung, trying not to step on anyone's feet, or hit the several children that were excitingly wandering all over the already overcrowded kitchen-dining room.

By groups of twos and threes, more soldiers were slowly coming out of the grotto, but there was no sign of the lieutenant.

Nino and his wife Elena, were graciously performing their duties, smiling and talking to everyone and passing around trays full of wine glasses and homemade ciambelle, (hard doughnuts with caraway seeds). As the wine was consumed, the atmosphere and spirits warmed up, and soon, finding it too hot, all the kids were sent to play outside, where they would have more room to run, soon voluntarily followed by the grown up people that, as the crowd got more numerous, moved out to the wide smooth cement platform running all along the front of the semidetached one floor apartments of both Nino and Ferrari's.

At about six o'clock, on one of the regular supply truck, noisily blowing his horn to attract our attention, the lieutenant arrived with more men and women.

The music stopped and everybody went to meet lieutenant Schmidt, who right away very gentlemanly, introduced two of the many Italian girls that had come down with him, while Ruggiero and Ferrari, the inseparable friends, lent a hand to sergeant Hans to carry the new supplies into the house, consisting of more fiaschi of wine and boxes of feed.

Drinks were passed to the new comers, who even though they had just arrived, seemed to be well ahead of us.

Among the things they brought, were several new records that were immediately played, and to the bouncing tune of "Rosamunda" (Roll out the barrel) trying to polka, and clutched tightly in his arms, the lieutenant began dancing with Elsa, one of the new girls, but the monocle that he constantly wore, kept falling off his eye, forcing him to stop each time to replace it, much to the annoyance of Elsa who kept looking around with a derisive expression on her vulgar face.

Sandy, Carmine and myself, were not supposed to be there at all, because papa' forbade us to socialize with the Germans, but truly, first of all, he hadn't come home from work yet, secondly, how could anyone pretend to keep us away from music, dancing, women, wine, food? After we had to fast for such a long time of almost everything? Besides, even though, we hated their guts, even Sandy admitted that it was very wise to mingle with them.

Seeing Mrs. Elena and Ruggiero's wife unwrapping packages of cheese, ham and salami sausages things that we hadn't seen since God knows when, we decided to help.

There was a mountain of loaves of bread to be sliced, and while Sandy started on it, we moved to the pile of cold cuts. I didn't think that such an amount of food could be found anywhere at any time, but there it was right in front of us. Someone must have hated to part with it, but the Germans didn't take into consideration people's feelings. They looted where they could and when they felt like it. The tantalizing aroma of the cheese and salami that we were slicing up to make sandwiches with, made our mouths water, and in spite of ourselves, we couldn't resist temptation, so we began helping ourselves.

It was one chunk of cheese for me, one for Carmine and one for Sandy, than, one thick slice of ham for me, one for my brother, but when it came to Sandy's turn again, to my biggest surprise, he refused.

"Hey. What is the matter with you. Eat it, it is delicious," I said pushing it again in front of him.

"It is pork and they don't eat pork meat. You stupid," Carmine barked belligerently. "Who are they?" I asked somewhat resenting his tone of voice.

"Pipe down and stuff yourself. You know what I mean or do I have to draw you a picture? Jews don't eat pork meat."

Only then, realizing the big mistake I had made, feeling rather foolish, I asked Sandy to forgive me.

"Don't feel bad about it," he said quite relaxed. "I am not eating it because there is plenty of everything else, but if ham or salami were the only food on the table, believe me, you guys would have had a hell of a fight on your hands. Come on, pass me another chunk of provolone."

We both laughed at his remarks, and the incident was easily forgotten, yet, in the back of my mind I started searching, and when I found what I wanted, I realized that the last time we had pork at the table, it was more than four months ago, when we got some sausages at Alibrandi's at Piazza Vittorio.

Piece after piece of the delicious and succulent delicacies found their way furtively into our stomachs, until we were finally caught red handed by sergeant Hans, the Austrian, who seemingly was having lots more fun watching us, than taking part in the revelry going on outside, in fact, laughing heartily in his good Italian he said: "Don't eat so fast, you might choke yourselves. Take your time, we brought lots of food for everybody."

"This is much better than Easter," Carmine answered a little embarrassed.

"Easter?" Repeated the sergeant questioningly. "Oh yes. Easter, last Sunday."

"The past four Easters have not been very good for me either, I missed my family. Did I ever show you the pictures of my children? I happen to have them with me, would you like to see them?" He said pulling out his wallet and leafing through the different compartments.

We had already seen them more than once, but sensing his loneliness, we reached for them and naturally made the right comments, such as: "What a lovely family you have sergeant. Is this your wife behind the kids?"

Beaming now, smiling from ear to ear and drawing closer to us, he pointed to one particular figure in the snapshot saying: "This picture was taken when my oldest boy was seven years old. See how tall he stands near his mother? I wonder how big my Gustav would be now, it has been four years since I seen him last," he said with a dreamy look in his face.

In a detached sort of way, noticing a stock of sandwiches already prepared, waiting to be passed around, and seizing the opportunity to change the subject, Carmine reached for them and passing the plate over to him, in a consolatory way he said: "Never mind Herr Hans, maybe next Christmas will be better for everybody. Have a sandwich now, this salami is delicious."

Pushing the sandwich away with his big hand, and heaving a big sigh, he was just about to leave, when from the other side of the table, walking away from the lieutenant, Mrs. Elena yelled:

"Would you like to help sergeant? Here," she said handing him a tray loaded with glasses full of wine. "Pass them around like a good boy, will you?"

While Sandy now completely satiated, abandoned his post and started chatting with Ada, Ruggiero's oldest lovely daughter, we began passing sandwiches around. Everybody was hungry and for the next hour or so, we kept hustling back and forth for fresh supplies, trying to keep up with them.

The sound of the music and the smell of food, seemed to have attracted all the people of the surrounding area, because they came down as far as the farm.

At any rate, the party had enlarged considerably. Almost all the soldiers from the grotto must have been out now, and with ten men to one women, the party got louder, noisier and more dangerous, so to avoid any trouble, mostly of our close neighbors and many others, quietly assembled their families together and silently, one by one left, heading for their homes.

After we saw Ruggiero's wife stuffing her coat with all kinds of goodies, we didn't hesitate to follow her example, we filled our kid's pockets with as much food as they would hold, and sent them home. After all, everyone seemed to be helping themselves, why shouldn't we? Lots of it would be thrown out anyway.

At ten thirty, when the lieutenant decided he had heard enough lamenting from Elsa and her companion, who had been bothering him by asking too soon and too many times to take them home, with a noticeable irritation in his voice, shouted: "Sergeant Hans? Please get them out of my sight." Then turning angrily to his soldiers, ordered them to leave immediately, thus ending the party on a sour note, and to our chagrin the chance to steal whole salami.

Sandy had disappeared with Ada long time ago, so instead of going straight home, Carmine stopped to see how things were with our grandparents, but mostly to unload some of our pocket's contents.

At their loud exclamations of surprise, of how we came to have all those goodies, we couldn't help but burst out laughing, and while they listened very pleased, we related to them the whole story.

Right after Carmine went home, and I had hardly finished undressing, when suddenly there was a heavy knocking at the door that could be heard through the whole house.

"What in hell is that?"Asked nonno Agostino getting up and rushing to see who it was, then, "Santa Madonna" He exclaimed "Signora Elena...what's happening?"

"Please let me in. Please help me, cried out in despair Mrs. Elena standing in the middle of the door in her nightgown and bare feet, holding her scared little boy Fausto in her arms.

"What is the trouble?"Asked nonno taking the baby away from her and drawing her into the bedroom. By this time, Piero, Rosa and all my family were rushing in.

"Oh my God. Oh it is terrible. What am I going to do. Please help me," Mrs. Elena kept repeating, big tears streaming down her beautiful face.

" Come. Come woman. Pull yourself together," said nonno Agostino brusquely. "Tell us what the trouble is, maybe we can help you."

Between sobs and tears, the story came out in bits and pieces, and putting it all together, the sequence of the drama was this: In her late twenties, Mrs. Elena was a beautiful woman, tall, well built, long blonde hair, that evening she had been the heart of the party, she seemed to be everywhere and at the right time. More than often she had been invited to dance and she had never refused anyone.

Even though he was in company of his friend Elsa, Lieutenant Schmidt had asked and danced with Mrs. Elena quite a few times, as the evening was progressing, and even though she was trying her best to avoid him, he made it so obvious that everybody present could see that he was imposing quite heavily on her host.

It seems that after the party was over and everybody was gone, clutching a five liter bottle of wine drunkenly to him, Lieutenant Schmidt came back with sergeant Hans, and began pounding insistently at Nino's door.

Ferrari who lives next door, curious as to what the noise was all about it, opened his door and peered out, but was immediately knocked unconscious to the cement floor by the lieutenant, who after this slight interruption, began pounding at Nino's door once again.

Nino, who had just retired in bed with his wife and child, still a little drowsy from the evening's drinking, got up, staggered toward the kitchen and opened the door, surprised to see his guest so soon.

"Let me in Nino." Said the lieutenant. "The party is not over yet. See? I brought some more wine. Let's have another drink. Shall we?" Slamming the bottle on the table, he reeled toward the cupboard and taking down four glasses, noisily he placed them on the table.

Nino's eyes couldn't see too straight, as everything spun in front of him, but began getting more sober by the second, as he realized the implication of the fourth glass.

"Where is your wife?" The German asked tottering in his heels.

"Oh my wife? She is not here. She went to spend the night with some friends," he answered, raising his voice enough, so it would carry to his wife's ears in the other room, and hoping she would understand what he meant, stalling for time he began pouring the drinks, then: "Come on," he said to his guests, trying to hide the sudden fear in his voice. "You guys came to drink, so let's drink, and I propose a toast. Here Sergeant Hans? Lieutenant Schmidt? To happy times," clinging the three glasses together and raising them up in the air, they repeated after him: "To happy times."

Emptied, they were immediately refilled by the lieutenant who this time said:

"Call your wife out Nino and we will have another toast."

"How can I call my wife if she doesn't sleep here tonight," answered Nino trying to keep calm, but at the same time thinking fast how could he distract his attention, and desperately hoping that she had already left, pointing at the bedroom door he added: "If you don't believe me, look for yourself.

"I had already jumped out and I was going to close the window behind me, but when I heard their footsteps entering the bedroom," Mrs. Elena said, "I knew that they would notice the open window, and without any delay, I ran and came up here. What shall I do now?" She asked anxiously. "Do you think they will hurt Nino?"

"First of all," said papa', "I think you better spend the night here, second stop worrying about Nino, he is a man, and once they get tired, they will leave him alone, and he will know where to find you. You will see, he will be here any minute now."

But the minutes dragged into a long hour, and still no sign of Nino. Rosa and her husband Piero, had been with us to keep the desperate Mrs. Elena company, and were trying their best to keep her calm, because she was threatening to go down herself if her husband didn't show up soon.

It must have been around one o'clock, when with a wet towel covering his right eye, short of breath and panting like a bellow, Ferrari walked thru the door with his terrorized wife and daughter behind him.

"They have taken Nino down to the grotto, they are going to kill him." The roaring of a wounded wild beast and the cry out of pain of Mrs. Elena, at that moment sounded exactly the same, and before anyone could stop her, she flew out of the door and started running down toward the grotto screaming: "Nino. Nino" By the bend, Carmine and Sandy overtook her, and by force brought her back into the house.

"Calm down," said papa' kneeling down and holding her firmly on the bed where she was restlessly jumping up and down. "Nobody is going to kill Nino. Let's not forget that you personally are the reason for this maniac to behave as he is. By going down there, no one knows what his reaction could be, intoxicated as they all are, their bestial instinct surely would prevail, and only God knows what could happen next. Armando. Carmine." He ordered getting up. "You two, go you know where and check what they are doing. Sandy. Come with me to the office. We are going to call the German Headquarter to see if they can send someone to stop all this senseless brutality once and for all. Damned. Damned bastards. How many times have I told you people not to trust these barbarians? Now we pay. Come on Sandy, let's go."

Right away we all took off in different directions and when we got there, Nino and his escort were just arriving in the main room. Something must have happened along the way down, maybe Nino had tried to resist them and they had to use force, because beside sergeant Hans and the lieutenant, two soldiers, Tommy guns leveled were pushing Nino in front of them.

Holding tightly the big bottle of wine, the lieutenant let a roar out of him that awakened every man on the compound, in a matter of minutes, more wine appeared, someone brought out an accordion and the music started.

Meanwhile, being the center of attraction, it was quite evident that among them Nino was out of place, becoming more frightened than ever when they began poking fun at him, forcing him to drink wine he didn't want to, and stuffing his mouth with several cigarettes at the same time saying: "Smoke comrade smoke."

As the cigarettes burned down, instead of letting him throw them away, they kept putting more lighted cigarettes in his mouth until the pain was excruciating and when he complained they forced some more wine down his throat.

Suddenly someone appeared with a wig and planted it on Nino's head, someone else came with two balls of wool that were stuffed inside his shirt, giving him the appearance of a woman. He tried to protest and struggled to get free, but in vain, they brutally struck him on the face, on the body and everywhere.

"So we are no good for the Italian women are we?" Asked the lieutenant with a sardonic smile. "Come on move. Give us a demonstration of your dancing ability then, unbuckling his wide belt and letting it fall heavily on poor Nino's shoulders.

While the men around him highly amused at his act of bravery, began laughing uproariously, the music started up another lively tune.

"Dance Nino, dance. Dance for us," went on the lieutenant striking Nino on the legs to make him move.

"Here sir. Make him wear it." Someone from the circle shouted, throwing at him an Italian soldier uniform jacket, all dirty and ripped at the right shoulder The lieutenant stopped to pick it up, then grabbed Nino by the arm and forced him to wear it saying: "Now let me have a look at you.... Good. Good. This might be just what you needed to complete your appearance. Now come on dance, dance."

This went on and on. At one time, they moved away from the main room, and we lost sight of them, but by the burst of laughter that resounded in the grotto, we knew they had done something new to him.

It is unbelievable how cruel and vicious people can be. For Nino, it was like a terrible nightmare, the raucous voices, the blows, the wine poured into and over him, and I am almost certain, that he did not know when he lost consciousness or what other obscenity were committed on his body.

They stopped torturing him only when they realized that he was completely lifeless, just like a vegetable, then, not yet satiated, to complete his revenge, Lieutenant Schmidt kicked him in the ribs for the last time and gave the order to take him away.

Immediately we left our lookout spot, passed by the house to inform Mrs. Elena and all together we rushed down to the grotto entrance.

Sure enough that is where we found him, but how. Laying unconscious, with the whole Ferrari's family trying to rouse him but without success. Papa' and Sandy were still in the office talking to someone on the telephone, but when they heard all the commotion dropped everything and came out to find Piero doing his best trying to lift up Nino, but with only one arm he wasn't much help, then papa' with Ferrari who was still not too steady on his feet himself, Carmine and Sandy, carried and dragged Nino the best they could, all the way into nonno Agostino's apartment, and laid him on a bed.

Mama mia! What a sight he was. Just taking a look at him, Mrs. Elena fainted. His face covered with blood, severe burns around his mouth and no sign of life at all. At first glance, we thought he had been shot, because there were bullet holes though from a machine gun right across the chest of the soldier's jacket that he was wearing, stiff with dried blood.

In undoing the buttons of the uniform though, we found out that he had not been shot at all, the only blood on him was what had dripped from the severe cuts behind one ear, and strangely enough, we did find the two balls of knitting wool stuffed inside his shirt. Carefully we tried to undress him, but discovering that both arms, as well as his chest and shoulders were black with livid welts, we cut his clothes off with a razor blade. After further examination, we found out that both legs were just as badly bruised and lacerated.

Gently we wrapped him up in a warm blanket and tried to make him as comfortable, as possible. How he did it I don't know, but at one point, he opened his eyes and didn't seem to be too bad, he even drank a little bit of toasted barley water, talked to his wife and fell asleep.

He rested until daylight and when he awoke and unbelievably was able to talk clearly with a big effort, little by little he told the whole story.

After the Lieutenant had looked into the bedroom, and found that the bed had been slept in but empty and noticed the window open, he became possessed with a cold fury. Thwarted in his plans, he walked back into the kitchen outwardly calm, except for his monocled eye that was gleaming malevolently. "Well," he said seemingly all relaxed, "let's drink my friends. Let's have another toast, to your wife this time." But as they raised their glasses to their mouths, Lieutenant Schmidt let fly with the back of his hand still clutching the glass that hit Nino a stunning blow and sent him sprawled on the floor. Then without hesitation, grabbed him by the shirt front and with an unusual strength, literally pulling him to his feet, brutally struck him again and again, under the reproachful eyes of sergeant Hans who had stood silently watching.

The first moment of rage passed, and making visible efforts to compose himself standing in the middle of the kitchen like a frustrated giant, he certainly made a terrifying spectacle to Nino's frightened eyes, that wondered what to expect next, as though nothing had happened, lieutenant Schmidt ordered: "Now get your black book out and find some girls for us."

"But it is late lieutenant," protested Nino. "At this hour"

"I don't care how late it is, get on the phone and you better succeed." They moved into the little office, and there, frantically, Nino tried calling number after number and when he didn't get any satisfactory results turning to the lieutenant, he said: "I am sorry, but I have already told you it is too late."

"Oh... Never mind," said the other, "We will have to amuse ourselves in other ways. Here, have a cigarette." Then turning to sergeant Hans: "Let's take Signor Nino down to the grotto. He won't entertain us, so we will entertain him"

"But Sir, it is kind of late, the men are all sleeping," suggested the sergeant. "Yes, the sergeant is right, the hour is late and I am very tired," protested Nino.

"Now, who in the hell asked your opinion?" Shouted the lieutenant, grabbing him by the arm. "Come on, let's go."

Thinking to humor him and hoping he would abandon the idea, Nino suggested to go into the house for another drink.

"You want another drink eh. Don't worry, you are going to get all you want down there. Now move," answered the lieutenant pushing Nino in Front of him.

Having lost all hopes, Nino tried to resist, and that is when under the specific order of their superior, the two guards on duty at the door took over, first they worked him out pretty good, then they escorted him down to the grotto, where all was quiet, but not for long. . . . .Nino couldn't remember when they carried him out and how long he stayed laying on the ground, one thing he remembered clearly though and we agreed with him.

When they arrived down to the grotto's big room, sergeant Hans disappeared, and as far as he recalled, he never showed up again, in spite of the lieutenant's efforts to find him.

I don't know if it was because Nino forced himself to sit on the bed or what, but suddenly his conditions worsened and began spitting blood. Piero had been on the phone for quite a while trying to get a few doctors to come, but seemingly at this early hour, either didn't want to answer or they didn't want to be bothered As soon as the curfew was lifted, I went to get papa's doctor, an old friend of the family, but he was already out on a call, so I left the message and came right back, just in time to see Nino heave his last breath.

With a convulsive jerk of his poor body, bleeding profusely from his mouth, nose and ears, he murmured something and died.

While amid tears, sobs and wild screaming, his wife Elena pathetically was trying to wipe away the blood from the corner of his mouth, we silently stood grouped around him with our heads bowed in grief.

A couple of hours later, the doctor arrived, but there was nothing further he could do, but pronounce Nino dead, caused by internal injuries and sign his death certificate.

From somewhere, four candles were brought in, lit and placed at each corner of the bed, and the watch began.

Nino was well known, news travelled fast and many friends came to see him for the last time. People wept and swallowed hard as though physically ill, or looked at each other in shocked disbelief when they were told what had happened.

Even Miss Cora and Mr. Spinelli came down to pay their last respects. They were both dressed in black. She had lost lots of weight and had a very unhappy look on her face. From the corner of my eyes, I kept staring at her, and the more I looked, the more I asked myself, what I could have seen in her that made me like and love her so much. Definitely she was not ugly, but neither a standout beauty.

Of course, the fact that there was still some rancor and a bit of jealousy in my heart, knowing that I would never possess her again, I was doing like the mouse that unable to get at the cheese because the cat was there, was saying that the cheese was rancid.

Mr. Spinelli looked old and tired. He took Mrs. Elena into one corner of the room and spoke to her for a good half an hour, then he walked toward the bed, caressed Nino's face, looked at him for a long time, then kissed him on the forehead, kneeled, made the sign of the cross, murmured something and left, his stone face completely wet with tears.

The next day, a quiet funeral service was held at nonno Agostino's house, when it was over, all the men present helped to put his body into the coffin, then while the heart rending sobs of his beloved wife, and the wailing women mourners could be heard, Ferrari looked at Nino for the last time, then put the top over him, nailed it and the casket was carried to the funeral wagon.

The usual black shiny hearse drawn by two well groomed matched pair of black horses were not being seen that day, in their place, they had sent a mangy sway back brown horse with a skinny brown tail, hitched to a make shift lighter cart. Once the coffin was placed on the cart and everybody had taken their place, we started moving slowly down the muddy road, with the procession of mourners following behind praying, the women with their black shawls over their heads, and the men carrying their hats in their hands.

As we went by the grotto entrance, there was no sign whatsoever of the tenants that lived within, not even the guards were there, they were too ashamed to show their guilty faces.

A few yards further down we stopped for a couple minutes to say a prayer in front of Nino's house, then we proceeded as far as the Appia Highway and stopped it would have been too far to walk all the way to the cemetery, so while the cart continued on its way, lined up on both sides of the road, we watched it disappear toward Rome.

We had heard of so many crimes and atrocities committed by the Germans, but this one, was the first time we had been hit directly by them. Death had been brought so abruptly to our small community and it didn't seem real.

On the way home, mama begged Mrs. Elena to come to our place and stay with us for a day or two, until some better arrangements could be made, but she insisted on going back to her own apartment. She wanted to be alone, she wanted to rest quietly she said. So we let her be.

That same day, around seven thirty in the evening, just about time for us to sit down for supper, mamma asked me to take to Mrs. Elena a basket full of food, she had just finished preparing for her. There was plenty of daylight left yet and, as I went by the grotto entrance, I noticed that the Germans too were ready for their supper, with large steaming kettles of food being loaded on the supply truck, soon to be taken to their troops on the lines.

Since the incident of the party, that was the first time I saw them. Lieutenant Schmidt too, was just coming out of the grotto to check the load, when suddenly, I noticed Mrs. Elena opening the door of her apartment, rushing toward the lieutenant like a tornado, and before anyone present could guess what she was about to do, pulled out from under her black shawl a small revolver, emptied six shots into him, then threw herself on him, and like an enraged tiger, began tearing at his face with her claws. As she kept digging and tearing at him in her fury, the sounds coming out of her throat were more animal than human.

Petrified and shocked with surprise at her audacity, the soldiers stood there momentarily stunned, then as one man, they were galvanized into action, as several hands reached out to pull her off the prostrate body of the lieutenant.

Tearing and fighting, she turned on them like a wild cat, somehow she freed herself from their grasp, and with her rage somehow spent, she began to run, but she didn't go very far. Simultaneously, four guns spoke at once and hit her in the back. She paused, stumbled a step or two and collapsed on her face into the mud

Everything happened so fast, that I stood there wordless, when suddenly her little three year old boy Fausto, dashed past me crying piteously in his baby voice: "Mamma. Mamma."

I put the basket down and reached for him, but he eluded me, and before I could get hold of him, he was on top of his mother's body.

"Mamma. Mamma." He was crying, trying to shake her by the shoulders, as he must have done many times when she was asleep. But his cries were unanswered. "Mamma. Mamma." He called again and again. But never again, would his mother answer his pitiful cries, or reassure him with kisses and soft words, never again would she kiss his hurts or dry his tears.

She was dead. She had left him forever, like his father did two days before.

This thought rushing through my mind, with tears streaming down my face, I gently picked up his frail little body, his clothes stained with his mother's warm blood, and cuddling him in my arms, I turned away from this gruesome sight.

As I walked away, a path was cleared for me by the soldiers who were all out in the grotto, as well as all our neighbors.

It seemed so natural, it seemed as though it had been rehearsed, with all the civilians on one side, the tragedy mirrored in their eyes, and all the soldiers with solemn faces, standing on the other side.

I couldn't think too clearly, I didn't know exactly what I was doing or where I was going, my legs were moving, and that is all I knew. While I was talking gently to little Fausto, I finally realized that they were taking me home.

"Please Fausto. Don't cry. Please, don't cry anymore," I whispered in his delicate little ears. "I got something to show you," I said in an effort to quiet him down. "My sister Maria has a lovely doll with big eyes that move up and down. Would you like to see it?"

The word doll acted like magic on him, because suddenly he stopped crying, rubbed one grimy little fist into his eyes, and with a shy smile he nodded.

After I had told them what had happened, I left little Fausto with mamma and nonna Teresa, who were completely shocked by the bad news, and rushed back to the scene, where now the two bodies laying side by side, had been covered with blankets

After shouting on the telephone for good five minutes, sergeant Hans came out of the little office as red as a lobster, gave the order to the drivers of the supply truck to leave and furiously began pacing up and down the cement floor, from time to time, looking inquisitively toward the Appia Highway. Obviously he was waiting for somebody and it didn't take them long to arrive. In fact, shortly after, a car with two officers aboard, and a truck loaded with S.S. soldiers, arrived on the scene and immediately, to our dismay, surrounded all of us standing there. Caught by surprise and never expecting them to do what they did, many of us, vainly tried to leave the scene in a hurry, while many others, remained there motionless, and amid the hysterical screaming of men and women, we were pushed by their rifle butts against the house wall and searched.

As time went by, the situation worsened, they were getting madder by the minute, their shouting grew louder and louder, and while a terrifying suspicion was growing among us, all we could do, was watch and pray silently. We knew that it could well be the end of all of us, only a miracle could have saved our lives, but miracles didn't happen while the Germans were around, so we might as well face it and resign ourselves to our fate.

But that was not our day, Lady Luck, must have been on our side that time, because after the two S.S. officers had conferred for a long time with sergeant Hans and the two sentries on duty, suddenly and to our surprise, reluctantly we were released by our captors and allowed to go home.

We couldn't believe it though, something was definitely wrong. Were the Germans getting soft hearted? Were they losing their touch? Were they the same Germans that only a few weeks ago, barbarically killed more than three hundred and twenty innocents of Via Rasella? It might have not sounded very unrealistic, but it was true. We were free for a change and thanks to sergeant Hans, the Germans had been fair minded, and even though they were Germans, at that moment we were very grateful and even admired them, because finally, even though at the cost of three lives, one guilty and the other two innocent, finally justice had triumphed.

Chapter 17

When we first moved to this house, our family consisted only of four people, but since then it had grown considerably including Nino's son Fausto, who had become one of us as of the night before, we were twelve now.

Three of them had lost their parents; my two cousins lost theirs by the hands of the Americans, little Fausto lost his by the hands of the Germans. What a sad, sad affair, yet, it was remarkable to watch the way these two sets of orphans were drawn to each other instinctively by their common misfortunes.

In spite of her tender years, Angelina, had taken to mothering little Fausto while Aldo, her older brother had assumed the responsibilities for both of them. Obviously the time would come when they would have to separate, maybe sooner than we expected, since that was just a temporary arrangement, until other plans could be made. My parents and everybody else had already made inquiries among their friends and neighbors, in an effort to locate relatives of the deceased couple, but so far until now, with very little results.

Conflicting stories were heard from various members of our neighborhood, especially Ferrari, making it appear that there was a small mystery concerning the late Nino's parentage. It seemed that at times when Nino was drinking, he would bitterly talk of his family. He never said anything specific or mentioned any names, but it was assumed that he had a stepbrother somewhere.

According to rumors, Nino's mother, was widowed when he was about thirteen years old, and in order to earn a living for herself and the child, she found a position as a domestic servant for a wealthy family.

After a number of years of loyal service, the master of the house in turn became widowed himself, in a short time the two widowers were drawn to each other for a mutual need and married. Thus she became a step mother to her new husband's son, who was quite a few years older than Nino. Many springs went by, but there was never any big love or harmony between the two brothers.

The oldest one, never forgave his father for marrying a common servant, and as soon as the war in Abyssinia broke out, he joined the army and made it his career as an officer. Years later, he returned for a brief visit to attend the funeral of his parents, who had died in a plane crash. There, the two brothers met again, and for a while it seemed that the old rancor, the old resentment had vanished, but it was only a surface appearance, they had nothing in common, their ideas, their ambitions, were as far apart as the poles.

One year before the war broke out, the older brother came back from Africa and quit the army altogether. Never drafted because he was born with one arm and leg shorter than the other ones, just around that time, Nino had married Mrs. Elena and both had moved to Rome.

Meanwhile, no clues were overlooked, the search was continued. Rosa, Piero's wife, came from the same village up north of the late Mrs. Elena, and knew her family very well before she moved to Rome herself, so a letter was sent to little Fausto's grandmother, and we hoped that it got there. From there on, there wasn't much else we could do, but sit, wait and keep the boy happy.

It was past the middle of April, the rainy and foggy unpleasant conditions that we had had for several weeks, had lifted, and with the good weather coming up, the almost dormant American Air force, began waking up.

Day after day, from morning till night, closer and from the distance, we could see their constant patrol from the air of all the main highways, but a special priority was given to the stretch of railway going from Colonna to Ciampino, used lately almost every night by the Germans to move the monster gun mounted on the armor plated train. In fact, taking advantage of the dull weather in their favor for a while, they were bringing it out even in broad daylight.

Usually in small formation of three or six lighter bomber planes, the Americans kept harassing the Germans by dropping bombs and destroying the railway tracks at different points along the line.

To us undisturbed spectators, the whole affair resembled the great game of hide and seek, or better yet, it looked as though the American pilots were playing cat and mouse with the German railroad men. In fact, the American airplanes stayed away just long enough to give the Germans the time to repair the tracks and then, bang. They circled their prey once, twice, then, down they came like a bunch of vultures and the deadly carousel began. It was unbelievable how precise they were. Keeping the same distance between one another, and coming almost straight down at a fantastic speed, first they dropped the bombs, and as the wham, wham, wham, of the explosions resounded like the crush of the thunder, continuing on their descent and flying as low as possible, they finished the job with the rattling of their machine guns.

The noise of their roaring motors working harder to regain altitude, completed the terrifying picture.

Needless to say, that after that exhibition of power and destruction, and the steady interruption of the railway tracks, the armor train was stuck in the tunnel of Colonna, and no one ever heard the sound of the big gun again. In fact we made it a point to find out what had happened to it. During two bad, bad days of nothing but rain, the Germans worked steady to restore the line, and one night the whole convoy was rerouted toward Rome and shipped north of Italy.

After the lieutenant incident, unless it was really necessary, the soldiers stayed down in the grotto, and besides the coming and going of the supply trucks, we very seldom encountered them.

Yet, lately we noticed the arrival of isolated and groups of fresh new troops, that by the looks of it, rested a couple days after which, they were regrouped and ten, twelve men at the time, they were loaded in the trucks and before dark, taken to the front line.

No one was aware of our clandestine activities, and lately the flirting going on between Ada and Sandy, and Marina, Ada's younger sister with my brother Carmine, at this time, came very handy, because with the excuse for the two of them to pay their nightly visit to the girls, at the same time, from Ruggiero's house, they had a clear view of the grotto entrance and could control unmolested every movements of its tenants.

Then, one day, sooner than we expected, and whether it was because of the unpleasant incident caused by the lieutenant and the ensuing consequences of his death, or for other unknown reasons, the entire detachment stationed in the grotto, had been ordered to move out. Destination front lines.

It seemed like an eternity, it seemed as though we would never see the day, we had been anxiously waiting for this moment drop by drop, we had counted the hours, the minutes, the seconds, and finally here it was. We had been caressing the yearned thought of revenge for a long time, in fact, we had lived, slept, ate and drank with it, and now, as much as the waiting had been excruciating and exhausting, so much more sweeter the vendetta was going to be.

We were so excited, because at last, even if indirectly, someone was going to pay for all the German crimes, for all the vexations and injustices, for the death of the young lieutenant Alfredo, Nino and Mrs. Elena, for the atrocities committed on Sandy's family, Signor Spizzichino and his wife, and all the victims of the massacre of Via Rasella.

Once we knew for sure the exact date and time of their departure, we went up to the pump house and with our hearts in our hands, Sandy sent the message. Now there was no way back, the die was cast, the Germans were condemned to die. Nevertheless, if at the beginning on the whole, I was glad that they were going to be punished, when in bed, the more I thought of it the more I felt sick, because I knew that a good part of them would never see their homes again.

As we watched them with mixed emotions in our hearts, to prepare for the evacuation, we could see that their faces were not indicating any happiness either especially the younger ones, were making no efforts to hide their tears and fears when they talked to us.

Coming out of the grotto one by one, the carts were slowly lined under the roof of the long shed, we saw them preparing and eating their last meal, and once their supper was over, it was time for them to leave.

The days were much longer and warmer now, we watched them pack up the last of their equipment and personal belongings, then just before darkness settled, while we stood by waving silently, the children calling out their goodbyes to their friends, whom in turn smiled sadly back, the column started moving down the same road on which, with such dread and fear in our hearts, we watched them arrive several months before.

For the first time we were able to count them. All together, they had four trucks, thirty two carts, forty seven horses and mules, and ninety four men, plus three non commissioned officers.

When the last of the carts and men had entered the Appia highway, with a very unhappy expression on his face and trying to force a gay smile, sergeant Hans now in charge of the group, walked toward us, holding his hand out to nonno Edoardo the oldest of the group and said: "Well, as you see we are leaving, and I would like to express my sincere gratitude for myself and my men, for your many kindnesses. Please forgive us if we have caused you any pain or grief. When countries are at war, many, many unpleasant things happen, for which an individual cannot be blamed. He is but a part of a large machine called an Army. Sometimes he forgets to be human and acts like a beast. For these bad ones, we ask your forgiveness. Good bye now and God bless you all."

With his eyes glancing over each face, sergeant Hans saluted smartly, then turning on his heels, started back for the waiting truck. He had gone just a few steps, when he halted abruptly as nonno Edoardo called out: "Wait son," he said walking forward to meet the returning sergeant, then took his hand, shook it warmly and with a slightly trembling voice he added: "Goodbye son, take care of yourself. Maybe we will never meet again, but if this damned war ever finishes, you must try to come back to see Italy, our people will need men like you to make friends again."

Obviously touched, swallowing hurriedly, the sergeant put one hand on nonno's shoulder, nodding his head smiled, then with a happy bounce on his stride, jumped on the vehicle and once more waving to us in a final farewell, he drove out of our sight.

From then on we began the cruel wait, because we knew that sooner or later sergeant Hans and his men would be discovered and they would be in deep, deep trouble. Sure enough, earlier than we expected, at about ten o'clock that same evening, we heard the "Moscone" buzzing in the sky, flares were dropped from the plane illuminating the sky and the area below, till you would think it was daytime. When they died out, some more flares were dropped by the circling plane that unusually kept going around and around, seemingly changing his course very little.

Had he spotted the column or something else? Was he going to drop some bombs? These were the questions going from mouth to mouth, as we watched and waited in suspense to see the end of his mission.

The plane kept circling and dropping flares, circling and dropping more flares. Almost half an hour went by, as we witnessed one of the most beautiful and rare display of flares ever performed in the area which seemed so close to us.

Suddenly and scaring the wits out of us, coming from the same direction, nine airplanes, flying very low and at lightning speed, almost immediately began dropping their bombs, that hitting the ground, caused tremendous explosions, accompanied by the rattling of the machine gun fire, that could be seen so clearly in the dark of the night, as we followed the trajectory of their red bullets.

We couldn't say if they were American airplanes or not, but knowing how accurate they were, we felt sorry for whoever happened to be their victims.

Actually we couldn't see them because they were flying so fast, but we could hear them and how. Round after round, they descended on the target, then they raced their engines to regain altitude and back at it they went again, as furiously and ravenously as before, till their thirst for blood and destruction was sated, and finally with a deafening roar, they disappeared into the sudden darkness and quiet of the night as fast as they had come.

None of us could go to sleep after what we had just seen, and as we stood outdoors talking, shortly after, our worst suspicions were confirmed, when we found out that the airplanes target was our German column after all.

Somehow, sergeant Hans with a handful of his soldiers, half of them wounded and laying on the bottom of the truck, had found their way back to us. In the moonlight, we had to look twice to recognize him. He didn't seem to be the same man that had left us only four hours before, so confident, so full of life.

He requested us to help him and his wounded men, but he didn't have to, we all pitched in whole heartedly, spontaneously. Quickly we rushed to the truck and helped unload the poor broken bodies of our supposed enemies, who after all were human and made of flesh and blood like us, because they cried with pain, an agonizing pain that tore our hearts apart while we removed them and carried than under the long shed where we placed them on the ground over some old canvas.

Sergeant Hans seemed to be in a desperate hurry to leave, and when ready, whether we liked it or not, six of us, were unceremoniously ordered to go with him.

It was in the middle of the night when we arrived at the place where the Germans had been caught, a wide open area, completely unprotected just past the Ciampino airport and the little village of Frattocchie.

It was a real piteous thing to see. The scene before our eyes, was so ghastly, so hideous, that I will never be able to erase it from my mind. Under the moonlight, you could see pieces of dead bodies of horses and men and carts, scattered along the Appia Highway and all over the surrounding fields, like if the wind had gone through a pile of garbage, the odor of dead flesh mixed with the still warm guts of the animals, did emit a breath taking smell. It was so horrible that we could hardly stand it, it was nauseating.

Two ex Italian busses with a red cross design on both sides and on the roof, were already on the spot where the dead bodies and the wounded alike were being loaded.

After a quick counting, it seemed that of the ninety four men, forty seven horses and thirty two carts, forming the German column, seventeen men and nine horse, were the only survivors., as for the carts it's is not even worth mentioning, of the trucks, only one was road worthy, the one sergeant Hans was riding in.

Once the road had been cleared, there was very little else we could do to help, so with the rest of the able soldiers, that resembled more phantoms than men, we climbed on the back of the truck with them and silently we started toward home.

As soon as the truck gained velocity, we began feeling the cold wind and light dew of this early April morning, and we all bunched up together to feel a little warmer. Sitting next to the few soldiers and looking at them, with their clothes dirty and torn to tatters, their faces unrecognizable and still scared, gave me a deep, deep strange sensation in my stomach. I couldn't explain why, maybe because of my young age and I couldn't understand why, instead of being overjoyed for having contributed to the final success of the operation and their destruction, I was all mixed up, and couldn't get rid of the big lump on my throat that was actually choking me. Was the remorse already haunting me?

Why hate and pity played and weighed equally on my conscience? I knew that I could have repented as much as I wanted, but it was too late to say that I was sorry for having caused them such a terrible experience, or to bring back to life all those who had been killed, but why such a senseless slaughter? Was it necessary? I asked myself. It seemed to me that to rid ourselves of one devil, we committed a sin just as devilish, which made me wonder and doubt, of what was right and what was wrong. Yes, we certainly had punished the guilty ones, the wicked ones, but at the same time we had also slaughtered many, many good ones.

I guess this is what all wars are all about, I bet, no one really knows why they are fought for, in the meantime, millions of innocent people pay for the wickedness of a few sinners.

When we got home, four ambulances had just arrived from Rome to pick up all the wounded, and with the truck following behind with its cargo of human derelicts, they slowly moved out once more, this time though in the opposite direction that they had gone the night before, toward Rome and maybe safety. Once again, my heart was tightened with sorrow and pity. They were Germans, they were our oppressor it was true, but at that moment, I didn't think of them as such, I only saw them as human beings made of flesh and blood like ourselves, far away from their homes, without any affection of any kind around them, dying for a lost cause the third Reich and his foolish leader Hitler.

That same afternoon I was in bed trying to catch up on some of the sleep I missed the night before, when like in a dream, I could hear the voices of Miss Cora and Mr. Spinelli talking to my grandmother Teresa.

"If I am not mistaken, you are Mr. Viselli's mother in law. Aren't you? Is he home?" I heard Mr. Spinelli asking.

"No. He is not, he is at work." Nonna replied.

"Well. It doesn't matter," he said a little disappointed. "I understand you folks have been taking care of Nino's little Fausto."

"Yes. Yes. He is staying with us," Nonna said animatedly. "But right now he is outside playing with the other children. Why do you ask? Is there anything wrong?" Asked nonna with a mounting curiosity in her voice.

"Oh no. Do not be alarmed my dear lady. We came to get him."

"The boy seems to be very happy here with us. Why do you want to take him away?"

"Well. I think I have the right to, after all he is my nephew." He calmly dropped his bombshell.

"What? Fausto is your nephew?" Exclaimed nonna with deep surprise registering in her old voice. "Why then have you never said anything before?" Hardly believing my ears, I hurriedly got up, and still half undressed, walked into the kitchen where the conversation was taking place, to find them standing just inside the door, with nonna staring at them, a hand to her mouth in a stunned silence.

"Oh. Meno male. There is Armando," yelled Mr. Spinelli, as three pair of eyes turned to look in my direction.

The two seemed so changed since I saw them last at Nino's funeral. The hard drawn lines in his face were not there anymore, they had been replaced by a soft kind expression, even his voice had changed, he had lost the arrogant attitude he always had, while Miss Cora on the contrary, despair showing in her worried eyes, didn't resemble the gay happy woman that I thought I loved once.

In a polite formal manner, we exchanged greetings, and after that, I went to get my mother, which, since my father was not home, she urged me to go get Ruggiero, Ferrari and if possible their wives, and as soon as they arrived, an impromptu conference was held right there and then as to what to do.

"Excuse me if I Interrupt, but could you please tell me what is going on?" Asked Mr. Spinelli obviously annoyed, showing a little of his old arrogance.

"It is not very easy to explain," began mamma hesitantly. "You see, we have been making every effort to locate relatives of Nino and his wife, bless their souls, and we are kind of surprised and confused to find someone so close to home. We never suspected you were related, but if that is the case, we are delighted."

As mamma spoke to Mr. Spinelli in her calm voice, he quieted down considerably, and finally in a very subdued voice he began explaining: "I am sorry for losing my temper. In the past, I didn't want it known generally, but Nino was my stepbrother. I have known of his wife's death only yesterday that's why I never came before. Now by claiming their son, it is the best I can do to make up a little for all the pain and heartache I caused them both with my selfish and unjust attitude, by making a home for their son who is really my nephew, and I want him as much as she does," he said nodding to Miss Cora.

"My wife just lost her first child and now we need him just as much as he needs us. I am sure we can make him very happy."

In the silence that followed this disclosure, we were all touched and as the women surreptitiously wiped away a few tears, Ruggiero went out to get the boy. Shortly he returned with a very dirty four year old boy by the hand, who, when seeing so many people, became frightened and was about to burst into tears, when Miss Cora, who up to now had said very little, came forward with arms outstretched, stooped down, picked him up and said: "This is your new mamma Cora. Aren't you going to give her a big kiss Fausto?"

"And this is your papa," added Ruggiero, pointing his finger at Mr. Spinelli.

"They came to take you home with them. Would you like that?"

But the poor boy confused by this sudden turn of events, remained silent and kept staring at the strangers.

While we watched silently, kisses and caresses were profusely administered by Miss Cora on the little orphan, then, to break the uncomfortable pause that followed, mamma said brightly: "Of course, while you people are here you will stay for supper with us, won't you?"

"Oh no, thanks." Answered Miss Cora smiling, and trying to be as gracious as possible: "Not today, perhaps some other time. It is getting late and we have to get going, besides we have a thousand things to do especially now that we have a baby to take care of."

At their refusal, I heaved a thankful sigh of relief. For the life of me, I couldn't imagine where on earth mamma was going to find the food to feed them. Mr. Spinelli's confession must have been good for his soul, as the saying goes. Well besides Fausto, who got himself a brand new set of parents, it turned out that Ferrari also benefited from the whole deal, because he became the new foreman of the grotto and all the adjacent properties.

After thanking nonna Teresa, mamma and all the neighbors for all they had done for little Fausto, promising to bring him back someday for a visit, the two left.

As we followed them with our eyes, we were glad to see that the boy had found a good home. Soon, since he was so young, and did not understand what it was all about anyway, he would forget the tragedy of his parent's death, in no time would adjust himself and transfer his love and affection to his new parents, that possibly could do much more than his real parents ever could.

Thus, a happy ending, resolved itself from on unfortunate tragedy.

Chapter 18

At home the food situation was near starvation point. By the time the six hundred grams of bread we got at the store was divided among the members of our large family, it became barely a mouthful for each one of us, and this happened only if the kids were not present at the time of the arrival otherwise, all we got was just the smell of it. In fact mamma didn't even get that.

Although she was a very healthy woman, she had never been what you call a plumpish person, but lately she had become all skin and bones. Her unselfish personality was her worst enemy. She never complained of being hungry. She always waited for the last person to get up from the table, and if there was anything left over, then, and only then she would sit down and eat. Poor mamma.

She did miracles with what little she had. Onions, raw or cooked, turnip leaves, squash and dandelions green were our main diet, very good at any time, but without oil and salt, and at least a little piece of bread to go with them, not only were they not very substantial, but at times, not even the stomach wanted any part of them.

I found that out the hard way one morning when, hungrier than a dog, I made myself a green salad out of dandelions and radishes just picked from the field. Fifteen minutes if not less, after I finished eating it, if I didn't bring everything up and vomited my whole guts out, I would be still rolling on the grass like an animal for the excruciating pain.

Even on the black market there was nothing to be found anymore.

Having a large family of his own and exactly in the same predicament of ours, lately, Ruggiero and his younger son Gino sixteen like me, had just come back from a fruitful trip around Perugia, from where they had brought plenty of flour.

Naturally; since the need was urgent, every time we sat around the table, the main subject of our talk was food and Ruggiero's success.

Everybody agreed that something should soon be done about it, but papa' was very skeptic and completely set against the idea of any of us going anywhere, until we were almost in the middle of May and had hoped that the Americans would be here a long time before this, still they had not arrived and yet, we knew that very soon, something had to happen.

During the day, it would have been suicidal to adventure on any main or even secondary road. With the weather holding up beautifully, the American air force had taken complete control of the skies. The German air force and the antiaircraft guns from the ground, was now inexistent, zero.

We didn't know if it was pure coincidence or if the Germans had learned the lesson, but after the last carnage near Ciampino, there had been no more long convoys on the Appia highway, only well placed apart vehicles, traveling only from dusk to dawn. Nightly, we were steadily checking the traffic, and all we could report, was the passage of the odd truck with supplies going south toward the front lines, but quite a lot of isolated trucks carrying pieces of heavy artillery, tanks, and all kinds of equipment, coming from the opposite direction.

From our part, Sandy had already sent more than one message, and by now, the Allies Command, must have been well aware of what was going on, because in spite of their air superiority, they could not stop completely this steady flow of armaments moving north.

Nobody knew for sure, we could only guess, but it was very obvious that when the Allies would launch their offensive, unless the Germans decided to fight for the city of Rome itself, which was very improbable because of the Pope and the Vatican, plus all the art treasures that were in it (Once destroyed, they could never be replaced) the allies march northward was going to be a very quick one.

On almost flat and open country, the Germans had no leg to stand on, they were cooked, but they couldn't run forever, they had to stop somewhere sometimes.

Now, where was going to be their next line of defense? Perhaps on the next chain of mountains along the Passo della Somma behind Terni? This could have been the next biggest concern of the Allies, and the reason behind Sandy's new mission, who, was to find out if up there was any indication of German preparedness and let them know as soon as possible.

It seemed that what was needed to help papa' make up his mind in a hurry, was Sandy's new mission, and even then, at first he wasn't going to let us go at all, but finally after many conferences, and under Sandy's pressure, gave in, and consented to give us some money and let us try our luck on a food search trip up north, naturally by way of the Flaminia Highway, Terni and the Passo del la Somma.

"Maybe you guys are going to kill two birds with one stone, it is possible, but do not hope for miracles. Ruggiero and his son, were very fortunate," papa' said at the last minute. "All I am interested in, is to bring back yourselves in one piece. Stick to each other at any time and don't take any useless risks, because the road is going to be full of dangers. I entrust to you my son Sandy. Be careful." He kissed and hugged us both, then, with tears in his eyes he ran into the house saying: "Maledetta guerra. Damned war."

For the last couple of days, Sandy had been teaching me how to read maps, and I couldn't say that I had become a specialist on the matter, but more less, I knew where we were going, so that afternoon, each with a large army knap sack, tied across our shoulders, we bid farewell to my family, and started on our journey for the unknown.

From all the information we got from Ruggiero, the best place to hitch a ride was the square just over Ponte Milvio, the bridge over the Tiber River, where all the trucks stopped before heading north.

"Don't tell me all those people are waiting for a ride." I exclaimed really surprised as we got there, dropping the army sack on the cobblestone and looking around in dismay. "Do you think we should start walking?" I asked stupidly.

"Are you crazy? We will never get anywhere if we do," replied Sandy. "Do you realize that we have more than one hundred kilometers to go? Besides, we better wait and see what the rest of the people do, none of them seem to be in a hurry." As time passed, we entered in conversation with other groups, and learned that lots of them were veterans of the highway, in fact for the majority, mostly women, and few men of all ages, this was their third or fourth trip they were planning to make. Now and then, a local truck went by, and while we got all excited for nothing, they remained calmly at their places laughing at us, until someone shouted in our direction: "Sit down and don't waste your energy. If they are going any distance at all, don't worry, they will stop here."

Around five o'clock, we noticed a big truck and trailer lumbering toward us, slowing down, then, stopping completely near the fountain standing in the middle of the square. Two German soldiers, getting out of the high cab, walked toward the public fountain, pulled up their shirt sleeves and began refreshing themselves with the icy water.

Swarming toward them like bees to honey, everyone in his own way and at the same time, we asked what their destination was and if we could have a ride, Surprised at first, then laughing heartily, the two elderly men looked at each other, then at us, holding a private conference, and finally the spokesman of the two said in a very crude Italian: "We go as far as Narni. Fifty lire per person." Then they both walked back to the fountain, drank some more water and waited for an answer.

It seemed that the price they were asking was not too much, because instantly everybody agreed with them.

Both truck and trailer were carrying a load of beautiful windows and doors. Once we were all seated wherever it was possible, money began changing hands, and as the collection ended, the two drivers in a very emphatic way warned us to be on the lookout for American airplanes, then climbed into the cabin, started the engine and we were on our way.

As the truck rolled along the Flaminia Highway, like everybody else, Sandy and I, grateful for this opportunity of a ride, kept a sharp surveillance for any aircraft, but with the sun facing us low in the heavens, and a beautiful clear sky, it made our job twice as hard.

We had driven about twenty miles and everything seemed to be nice and dandy, when suddenly someone from the trailer cried out: "There is a plane. There is a plane." Pointing into a northwest direction, while someone else, closer to the cabin, without even looking, began pounding on the roof. Immediately the brakes were applied, and with a big jerk throwing us forward, both truck and trailer came to a dead stop, but fortunately it was only a false alarm. The two drivers a little annoyed by the interruption, but at the same time pleased that it was only an innocent big bird, reached for their seats and took off once again on their course.

Five minutes hadn't passed, when the signal was given again, but this time it was for real. Three American fighter planes, their wings glistening in the sun, were coming toward us at a terrifying speed.

Amid terrorized screaming and yelling from the passengers, the squealing of the brakes could hardly be heard, and in the confusion that ensued, we all jumped off and made a swift dash for any shelter the roadside could provide.

Relentlessly the planes bore down on us, coming lower and lower with their machine guns chattering a staccato: Ra,ta,ta,ta,ta, whistling as the bullets hit the ground and the asphalt pavement.

In the excitement I had lost Sandy, and when I became aware of my surrounding, found myself alone inside a big cast iron water pipe, where instinctively I had crawled for protection.

Twice the planes swooped down on us, with their ferocious song of death; while scared stiff and afraid to move, I prayed and waited for the third onslaught, but it never came. When at last, it seemed as though everything had gone back to normal, cautiously I came out from the pipe, and to my bewildered eyes, noticed that un insurmountable fence was standing between me and the highway.

"How did I ever get in here?" I asked myself. There was literally no gate or any other visible means for climbing it, so I must have jumped over it. But how?

And how was I to get out? I tried my best, I tried hard, but after several attempts to climb the fence I gave up. Through the cracks between the planks, I could see people getting up from the ditches and heading back to the truck, that is when, afraid of being left behind, I yelled for help "Were are you?" Sandy called back.

"I am here behind the fence."

"Well. What is the matter with you. Jump out." Then "Are you hurt?"

"No damn it, I just can't get out."

In a matter of seconds, a human chain was formed from the outside and a couple guys jumped in, then we formed another chain from the inside and finally sweating and swearing, they dragged me out.

"How in the hell did you ever get down there?" Someone asked. "Did you fly?"

It was fantastic and unbelievable, but only one answer could be found. It was one of those things that only fear could make possible.

Still wondering how such a feat could have been performed by any human being, we went back to the truck and there another unbelievable miracle was that no one was hurt. Also there was no perceptible damage done to the vehicle and trailer, that once more loaded with its live frightened freight, continued northward.

As the night descended on the countryside, we proceeded steadily toward our uncertain destination, and without any further incident, we reached the little city of Narni, situated on a very high hill. We left it behind us, proceeded for another mile or so downhill, then at a crossroad, the

Germans stopped the vehicle to let us off and continued on their own.

By that time, it must have been around midnight, the air was quite chilly and with no specific place we could go to warm ourselves up, since the Germans traveled mainly in the dark of the night, there was still a good possibility to get another ride, so we sat on the grass at the edge of the road and waited.

Unfortunately we had no luck, very few trucks went by and none of them stopped, so dawn found us sprawled in many different positions, trying to get whatever rest we could get, with one eye closed and the other one open in expectancy.

As the sun slowly rose above the horizon, the chances of catching a ride vanished with the daylight, and the groups began dispersing.

Stretching our cramped muscles, we too began collecting our things, strapped them on our backs and looked around. From the junction, three roads could be seen winding off in several direction and offered quite a choice, but knowing our goal we continued on the Flaminia Highway. We had gone just a few hundred feet, when a man on a bicycle overtook us, stopped, got off his bike and greeted us in a friendly manner. We answered back the same way, then Sandy asked: "Is there any place along the highway where we can have a hot cup of something?"

"No. No, nowhere. Either you go back to Narni and still you won't find anything open yet, or you have to go to Terni," replied the stranger. "But if it is only for a cup of coffee, I can offer you one. As a matter of fact, I am going to have some myself, if you guys care to join me, you are welcome."

Needless to say that we immediately accepted his invitation and thanked him.

"I imagine that you two are up here for the same reason as everybody else, looking for food, but my dear friends," explained the farmer, "you won't find anything around here. Between the Germans, the fascists and the Romans, the place has been stripped bare, and your best bet, is to cross the mountain and head for the fertile valley on the other side of it, but even there, I doubt very much if you will have any better luck. Don't forget, this is the month of May, and until the new harvest comes, there won't be very much to be found anywhere, because the farmer's supplies must be running very low by now, but since you have come this far, you might as well see for yourselves, as you never know, you might get lucky. In fact, I have a little bit of corn flour myself, but it is expensive, and if you are interested at sixty lire per kilo, maybe we can do business." Right away we thought the price was outrageously high but we made no comments and followed him.

During winter months, the farm house, was used only for storage, him and his family lived in Narni, therefore, when we got there, there was nobody around.

He put the fire on and while we were waiting for the kettle to boil, instead of buying outright, I tried to exchange the two bicycle tires that we had brought with us, for fifteen kilos of his precious flour but while he wanted our tires very badly, he only offered five kilos in exchange, and I refused saying: "You are asking top price for your merchandise as if it were gold, but you won't give me anything for my tires. Look, they are brand new, never used. Let's split the difference then, give me seven and half kilos and we close the deal."

"No. No. Five kilos, take it or leave it," the farmer answered coldly.

Right away, I could see that we were dealing not with a simple good old easy going farmer, but with a shrewd business man, so I dropped the subject.

While we were drinking a cup of toasted barley, very nonchalantly, Sandy inquired if lately there had been any new activities in the area by the Germans, but he reassured us that there had been none.

Soon after we finished drinking, we thanked and told him that if we could not make a deal somewhere else, we would return and save the tires for him.

Once again on the Flaminia Highway, we got a ride on a cart from another farmer who dropped us off at the outskirts of the industrial city of Terni, where thirsty and hungry we decided to look for a place to eat, but only to find out, that here too, conditions, were not better than those of Rome. In fact, maybe worse, because wherever we went, we could see nothing but ruins and destructed buildings.

Not a crust of bread could be found, not even wine, while the people seemed to be different, cold and unfriendly.

With our spirits completely dampened, we kept going out of town toward the foothills of the mountain that now could be seen in the near distance.

It wasn't midday yet when we came to the first steep hill, and by then, my shoes seemed to be two sizes too small for my feet that were aching and burning.

Sandy was having the same trouble, as a matter of fact, it must have been worse for him, with his high riding boots that must have been like an oven, but he never complained.

We kept going up and up under a real hot sun that at times, became almost unbearable especially when we were enclosed between the high walls of places, where the road was cutting right through the mountain.

As we kept climbing, we saw that along the side of the treacherous winding road that must have cost the Germans and Italians many lives and much expensive equipment, where cars and trucks had missed the sharp turns and gone over the embankment into the deep gulley's hundreds of feet below.

We had already past the halfway mark quite a while back, when we decided that we deserved a well earned rest. Even though the sun was shining and cooking us most of the way, when we encountered shady spots the air was much cooler and breezy.

Looking below us, the roofs of the houses of Terni, that just one hour ago seemed to be on our feet, now were becoming smaller and smaller multicolored spots on the ground. The look in front of us, wandered undisputed on the surrounding area as far as the eye could see.

By the time we had reached the summit, the sun hadn't started to go down yet.

On the plateau-like top, there was a cabin with fresh water, where we drank thirstily and again we enjoyed the scenery below while we rested. The view was magnificent, but the beautiful scenery, could not fill our stomachs, that had not tasted food for the last forty eight hours, and the prospect of getting any, seemed just as far away as ever.

We had ascended one of the roughest mountains this side of the Alps, known to the world as the "Passo della Somna". Now, if here, there was going to be some kind of a German defensive line, certainly we should have been able to detect immediately some type of emplacement in the rock for their artillery pieces and machine guns. Also, the area should have been infested with Germans and Italians working, with tractors, bulldozers and other heavy machinery, in short, the place should have been buzzing with activity instead nothing, completely nothing.

We climbed the embankment on both sides of the plateau, and walked quite a way into the woods, and there, nature, looked as virgin as the day it was created, therefore, once we got back to the fountain we concluded that the "Passo della Somna" was completely clear, and the first part of our mission had been accomplished. New with this thought off our minds, we were going to concentrate our efforts, to the second part, food, and get back home as soon as possible so Sandy could send his message to let the Allies know of what we had found.

Away from the sun that was fast going down, I was getting cold and looking at Sandy who had taken his heavy boots off to give a momentary relief to his feet I suggested to get going.

"Yes. We better. The sooner we reach the valley the better chance we will have to find something to eat, besides, if we stay up here any longer we are going to freeze to death." He said getting up.

Unexpectedly, for the first time since we began climbing the mountain, we heard the labored roar of a heavy motor coming up the steep hill in low gear.

Our hearts quickened with anticipation of a ride, as we looked at each other with broad grins and stood on the middle of the road waiting hopefully. The miracle happened. Puffing and steaming from its long climb, the big truck pulled off the road and came to a stop, as the lone driver descended, walked toward the fountain, drank, refreshed his face and turned to us. He was just a young man of medium height and very fair, and for a German, he had the friendliest face I ever seen. He seemed to be tired after the long ride, because he stretched first his arms, then his legs, then turning toward us he smiled and beckoning with his hands he asked: "Going down?"

"Yes." We nodded eagerly with our heads, returning the smile.

"All right, come on then," he said heading toward the cab, opening the door and gesturing with his hands at us to get in.

As I said, his manners were very amicable, and I couldn't help liking him instantly. I tried to start a conversation, but when I saw that we were getting nowhere, I stopped and let him concentrate more on his driving, which at some points, was very, very frightful.

Now and then he would turn his boyish face to us and smile, as though he was very pleased about something as for myself, I felt comfortable and relaxed, for a chance, it felt great to be seated and enjoy even the silence of the cab, while Sandy was tight, cold and ill at ease and kept staring outside the side window

While going down very slow, we kept inspecting both sides of the road for any particular changes in the scenery, but everything seemed to be untouched. This side of the mountain, was much nicer than the other side, with tall trees rich with their beautiful green foliage, the odd bird flying freely, and a solitary jack rabbit, who, scared by the sound of the engine, ran away hiding into the woods, were the only inhabitants of this immense natural kingdom.

It was pitch dark now, and the more we kept going, the more grateful I was becoming toward this silent Teuton, because I realized how far we were from the lowland, and if we had to walk it we would have spent most of the night coming down the mountain.

Once down in the valley, we entered the city of Spoleto and he asked if we wanted to descend, but at our negative sign, he proceeded. When we had the opportunity of a comfortable ride, we thought that we might as well enjoy it, besides, the further we went, the better chance we would have to find some food, but our luck couldn't hold forever, in fact we didn't go very far.

Around thirty miles past Spoleto, at a village called the Fonti del Clitunno, there was a concentration camp, where the Germans kept their war prisoners, and unfortunately for us, our friend's destination. As he slowed down there were all kinds of signs indicating to the camp that could be seen in the distance with the high barbed wire fence all around it, the watching towers on each corner where the shiny metal of the machine guns, reflected under the moonlight.

A few hundred feet from the gates, he stopped to let us off and we thanked him a million times. As we separated, I felt as though I was leaving an old friend and I couldn't help saying to Sandy: "He sure was a swell guy. Wasn't he?"

"Sure. Sure." He answered back with a sarcastic tune in his voice, and actually opening his mouth for the first time since we left the top of the mountain, "the trouble is that there are not too many like him around. Come on, let's get the hell out of here, this is no place for freedom loving men like us," as he lead the way across the road and into the fields.

There were lots of willow trees around and helped by the moon light, following a white shining path for a good half a mile, we were hoping to find a residence of some kind, but when we couldn't see any houses around we decided to stop and call it a day.

We only had one choice, to settle down in the open with the sky above for a roof and the earth below us as our beds, so we began looking for a good spot, and finally I thought I had found it, under two great big willow trees not even fifty feet away.

"What do you think of that?" I asked Sandy, pointing at them.

"Certainly. They are just as good a place as any, I guess," Sandy answered starting to walk toward them.

As we approached, we could see another white narrow path dividing the two trees, so, being closer to the first one, I got right at the foot of the tree, dropped my sack to the ground and flopping beside it, I said to Sandy: "Well. This is it. Good night and sweet dreams."

"Good night," he replied, walking toward the other tree, but suddenly the silence of the night, was shattered by a big splash and almost instantly, I heard the crying voice of Sandy imploring for help: "Mamma mia. Aiuto. Help me Armando help, I am drowning."

Naturally I got up as quickly as I could and looked, but Sandy was nowhere in sight. "Help Armando help," he kept yelling.

"Damn it. Where are you?" "Here. Here," as he thrashed madly about in the water over his head.

Then I saw him, with his head bobbing in and out of the water. I rushed toward him, immediately lay down on my stomach along the bank of the path that was not a path but a deep canal, and reached a hand out to grab him and slowly dragged him out of the water, as he kept lamenting in a frightened voice: "Mamma mia. Mamma mia. What happened?"

I couldn't help laughing my head off, and the more I looked at him, the more the more I laughed.

There he stood in the cool night air, soaking wet from head to foot, and completely covered with the white blossoms of the willow trees that had fallen and covered the surface of this apparently very deep irrigation ditch, making it look like a gleaming path in the poor moonlight.

"What are we going to do now?" Muttered Sandy between his clattering teeth and shivering like a leaf.

Actually it was not very cold, but the dew had already started falling, and the rigidity was beginning to set on the nightly air.

"Well. What do you suggest? I guess we will have to find a place for you to change and dry your wet clothes, before you catch yourself a case of pneumonia. Come on, let's move."

I jumped on the other side of the path, picked up his sack, jumped back, picked up my own and once more we started across the fields, with Sandy's riding boots squishing, squishing at every step and supplying the music.

The more we got into the interior, the harder we had to work to find a way out. We had stepped into a vast vineyard, where the several wires that ran from pole to pole hidden behind the leaves, was catching us on the face, chest and legs, not to mention the many more irrigation ditches that we both kept falling in to, making us wetter and madder by the minute in our frustration. By then, it didn't seem funny to me anymore, we were both swearing in exasperation, and to top it off, suddenly scaring us half to death, somebody yelled: "Stop or I will shoot."

Needless to say we did stop and in a hurry too.

"Who goes there?" The same voice called again.

"Please don't shoot." We implored them. "We are friends."

"Who are you, and what are you doing here at this time of the night? Don't you know you are trespassing?" The same voice spoke, as three men approached cautiously toward us, each armed with a hay fork.

Once reassured that they had no guns or rifles, we walked toward them and began explaining:"We are not trying to steal anything. Actually we started out trying to find a house for shelter, but when we lost our way, and fell into these damn ditches, being all soaking wet we had to continue our search."

"Jesus Christ," the oldest man swore vehemently. "You could have drowned and no one would have ever found you.

Some of those ditches are fifteen to twenty feet deep and always full of water, spring water. Come on now, you will be catching cold. We will take you to the house where you guys can get warmed and dried out."

Gratefully we followed them, as they led us around a large house surrounded by all kinds of trees, and into a barn where it was nice and warm.

"Take off those wet clothes," ordered the old man, then turning to his two boys more or less my age but well built, "bring down some of your own clothes to them," and before they were out of sight he yelled: "Just a moment," and turning again to us, he asked, "have you had your supper?"

"Supper?" We answered in unison. We haven't touched food since we left Rome, and that was two days ago. "

"Ooooh. Poveri cocchi! My poor dear ones. He exclaimed really touched. "Bring down some food and lots of it," he ordered his sons. "I bet they can sure use it."

Very soon, his two young boys came back, one with an arm full of clothes, the other one with a big clay jug of wine, a good half loaf of bread and a chunk of cheese.

"There," he said tossing a couple of blankets to us. "You will be comfortable here tonight. Sleep in the hay, it is soft and warm, and don't be afraid of Cecilia, she won't hurt you, she is a well mannered cow."

After we had switched into the nice dry clothes, they picked up the wet ones and left. Closing the barn door behind them he yelled: "See you guys in the morning."

Once alone, we devoured the food like two hungry wolves and drank the wine with relish, then as a delicious drowsiness came over us, taking a blanket each, we curled up in the warm clean hay and within minutes we were asleep.

We slept the sleep of the dead, till we were abruptly awakened by the sound of German voices. At first I thought

I was dreaming, but when I saw Sandy peaking through the barn door, I knew I was wide awake.

"What is it?" I asked in a whisper.

"Shh. Shh. Come and see," he said.

There was quite a commotion outside. We counted five trucks parked under the trees unloading German soldiers, with more loaded trucks coming in and stopping in the back yard. The uniform they wore, was a mottled green of the paratroopers.

"What do you suppose they are doing here?" We asked each other frightened and bewildered. "Are they taking over the place?" "If they are, we are in a hell of a fix."

Silently, we watched then get off their vehicles, but as we noticed that they were not rushing anywhere and all of them unarmed, we felt relieved, still we didn't dare go out, and waited for the farmer that soon entered the barn with our own clothes, and once we had slipped into them he escorted us into the house to have breakfast with his family, but to our surprise, we found other guests sitting at the big kitchen table and reluctantly, we drew back with fear and embarrassment.

"Don't mind them," said the farmer briskly, pushing us into the room. Come on, find yourselves a chair. They won't bother you, They are just in transit, and stopping here only for the day. Isn't that true sergeant? These two boys are good friends of mine from Rome." The farmer said introducing us casually.

"Rome eh. . Nice to meet you," replied the non commissioned officer speaking fluently in Italian, and getting up to shake hands with us.

After that, even though none of the officers looked up at us, it was much easier to sit and enjoy our breakfast. In the course of the conversation that followed, while we ate, we learned that the sergeant had a classical education in an

Italian school, and before he was drafted into the army, he was a teacher in a town near the Italian-Austrian border, he knew Rome as well as we did, and was very anxious to see it again.

After the officers left the table, for whom the sergeant acted as interpreter, instantly he became another man. He spoke less guardedly and sometimes despairingly of the Germans in general and their army in particular.

We were surprised and pleased to hear him talk like that, making us feel as though we had an ally in him, so taking advantage of his friendliness, audaciously and making it sound like a big joke, I asked him, "Sergeant, I don't want you to divulge any army secrets, but may I ask where you are going when you leave tonight?"

"It is no big secret, we are going to Rome." He replied with a noticeable satisfaction in his voice.

"We are part of a big family, and came up here to scrape some flour or whatever we can find. If everything goes as planned, we should be going back too. Would it be asking too much to give us a lift?"

"Sure. Sure. Why not? We are leaving tonight as soon as it gets dark. So make sure to be here on time."

"Thank you sir, we will try our best," and turning to Sandy who in the presence of Germans, always left everything up to me, I added: "We have all day ahead of us, if we are lucky, we should be able to buy all the provision in the world, and with God and the sergeant's help, by tomorrow morning we should be back home."

At that, we saluted the sergeant, we stepped into our still damp shoes, we thanked the farmer, his wife and their two sons for their many kindnesses and left.

On our way out, to our surprise, we discovered that the Flaminia Highway, was just a few hundred yards from the farm house where we had spent the night. All we had done the night before, was to make a large semicircle around a basin of water, fed by natural underground springs, completely surrounded and almost hidden by hundreds of weeping willows trees. The little lake, in turn fed all the deep irrigation ditches that branched off into the countryside, and this is how the place got the name "Fonti Del Clitunno" from.

Moving as fast as our feet would permit it, we scoured the whole area as thoroughly as we could, from farm to farm, following paths, dirt roads, at times the highway, where we even separated and went in different directions, back to the highway once more, back into the country through fields and farms, but without success. There was just nothing to be had. The Germans and the fascist troops of the Social Republic, had stripped them of everything but the bare necessities, and now the farmers were all waiting with hope for the early crop, but they too did not look very promising, as the fields were suffering from lack of care and cultivation because of the shortage of help.

Around noon, we asked for a slice of bread, but even that was denied to us. Courageously we kept going, hoping to be rewarded at our next stop, but we made many of them and the same negative answer was given to us.

"Sorry, we have nothing to sell, trade or give."

Judging by the sun, it was beginning to get late, soon it would be dark, now, it was either wait for another day and go further north to Perugia, or give up the search and go home empty handed. In the desperate mood we were in, it was easy to vote for the second option, beside, it would have been almost impossible to find again another splendid opportunity to get an easy ride directly to Rome, like the one the Austrian sergeant had offered us that morning, so, disappointed and discouraged, the futility of continuing the useless search was abandoned, and if we were to make the German convoy, we had better hurry on our way back.

More or less, we knew our position, and half walking and half running, we covered the five or six miles that separated us from the farm from where we had started earlier in the morning.

The trucks had already began to roll, as we could see them lining up slowly along the winding driveway. With anxiety we searched from the first in line for a sign of our friendly sergeant, and there he was, right on the last vehicle of the column. To make sure that he would see us, we crossed right in front of his moving truck, and as he recognized us, without saying a word, he made a sign to us to jump in the back.

Panting and out of breath, we threw the empty sacks on the truck and leaped up behind, finding ourselves in the midst of a dozen soldiers that looked at us strangely and resentfully. For a second, we thought they were going to toss us back on the road, but the yelling of the sergeant was heard just at the right moment and we were left alone. We cowered on the rim of the tall gate preciously like two forlorn little orphans and kept silent.

Out on the highway now, the column began moving at a regular speed of twenty five to thirty miles an hour, the sounds of the wheels lulled us into a sense of security, but the trip, beside Sandy's mission considered the only success of the operation, it had been a dismal failure, and the thought of the disappointment plus the fact that I had to face my parents bare handed, occupied my mind.

And it wasn't for lack of trying, we had endured many hardship and discomforts, and I was hoping they would understand. Next morning we would be home, and by the time evening arrived, everything would be forgotten, as any unpleasant incident are always soon forgotten.

Once again, we drove through the ruins of the town of Spoleto, with its dark street and no sign of life anywhere, then once more we were in the open country and we must have travelled a good distance, when suddenly the column stopped.

Quietly we waited, wondering what the delay was all about, silently a couple minutes went by, when we heard footsteps approaching and someone addressing the sergeant who answered back, then unexpectedly a flashlight blinded us with a glare and blackened out everything behind it. Angry words were passed back and forth for a few seconds between the new comer and the soldiers on the truck, and I gathered they were discussing us, then suddenly very unceremonious the man from the ground shouted: "Rowse. Rowse"

It was too clear by then that he wanted us down. Frightened, we grabbed our sacks and jumped to the pavement, to find ourselves facing a couple of German S.S. soldiers, all dressed in black, one of them holding a Tommy gun at our bellies, gesturing and shouting hysterically to walk away in the direction we came from.

There was no sense in talking, and even less arguing, so we started walking expecting any second to feel the impact of bullets in our back.

Without daring to turn around and look back, not only did we kept walking, but we kept going till we felt certain there was no one following us, then stopped, sat on the side of the road and we both wept with rage and frustration.

It is funny though how in such moments, we always forget to look at both sides of the coin, true, we were stranded once again which was very bad, but we never stopped to think just for a moment, that instead of going as it did, it could have been a lot worse. We had escaped death by a hair's breadth s or maybe deportation by the S.S. Anyway, there we were again, in the middle of nowhere, hungry, tired and depressed.

There was no sense in going back toward Spoleto, because we knew that the food situation was always worse around populated areas than farm country, where we just came from, so our best bet, was to continue heading toward the mountain, following at a much different speed now, in the tracks of the German convoy that had quickly disappeared from our sight, and with it, our hopes to go to Rome and our home.

Swearing and cursing all the Germans, who were responsible for this big mess we were in, we walked and walked till it seemed we could go no further.

It was completely pitch dark, even the moon had forgotten to come out, now and then we attempted to stop the rare vehicle that was going our way and hoped they would give us a ride, but no luck. It must have been around midnight when, finally our efforts mixed with a barrel full of curses, paid off, as a light army truck passed us by at full speed, pulled hard on the brakes and backed the few hundred yards to where we were.

"Where are you going?"Asked the driver in plain Italian.

"Roma. Roma."

"I go as far as Narni. You guys want a ride?" The driver asked.

"Sure. It is very kind of you. Thanks." We both replied heading for the back of the truck.

"Hey. Hey. Not so fast." The driver yelled. "Fifty lire a piece."

"What? Fifty lire?" I exclaimed freezing on the spot. "You are only going over the mountain. Come on man be reasonable."

"Fifty lire each. No arguing," said the driver racing the motor with impatience.

Dirty son of a bitch of a fascist renegade, I muttered between my teeth.

Money meant a lot to us, especially at this moment, when there was nothing in our sacks, but the thought of being left on the highway was too painful, so reluctantly we handed over the hundred lire, imprecating a thousand curses upon his head, we lifted the tarpaulin hanging on the edge of the truck and jumped in.

In the pitch darkness, we could hear two people talking on the right side of the truck, so we tried to find a place on the left, and while I made myself as comfortable as possible between a big suitcase and an army sack belonging I Imagine to the other occupants, Sandy sat a few feet next to me closer to the tall gate.

As the truck wound its way up the treacherous mountain road of the Somma, we in the back were lurched from side to side, and unexpectedly, my hand landed in one of the pockets of the army sack near me, which to my surprise, felt quite greasy. At first, I didn't bother, but after a while, my curiosity aroused, I explored further. I swear in my honor, it was just plain curiosity, I had no other intentions whatsoever, but after a long, long day without food, and coming into direct contact first with a generous supply of salted bacon, then with three large round homemade loaves of bread, I couldn't resist temptation.

With my eyes half closed, and being invisible to my travelling companions still busily talking, furtively broke off a chunk of bread, took a bite at the not too tender slab of rinded bacon, and from there on, had the time of my life all by myself.

I don't know if it was because I was too scared to move, or make any kind of different noise that would attract the attention of the owners, or because I was just plain selfish, but only when my appetite had slightly been sated, did I think of sharing my good fortune with Sandy who had been snoring peacefully.

Playfully I rubbed a greasy peace of bacon under his nose, at which, he almost gave the show away by his ejaculation of surprise, but quickly I smothered it with my hand. After that, the pork meat, didn't make a damn bit of difference to the poor starving Sandy, whom, while I continued to explore the rest of the contents of the knapsack, took his turn to feast.

When we got to Terni, the truck stopped to pick up a crowd of mad people who yelling, shouting and pushing, poured on the back of the vehicle like an avalanche, and it was then, when amid that great confusion that I decided to steal the whole knapsack. Immediately I informed Sandy of my plans, whom, to my big surprise, cowardly refused to go along with me, claiming that he was no thief. I begged, and begged, but when I saw that he wanted absolutely no part of it, he made me so mad that I swore that if I succeeded, he would have not even a crumb of bread from me.

Time and miles flew swiftly, and since I had to work alone, as the truck started going uphill and neared the town of Narni, I gradually moved the sack near the tail gate and waited for the truck to slow down. Once it did, there was nothing to it, without hesitation, I threw both sacks, mine with the tires in it, and the full one, then jumped myself, touching the pavement almost together, then, with the agility of a cat bounded to my feet, I grabbed the two sacks, and with the speed of a gazelle, I sped downhill.

At the last moment, Sandy had jumped right behind me, bringing up the rear and yelling desperately: "Armando. Wait. Wait for me."

But suddenly deathly frightened at what I had just done, I kept going down as fast as I could, as though, I was trying to put distance between me and the devil.

Still running, we retraced our steps to the very bottom of the hill, where not too sure of which way to go, we kept going till we came to a familiar sight, the junction where we had stopped on our way up a couple nights before.

Recognizing the familiar place, I felt a little more sure of myself, and for a split second the farmer with the corn flour came to my mind, but for the time being, I discarded the idea, because we were right in the middle of the night.

The best way to lose ourselves in case we were being followed, was to mingle with the crowd that always seemed to be waiting at this very important crossroads, and that is exactly what we did.

I wasn't talking to Sandy because I was still mad at him, in fact he could sense my coldness and kept following me like a beaten dog.

During the following hours, several times we attempted to flag a south bound truck, but they didn't stop, and when dawn came, tired sleepy and cold, hoping to find him there we decided to return to the farmer's house. He was not there though and since we had no other place to go, we sat by the house and waited.

The sun was already up when we saw him on his bike turning into the driveway, and his first reaction at having such early callers was surprise, but faded into pleasure when he recognized us. In fact, greeting us warmly like old friends, he invited us inside, and once seated around the kitchen table, since these days food was constantly on our minds, seeing a bunch of cooked turnips on the stove, we offered some bacon and with a couple of his onions, we fried the whole lot together and with a good chunk of our bread, a succulent breakfast was the result.

Just as we were getting ready to devour this delicacy, someone knocked on the window and a huge head appeared behind the glass startling us.

"Who is that?" We asked in a hushed whisper.

"Oh. Don't be afraid of him," said the farmer cheerfully getting up. "He is my Russian friend, a deserter of the German army. I have been kind of looking after him for a good while now, he comes here for food and water every blessed morning. I better let him in, he must be starving the poor soul," he explained opening the door and stepping aside to let a towering giant of a man into the room.

"Good morning Ivan. How are you this lovely morning?"

Timidly the Russian came into the kitchen never taking his eyes off us. He seemed very frightened, but gradually he gained confidence as the farmer spoke gently and patted him on the shoulder, while we smiled trying to make him feel at home.

Judging by the length of his long blond beard and hair that was beginning to curl up like a woman's, on the collar of his dirty yellowish overcoat that hung below his knees, the poor man hadn't had a shave or a hair cut for months, and obviously he must have been of Slavic or Russian origin, because his coat was buttoned from the chin to below his hips, with the canteen across his chest.

As he sat at the table he spoke, but even Sandy couldn't understand a single word he said, so to distract his attention, I passed him a slice of bread.

With him sitting at the table, the meal didn't last long, he had an enormous appetite, which put ours to shame, and within a short time, there was no tiling left to eat.

I didn't know about the others, but I was still hungry, Ivan must have been too judging by the way he eyed the empty dishes, with seeming reluctant, arose from the table, walked to the pump, filled his canteen with water and without saying a single word, silently left the kitchen. As the three of us watched him disappear into the thick woods behind the house, the farmer said musingly and at the same time shaking his head sadly: "I wonder how many there are like him scattered in these hills." Then, sitting down at the table once more, "well now," he said cheerfully again and changing the subject completely, "What kind of a deal are we going to make this time? Do you still have those rubber tires?"

"Yes we still have them," I answered promptly. "You were quite right you know? We had no luck at all, the farmers over there are very poor and could sell us nothing, but if you will be reasonable this time, we might work out a deal."

He pushed himself against the back of the chair he was sitting on, smiled in a friendly way, shoved his hands deep into his trouser pockets, and deliberately crossed his legs as though sitting down for a long discussion.

Involuntarily a deep sigh escaped me as I looked at Sandy saying: "Away we go again." We all laughed at that, but inwardly, I made up my mind that I was going to get more flour than he had originally offered.

Unfortunately in spite of the fact that the haggling went on and on, in the end we had to accept his offer or go home empty handed. We only got five kilos of flour for the tires, but in the deal, he consented to sell ten extra kilos for cash money, which wasn't very much, but we were more than glad to get it.

Leading the way into a well stocked room, that had just about everything imaginable in it, while we looked at all the goodies with desire in our eyes and hearts, he opened a sack of flour and with a plain dish, he scooped out fifteen of them. When the transaction was completed, suddenly he seemed in a hurry, because after looking at his pocket watch, he pushed us outside and locking the door behind him, he said: "I have some urgent business to attend to in Narni at ten o'clock, and I better get moving. As for you boys, it is not wise for you to go to the junction, first because there won't be any trucks going by till after dark in the evening, secondly, the place is not too safe in the daylight any more, as the American planes have been flying over it almost every hour lately. Do as you wish, you can remain here till it is safe or go away, it doesn't matter to me either way. It shouldn't take me long anyway," he added, throwing a leg over the bicycle bar and starting with a little push down the road leading to the highway.

I was still kind of mad at Sandy and didn't feel much like talking, therefore, with nothing to do, time seemed to drag, and to relieve the monotony we both began walking and exploring around the house and the barn. Only a few minutes had passed, when Sandy's excited voice broke the silence.

"Armando. Armando Come here. Hurry up though."

Unwillingly, I rushed to join him and to my amazed eyes, he pointed to the stockroom window which had been left wide open.

"Look at that," said Sandy stretching his neck over the ledge to have a better view. "What do you think, should we help ourselves?"

"Are you crazy? I thought you said you are not a thief. Come on, get out of there," I said half heartedly, trying to convince myself more than I was trying to convince him.

But we had already stolen once, now it was easier to think about it and repeat the same mistake, so without too many qualms, quickly we jumped inside and began inspecting the contents of the room.

We decided for the white flour of which there was a lot more than anything else and not only would be less likely to be missed right away, but it seemed to be right, because we had paid too much for what he had given us and hurriedly we proposed forthwith to remedy that condition.

Working as fast as we could, we emptied our sack of the corn flour we had just bought into the former container, and while Sandy began transferring the white flour into the same sack, I filled all the pockets of our three knap sacks with rock salt, which was as precious as gold, then I jumped outside and kept watch, just in case the farmer would come back.

As the operation slowly progressed, my heart was beating at a hundred miles an hour, and when the first sack was filled to the brim and securely tied, I said: "That is enough now Sandy, let's get out of here."

"Oh no, let's fill up the other one too," he answered with excitement. "While we are doing the job, we might as well do it right. Same price you know."

"Come on, that's enough. Let's be satisfied with this. The farmer could come back any time now. Come on. Hurry," I urged him.

Fortunately he did listen to me, because when he tried to lift up the sack, he found out that it weighed a lot more than he expected and began to yell desperately.

"I can't move the damn thing. Come and help me"

"Damn it. That is what you get for being too greedy. And you wanted to fill up the other sack too."

With rage I jumped into the room and helped him to lift the sack on the window sill, then as I was ready to follow Sandy who had already jumped outside, my eyes fell on my rubber tires hanging on at nail:

"Just a moment," I yelled to Sandy, who was courageously trying to get the heavy sack on his back all by himself. "What do you think? Since we gave him back his flour, we might as well take back our rubber tires," and started to reach for them, but: "No no no, leave them there," said Sandy. "At least, he can't say that we were unfair to him. Come on, jump outside to give me a hand."

Hurrying now, we took leave, and in an effort to put as much distance as possible between us and the farmer's house, we started toward the highway, but just before we got to it, poor Sandy who was walking ahead of me, bent over double with the heavy sack on his shoulders, and before I could do anything about it, he stumbled over a stone, his right leg buckled under him and all of a sudden collapsed under the weight. Immediately I tried to help him, but after that he seemed helpless, I don't know what had happened to him, but he had completely lost his strength, and could hardly stand on his own two feet.

Damn it. This surely was not needed. Sandy was a lot bigger and stronger than me, but I think I had more determination, more guts, because once he started pleading me to leave everything and get the hell out of there, I answered with more determinateness. I wasn't going to give up so easy the precious booty, either I was going to make it or I was going to bust.

Panicky, cursing and swearing, I tried once, twice, I thought my veins were going to explode with the great effort, inch by inch, first I lifted the sack on my knees, then trying to get it on my shoulders, I struggled and struggled but finally I made it. Once it was up and in its place, it even seemed lighter, and without too much delay, leaving Sandy still laying on the edge of the road where he had dropped, crossed the highway, entered a corn field, hid the sack among the already high stocks and went back to get the other two sacks and helped poor Sandy out of the way.

From our hideout located on a little promontory we were in control of the Flaminia where just before noon, we seen the farmer going at full speed downhill, but not too long after peddling his guts out on his way back to Narni. Surely he must have found out and only God knows what he would have done to us if he could have put his hand on us.

We spent the rest of the day hiding, and while still not feeling very good, Sandy slept most of the time, I divided the flour evenly into two sacks, making it a lot easier to handle. When it became dark, we moved once again to the well known junction, but all the moving vehicles seemed to be going north, with very little traffic going south.

For three days hiding and four nights on the road, we waited desperately, hoping to get a ride back to Rome, but in vain. The morning of the fourth day, our supply of bread and salt pork that we had rationed so carefully, was exhausted, cold, dirty, with our empty stomachs again growling at us, regretfully we looked at each other and with a great big yawn, showing all his thirty two teeth, Sandy got up, stretched his whole body and growled: "Something had better show up soon, otherwise we will have to find a way to use some of this flour. Maybe if we go up into the town to a bakery shop, we could try to exchange some of it for bread," he suggested. But the idea went away as fast as it came, as the fear of being recognized and caught by the farmer, was still too fresh in our minds.

Slowly we began picking up our things and were getting ready to move to our hideout for the day time, when suddenly we heard the welcome sound of a heavy motor and saw a great big truck coming toward us, with a civilian sitting behind the wheel. In a matter of seconds, as though we all had the same idea at the same time, a mob of at least fifty people hurried for the middle of the highway blocking the road and yelling: "Stop. Stop."

Due to the steepness of the hill and the heavy load that was being carried, the truck, a great big Alfa Romeo with trailer climbing in low gear, came to a dead stop, while the infuriated driver came out of his cabin shouting: "Hey, siete pazzi? Are you gone mad? What is going on here anyway. Come on, come on, clear the road."

"We want a ride. We want a ride"

The mob answered angrily, while lots of then had already climbed on the truck and trailer and were helping others to do the same.

"Please. Please," Shouted the driver hysterically pulling his hair. "Take it easy, that is all live ammunition. We will blow up in a million pieces if you people are not careful."

At the word ammunition, the crowd stopped momentarily, and while some recoiled in fear, the more brave kept climbing, but with less enthusiasm, and looking at the driver who kept gesturing wildly, his arms up in the air and shouting, in an effort to make himself heard above the tumult around him.

Gradually order was restored and as he patiently explained the situation, we came to an understanding.

It seemed that back in Florence where he had arrived a couple of days ago with a load of beds and clothing for the fascist brigades, the same ones, had commanded him and his truck to take a load of their own to Torino, his home town, and gladly he accepted or he would have had to go back empty. Thinking that he had been real lucky at such an easy way to make a few extra thousand lire for himself, without the company he was working for knowing about it, he took off, but soon learned that it was only the beginning of his troubles. Just outside of Florence, he was stopped and this time by the Germans, who made him unload his cargo, and reload with the present one, which was to be delivered to Albano, not even fifteen miles south of Rome, near the front lines.

Thoroughly disgusted by now, and grudgingly on his way once more, he was stopped again, this time by us, but the crowd soon understood his predicament and willingly accepted what he proposed. He didn't want any money, but since we offered it, for fifty lire per person he would take us all to Rome.

Once more, he got rolling up the steep hill, with the entire crowd following behind on foot. The whole scene, reminded me of the pilgrimage we used to make every year at the beginning of may, to our Lady of Divine Love, with a great big difference though in the whole predicament and surroundings.

This time there was no imploring, no chanting or loud praying, just a silent, patient plodding along of a mass of weary people, anxious just as much as we did to get to our destinations.

Being in constant fear of being discovered, Sandy and I, we had a little choice if we were to get away from there, and we tried to make ourselves as inconspicuous as possible in the midst of the crowd. In Narni, the truck with its deadly load, was concealed under the foliage of the trees that overhung the highway, and we all sat around it and waited for night to fall.

By six o'clock, the sun was still very high, but the driver who was as anxious to get the distasteful job that he was forced to do over with, as we were to be on our way, suddenly got up and said: "Oh let's take a chance, let's go."

It was no sooner said than done, and with big sighs of relief on everyone's lips, we began rolling. The whirring sound of the wheels under us, lulled us into a sense of security once more, making us forget that we were sitting on a bed of dynamite. It was a good two hours at least before it would be dark, so we all kept our eyes wide open for any airplane that might be passing over our heads. Twice they did, three of them flying at a high altitude, but I doubt if they seen us because we were not molested. In a way, we even felt kind of reassured and almost forgot about the danger, because we were well protected by the large umbrella shaped trees lined up all along both sides of the highway.

After a good forty five minutes of steady driving, we were nearing the town of Civita Castellana, we could see the spires of the churches and the towers of ancient castle silhouetted against the skyline in the distance.

To bypass this ancient and historical city, constantly at war with its neighbors during the reign of the Borgia's, and considered by some experts contemporaneous to be impregnable, way down below, we had to cross a modern cement bridge that spanned the Tiber River at this point, and was now coming into perfect view.

The truck slowed down and stopped right in front of a barricade that had been erected by the Germans, with a big sign nailed to it, informing the travelers that the bridge was under repair.

Five days previously when we passed going north, it was intact, but it seems that later, it had been bombed by the American airplanes and damaged, now a crew of German engineers were supervising the repair, while the actual work was being done by Italian laborers. We could see that they were laying the cobblestones over the surface, and as one of the officers in charge explained to the driver, the repairs would have been completed within a couple of hours.

We had our choice, wait for them to finish and go through the bridge, or go back to Narni where we just came from, and from there take another road, which it explained to us, why we could not get a ride in Narni. But that was past history what mattered now was the future, and it was up to the driver to decide which way it would be. No matter what happened, we had to get away from there because we didn't have the protection of the trees to hide us anymore, and as, the long convoy began to swing around, all eyes turned skyward as the steady drone of many planes approaching could be heard, and believe me it didn't take them long to be on top of us. Nine in all Lightning type airplanes passed over us, made a wide circle and plummeted earthward in single file.

Before the driver had a chance to apply the brakes, half of us had already jumped, and scurrying madly in every direction seeking whatever cover this wide open area could provide.

Blindly I found myself running, without realizing that I was heading straight for the river, suddenly the earth shook as a reverberating shock struck a span of the bridge at my right. I looked up and saw a mass of the structure flying up in the air like so much match wood, while at the same time I lost my footing and tumbled head over heels down the steep embankment of the river.

Stunned and half conscious, I put my two arms around my head and huddled there, while, as though from a very near distance, I heard the terrifying ra, ta, ta, ta, and spatter of the machine gun bullets, as they hit the rocks around me where I cowered.

The raid didn't last long, but to me it seemed like it would never end. Long minutes after, it stopped and was all silent again, but I remained there too frightened to move, when suddenly I heard Sandy's voice calling my name: "Armando? Armando? Where are you?"

Cautiously I peeked out and peered around me. I guess I was born a coward, because I was still shaking violently and could hardly get to my feet. That was too close for comfort. While the laments and cries of the wounded could be heard among the people on the bridge, slowly I clambered back up the bank and onto the road, where at first glance everyone of our group seemed to be present and unhurt, so once aboard again, without anymore indecision, the driver took off on the first side road he came to, a winding white gravel dusty road.

From there on, it seemed as though the devils were chasing us, leaving a long trail of dust in our wake.

Apparently we were destined for further eventualities, because it could have not been no more than twenty miles we had covered, when our trip was interrupted again, this time by two German S.S. soldiers on a motorcycle with sidecar, which halted the truck and to our dismay ordered the driver to enter a lane that led to a near abandoned farm house.

Once there, swearing and cursing in their language, the Germans made us all descend, lined the men on one side, the women on the other and with drawn pistols they began asking for identification documents.

But who was carrying papers in those days? Not many people. Besides in the overall picture, mostly men except Sandy and another gentleman, were all very young like myself, or too old and we were not worth the trouble they were taking.

When they couldn't get too much satisfaction either out of the men or the women, they turned their attention to the truck, trailer and its contents.

The poor driver did his best to explain the situation and why he was on that gravel road, but the S.S. men either did not understand what he was saying or they didn't want to. In any event, he was ordered to turn around and go back all the way to Narni.

Now what? What was going to happen to us next? Stranded in the middle of nowhere once again, without any means of transportation and, worst of all, far away from any main highway, we all felt lost.

Some of the crowd decided to spend the approaching night at the farm house, but the majority, us two included, continued moving in the general direction of Rome. As we walked along the dusty gravel road, Sandy and I noticed a field of lima beans and we entered it, hoping to find some fresh beans we could munch on as we moved, but like old Mother Hubbard's cupboard, it had been stripped bare

As time went by, the sacks were getting heavier and heavier, forcing us to make frequent stops on the side of the road, and every time we had to restrap them on our backs, it was getting harder and harder.

It was quite dark now, and before long, even though we couldn't see it coming we could hear the sound of another truck approaching. Once again, hope mounted in our hearts as we began waving ours arms frantically in the middle of the road, but we didn't need to worry. As usual, traveling without lights and at a very low speed, the vehicle, this too a big truck with trailer, but not as big as the other one, stopped by itself, and two older German soldiers sticking their heads out of the window, in a halting Italian, inquired: "Comrade. This way Rome?"

All of a sudden everybody knew the way to Rome, and talking at once, directions began flying from every mouth. Laughing, the Germans held up their hands shouting: "Uno memento Comrade. One of you, sit in the cabin with us to show the way, the rest of you find yourself a place in the back."

The eagerness with which this invitation was accepted need not be described here, because we must have looked like a bunch of pirates boarding a ship.

Sandy and I like everybody else, found ourselves seated on a mountain of bags of flour of all things, with which the trailer was loaded.

The truck continued without stopping until midnight or near it, when at an intersection, we encountered the paved highway again, and since the would-be guide, didn't know where we were anymore than the rest of us, he had to get off to ask one of the villagers for guidance. At this discovery, hell broke loose, the German drivers became very angry and hostile and threatened to throw all of us off. While they had every right to be upset, we had no leg to stand on, and the whining, and moaning began, we begged and promised the wine, songs, money women and anything we could think of at the time to calm their rage, as long as they would let us proceed with then. Finally they fell for it, peace was restored and once again aboard, we rolled on toward Rome, and this time on the right road and direction.

It must have been an hour or more, when I noticed some guys at the back of the trailer, throwing off some bags of flour off the tail gate and jumping out right behind them.

"Look, look Sandy," I said waking him up. "Somebody is stealing the flour."

He didn't even answer me or move, meanwhile other occupants began getting the same idea, and a few more left the same way, then: "We still have one empty sack, haven't we?" Asked Sandy.

"We sure do, and I know exactly what is going through your mind," I answered. "But how are we going to carry them? We can hardly carry these ones," I said pointing at our loot.

"Ah. . . Don't worry about it. We will find a way. Come on, let's fill it up."

From there on, it was everyone for himself. Bag after bag was ripped and their contents emptied into smaller bags, bigger bags, till the truck load of flour was almost reduced to half.

By this time, we were all as white as phantoms, our lips were dry and our eyes were sticky, while our hair felt like wire but no one did mind it. What counted in that moment was that if we could get all this flour home, our families would eat for a while and at the Germans expense, which would be ironical justice, after all they were to blame if we were stealing our own flour.

While we were so busy, time flew quickly, and it must have been just around four o'clock in the morning, when we were stopped at the first road block guarded by the Italian Guardie di Finanza

By their disappointed look in their eyes, you could see that they would have been very happy to put their hands on us and whatever merchandise we were carrying, but being a German vehicle, they didn't even question the drivers who were allowed to proceed, but several miles further, at Prima Porta, right on the outskirts of Rome, we were stopped again, this time by the Germans themselves, and believe me, I don't know about the rest of us, but I was scared stiff.

It must have been our lucky night, because they looked around, they asked the drivers for their papers, they shouted something and without any delay they gave the order to continue.

"Oh God. Thank you," I said when it was over.

We weren't far from the street car stop now, hurriedly Sandy and I whispered our plans as to how to get away once the truck stopped to let everybody off.

There were hundreds of people with all their belongings, lined up on both sides of the road, some waiting for the curfew to lift to enter the city, and many more leaving it, heading up north and waiting for a ride.

The truck halted, laughing and joking the drivers came down and began collecting their well earned fare. As we had planned, I jumped off the trailer, Sandy handed me the largest and heaviest sack of our collection, and as quickly as my legs permitted, I rushed in the direction of the street car stop, where the crowd was the thickest. There, I sat it down and asked an elderly lady to keep an eye on it for me, as I would be back in a few seconds.

She agreed graciously, I thanked her and like a thunderbolt, back to the truck for the rest I went, where I almost had a fit, when I noticed that damn fool Sandy was still on the trailer.

"What an earth are you doing up there?" I asked greatly annoyed.

"I am looking for one of our sacks," he cried petulantly. "It is not here anymore."

"Damn you Sandy," I muttered between my teeth. It really bugged me sometimes. He was so smart in so many ways, and yet so slow in many others.

"To hell with that. Come on down out of there," I shouted with rage, grabbing the first bag that came to my hands. Then somebody passed down a small suitcase and another bag. I knew they were not mine, but in a moment of confusion like that, who cared. With my arms well loaded, I headed back once more to my guardian lady, deposited everything at her feet and, was about to turn back toward the truck again, when almost out of breath, and bent over under the weight of the big sack full of the German's flour, Sandy joined me. Right then pandemonium broke loose as a thundering shout was heard so clearly in the morning silence, then: "Ladri, ladri Italiani. Italian thieves. Scoundrels."

The two Germans were shouting so loudly now that their voices, could have been heard for blocks, as they kept circling and searching all over their vehicle with their flashlights, shouting more and more in an incomprehensible language.

To the contrary of Sandy who was laughing his head off at their cursing, knowing what we had done, a cold chill began running through my spine, and not caring to find out what would happen next, I urged Sandy to move.

Simultaneously we both grabbed all we could hold, and as though the devil was chasing us, we moved quickly further away and stopped only when we felt we had put a good distance between ourselves and the Germans, then, leaving Sandy standing guard over our precious loot, retraced my steps to pick up the rest and silently began the long wait. We waited and waited, finally half an hour later, amid a crowd of yelling, cursing, crying and shouting enraged people, the truck slowly pulled away, passed in front of us and disappeared toward Rome.

We knew that once the Germans had made the discovery, they would revenge themselves, but we never imagined that they would find out right there and how they would get even. To our surprise, truck and trailer had acquired a new load, that seemed to be overflowing at the sides and back.

Curious and wondering what had happened, cautiously, I returned to the scene of the crime, and what a pitiful sight met my eyes. The people closest to where the truck had parked, were the ones who bore the brunt of the German's wrath. In their rage at having been robbed, they exacted retribution by picking up every stitch of clothing, boxes, suitcases, bags and every bit of luggage that was to be seen, leaving those poor innocent victims in tears and without whatever precious possession they had.

My heart was filled with remorse for what we had done, as was Sandy's when I told him what had happened. The thrill we felt for what we had acquired so easy in the last few hours of our trip, was greatly diminished, because of the terrible unhappiness we had caused others of our kind, but unfortunately, that was the way things worked out in those days, the innocent paid for the sinner.

Our crocodile tears were just momentary though, because as soon as the tramway arrived, we had already forgotten about the incident. With the crowd pressing all around us, fighting all the way, inch by inch, finally we managed to get all our sacks and bags aboard. We knew that this was going to be the last struggle, the last penance before we reached our destination, and we didn't seem to mind it so much, in fact, for a change, it was a pleasure to push and get pushed.

For a change I found myself relaxed, peaceful and content. I didn't even seem to mind the fact that the tramway once it started moving, was going at snail's pace, stopping at every street corner, because I knew that it was only a temporary delay, it couldn't last forever because now we were in Rome, we were home. Sweet home.

Two hours later, we arrived at the Acquasanta, where nine long days ago, one afternoon we had taken off. Our last effort was to drop our precious provisions off the street car and we did it, then suddenly the strain of the load weighed down on us, it seemed we could go no further after that, it was all we could endure and no more, so while I stood on guard, Sandy went to get help.

A few minutes later, like a dream, the dear familiar faces of our friends and loved ones, were coming toward me, shouting greetings and crying with joy.

They had given us up for lost, but seeing us standing there alive and sound, made them forget the anguish and worries they had suffer during our long absence and welcomed us like conquering heroes.

After the hugs, caresses and greetings were over, they took over completely, they wouldn't let us touch a thing. We had done our share.

At nonno Agostino's place, we divided all the blessed loot. There was a little bit of everything. In the suitcase, we found two four quarts of oil, more salt and macaroni, the other little bag was all flour like the two big sacks, and all together amounted to more than hundred kilos. No wonder we had a heck of a time to carry it all.

Maybe we didn't pay the exact price for whatever we brought home, but believe me it was well earned. Maybe that food would not be blessed by our Lord because it was stolen, but maybe some of us, especially the children, would not be in good health today if we had not dared and learned how to steal.

At home they had a million questions to ask, they wanted to hear all about our experiences, but suddenly, the exhaustion that we had fought for so long finally seemed to descend on us with a rush. At the moment, sleep, not food, seemed to be the most important thing, and without any further delay, that's exactly what I did. I went to bed dirt and all, and there I stayed for a full two days. Not Sandy though, he stayed awake, and the same night, with Carmine, they both went to the pump house and at the usual hour, the message was sent to the Allies Command. The Passage of the Somma was completely unguarded.

Chapter 19

During our absence, a few things had happened to break the monotony in that small neighborhood of ours, that came almost all at the same time and brought us a little bit of everything. More grief, more fear, some joy and once again hope.

Two days after we had left for our unforgettable trip, bad news arrived to Mr. Fano and his family. His son, who months ago went up north with the Fascist Brigades, to fight the guerrilla warfare against the growing forces of Italian partisans hiding on the mountains, had been killed in action. Although nobody liked him, the news of his death had touched us. After all he was only a kid, and his parents as bad as they were surely would miss him.

In addition to all our problems, the Germans had made a fuel dump right at our doorstep. On the old cemetery of the Tombe Latine, protected by the shadow of the umbrella of the several pine trees all around it, they had piled hundreds of drums of oil and gasoline, that they came to pick up every evening after dark and slowly moved somewhere else. As soon as he was informed of it, and after checking it out personally, Sandy was all set for sending a message to the Allies Command, but after discussing it over with the family, he decided against it.

First because we could see that it was only a temporary arrangement, in fact more than half the pile of drums had already disappeared, secondly, the whole blooming mess was not more than three hundred feet from our house which was virtually a question of having a load of dynamite over our roof. If the American airplanes ever came, and either way, scored a hit or even missed the target completely, we could have had our share of troubles. They could have literally made a human torch out of us and all the people living around here, or they could have blown us all to pieces, and believe me, the very thought of it, was not a very comfortable one.

A very, very important news to us personally, was the fact that papa' had received word from the Red Cross, that my oldest brother Peppe, who had disappeared after the eight of September, was well and on the Island of Malta with his ship working side by side with the English navy.

When they told me, while my heart was filled with a great joy, I was also very grateful to God and wasted no time in thanking Him.

More, it was rumored that after heavy fighting, finally Cassino, the German stronghold on the Casilina Highway, had fallen into the hands of the Allies Forces who were still advancing progressively in our direction.

Lately, the traffic on the Appia Highway had been and still was in cool motion, as the German convoy of two, three trucks at a time of troops and equipment, tanks and cannons, moved steadily toward Rome.

Such movements by the Germans could only signify one thing, the Americans must have been getting ready to attack at Anzio where they had been since last January, and before they were trapped and destroyed, they would rather evacuate.

So we hoped that our conclusion were right and such a day would come soon, especially after what we had seen the night before.

For two consecutive evenings, the Germans came to the Tombe Latine with several trucks and worked all night long loading the drums of fuel and taking them away. Unable to take it all, a couple dozen drums remained, and when the morning came and they went away, they left the cemetery gates wide open and unguarded.

During that same day, some villagers living nearby along the dirt road and Tuscolana Highway, passing by the cemetery saw the drums and thinking that the Germans had abandoned it, and that for so little they would not bother to come back, not only decided to help themselves, but called their neighbors. Pretty soon, like a bunch of hungry wolves, a pack of madman came rushing to the Tombe Latine and shouting and yelling as though they had found a treasure, full ones as well as the empty ones, drum after drum, were rolled down along the dirt road and to their respective back yards, until there were none left.

That same evening at dusk, two German trucks pulled up at the cemetery to load, but to their surprise they found the barrels had disappeared. The most likely place to find their merchandise, was ours, therefore, quite convinced that we had the drums, enraged, they came flying down, cussing and swearing and bullying their way through, they began searching. They were going around like crazy, and when they couldn't get any satisfaction out of us, all ten of them, rushing up they went again, descended along the dirt road, started going from house to house, and when any of their drums were located, their contents were emptied on the ground and set on fire. That is when the fireworks began.

Lighting up the sky with a reddish glow, the high flames could be seen for miles around, as large clouds of black smoke drifted above our home like the pall of doom, and the screaming and wailing of the terrorized villagers were carried to us in the still evening air. In such a fashion about a dozen homes were burned to the ground. It was terrible. How can you forget things like that?

As the days passed by, we counted them. We were on pins and needles, we were getting impatient.

"Are these blessed Americans ever going to arrive?" We asked ourselves time after time. May twenty-eight, twenty-ninth, thirtieth. The hours dragged slowly, but nothing happened. It seemed we couldn't wait any longer. May thirty-first.

Like life, like daylight, the darkness of the night, the storm, like the Egyptians, like the Romans, the French Revolution and Napoleon, the Czar of Russia and many others things, there has always been a beginning and an end to everything on this earth, and that time, it looked like the end of the Germans and their tyrannical occupation.

On the first of June, preceded by one of the heaviest artillery firing we ever witnessed, the American troops had finally launched the offensive against the shaky German positions, and from what we had been able to gather, they were crashing forward at full speed. On the third day of the attack, when we learned that the Germans had been ousted from Albano, we knew that it wouldn't be long.

With the rough and treacherous hilly ground left behind them, the way to the Eternal city should be a cinch from now on.

Silently and with much happiness, we watched the bulk of the last German forces retreating helter skelter, yet what was very unusual and quite incomprehensible to us, was the fact that without a single cloud on a clear sky, and a weather that had never been nicer, beside the frequent visit of a single engine scout plane, better known as the grasshopper, the terrible American air force was entirely absent from the scene. The German retreat was completely unmolested.

The same night, what with the constant noise of the traffic of vehicles and tanks plus our delirious excitement, we were unable to find any rest, but nobody seemed to mind it very much. Morning found us tired and sleepy; but who cared?

It was Sunday, and this was going to be the great day, we felt it, and we didn't want to miss anything.

Rumors were flying thick and fast, we hardly knew how to sort out the facts from the fancy, yet never the less, we were elated, as the shooting got closer and closer to us. We were hoping, but it did not seem possible that the Germans would continue their head long flight without resistance of any kind, and in a short while, our suspicions were confirmed. Around ten o'clock in the morning, fox holes, shallow trenches, were hurriedly dug all along the edge of the dirt road that skirted the Tombe Latine, while machine guns and small mortars were being set up in strategic positions. The Tombe Latine was suddenly swarming with soldiers and armored tanks, and the place reminded us of the eight of September of the year before, when the Italians were going to use the same tactics against the Germans..

Were the Germans going to use these forces temporarily just to harass the advancing Americans and allow their own troops to evacuate, or were they going to fight inch by inch for Rome as they had done in Cassino?

Seeing all those preparations, our spirits were considerably dampened, and assuming they were, we too began to prepare for a long siege. If such things were to happen, once again, the grotto was our only hope to survive, and broken hearted, we started carrying down all our belongings that would help to make us as comfortable as possible, including bedding, mattresses, blankets, cooking utensils and the little food we had available.

For hours now, hundreds and hundreds of German soldiers on foot, were coming down in a steady stream from all directions, along the Appia Highway, our dirt road and through the fields. They were a pathetic looking bunch, young and mature men alike, with heavy faces, marked with deep lines of fatigue and strain, tired dirty, bandaged, walking with canes, some with crutches, leaning on each other, while the more seriously wounded, were transported on wheel barrows, hand carts, old baby carriages, bicycles, makeshift stretchers and every other conceivable conveyance.

It was only ten months before, from those dark days of September, when the mighty Wermacht soldiers, defiantly and arrogantly began pouring into our city and over our highways, roaring in every direction boldly and confident in the future under the protection of their armored tanks and their deadly guns. But things had changed since then, finally they were being forced back to where they came from, but much differently though, much differently. This time, they were crawling, their boldness was gone, and the fear and terror that was once in our eyes, now could plainly be seen in theirs, they were disorganized, demoralized, and they must have a bitter taste in their mouth: "The taste of defeat."

Once in a while an officer riding on horseback, appeared goading and prodding his men on to greater efforts and speed, but sadly, they only had one speed left: "Crawling."

While this was going on, we had been busy going back and forth to the grotto, where we had already brought down most of the beds and mattresses.

The bell of the near church had just struck one o'clock, when carrying an armful of clothes, Carmine had just stepped out of the house with Sandy and I right behind him, when a German officer coming down from the farm, and riding an old jade at a gentle trot, seeing Carmine with his blonde hair, blue eyes and fair complexion, possibly mistaking him for one of his men, brought the animal to an abrupt stop and with an angry, voice in his own language, he began shouting questions at him. Caught by surprise, bewildered and petrified, poor Carmine stood there gaping at him wordless, and I didn't know what could have happened if papa' called quickly by my younger brother Mario, had not come rushing out calling frantically: "No, no. That is my son. That is my son."

At which the officer seemed to believe him, shrugged his shoulders and rode away, leaving us all trembling and as white as a sheet.

"Mamma mia!" Exclaimed papa' very nervously. "That was a close call wasn't it?" Then turning to Carmine and shouting angrily "God dam it. Get down to the grotto and stay there. You too Sandy. I don't want to see any of you until this damn thing is all over. Understand?"

Only as he started back toward the house, I noticed the big Mauser sticking out from under his belt. I bet the way he came rushing out of the house, if needed he wouldn't have hesitated a second to use it, and I shuddered just to think of what might have happened.

To avoid the repetition of such unpleasant incident, soon after, we all moved down to the grotto, and when around three o'clock we came out again, the Germans had disappeared, as though vanished in the air. There was not a single sign of them, all around us was calm and quiet, and not a sound could be heard. Minutes later, we even climbed the little steep path leading to the dirt road, and to our delight, we found out that even all the tanks and troops stationed on the Tombe Latine had gone, leaving behind four lonely solemn faced soldiers with a machine gun entrenched in a fox hole, at the foot of the old Roman house right on the edge of the dirt road.

Once again, without questioning the reason for this change of plans, we were more than happy to see them gone, and we were just standing around gloating among ourselves, when suddenly giving the impression that the world was coming to an end, there was a tremendous blast that deafened us and threw us on our faces on the ground, followed by a gigantic cloud of black smoke that rose in the sky like a big mushroom, the old Fort of Acquasanta was blown to pieces.

"This must be the last destructive crime the Germans will commit," commented papa' gloomily, as we slowly recovered from the shock of the explosion.

When we came down, while the rest of the gang proceeded toward the grotto once more, like I had been doing all afternoon, I went to check the fire under the big pot were the beans were cooking, and again to my disappointment, I found that they weren't ready yet. In fact, even though the dry beans had been soaking in water for two whole days, and cooking slowly since early morning, they were still hard as a rock. Only God and the son of a bitch that sold them to us, must have known how old those damn beans were.

Once outside again, the incumbent silence was broken periodically by rifle shots that were less intensive but more distinct, and by the sporadic cannon fire and machine guns, then, as though going on a pleasure trip, the sky became infested with many tiny grasshoppers, flying very low and very slow. As they approached I noticed clearly their fuselage a bright silver star, the well known American insignia. I tried to attract the occupant's attention by waving at them, but they were too busy looking below for something else and talking on the radio.

Seemingly they were scouters working in cooperation with the advancing troops.

Amid the great confusion and excitement, no one had paid too much attention to the children, who like everybody else, hadn't touched food from the evening before, and lately had been pestering mamma and nonna, that they wanted something to eat. We were all gathered in front of the grotto entrance watching the coming and going of the "Cicogne" (grasshoppers) when tired of listening to the children's crying sing-song, cooked or not, nonna told me to bring down the big pot of beans.

With Sandy at my heels, on our way up to the house, the German soldiers entrenched nearer the old Roman house, suddenly opened fire on one of the scouter planes that had been circling overhead, and apparently must have had then spotted.

Scared by the shooting so close to us, we made a run for the protection of the house, and peeking through the bedroom window, we followed the plane disappearing in the distance toward the American lines, but suddenly and unexpectedly, hell broke loose, with all the fury that came with it.

Shell after shell began whistling and exploding around, then like a thunder had just struck the brick wall, several projectiles came zooming through the house, as if the wall were made of paper, making holes the size of a big pumpkin.

"Let's get the hell out of here," shouted Sandy, just before more shells came through, first higher through the roof, than lower than the previous ones, hitting the wall and the tall wardrobe mirror, filling up the room with a white dust, and sending flying in every direction, tiles, bricks, plaster, wood and thousands pieces of glasses.

"Mamma mia. They are going to kill us," that is all I remember saying, then, completely unnerved, forgetting why we had come, I flashed across the room and got out of the house, to find myself face to face with two very young German soldiers carrying Tommy guns in their hands and rushing down the side of the cliff, their dirty and sweat streaked faces, showing tenseness and a terrified expression.

Freezing in my tracks, I began murmuring my last prayers, but strangely enough, they paid no attention to me, and while the bombardment continued raging fiercely on the old Roman house, the two soldiers, holding their automatic guns tight in their hands like two badly frightened children, scurried toward the little shelter we had previously dug and disappeared into it.

Completely sure that Sandy was behind me, I began running, and devouring the distance separating me from the grotto, I finally entered it, while outside shell after shell kept arriving and exploding ravenously.

A circle of people immediately formed around me asking questions, but by the time I regained my breath and stopped shaking and stuttering, and explained what was happening, the infernal music quit playing, and the deadly silence that followed, was interrupted by the arrival of more "Cicogne" that kept circling and circling above us.

As time passed, our faces showed a growing tenseness mixed with fear, and waiting became a torture. The curiosity to know what was going on outside was unmeasureable, but at the same time no one dared show more than his nose past the heavy grotto doors. Not after they heard what I had gone through anyway.

Finally Ferrari got up enough courage to widen the slight crack between the doors, and peeked outside, while hushed, the rest of us watched intently, marveling at his bravery. Cautiously and silently we crowded behind him to see too, still seeing nothing, and hearing nothing, the big doors were pushed wider and wider, and at last we were all outside, and hurriedly we retraced our steps.

Two men aboard a strange looking vehicle with a tall antenna were rolling slowly along the Appia Highway, while on each side of the road, two soldiers, rifles pointed forward, followed behind advancing cautiously.

"They are Americans! They are Americans!" We all shouted enthusiastically trying to come out again. "Calm down, calm down", yelled Ruggiero nervously. "Maybe they are, but before we commit ourselves we better make sure. They could be the last of the German rearguard." "No, it's impossible didn't you see the different uniform?" Argued Ferrari impatiently, once again heading for the outside.

Our doubts were soon cleared, when with joy, we noticed another vehicle looking exactly the same as the one that had just gone by, then another, and another, while foot soldiers kept moving in more numerously.

Suddenly, coming from nowhere, a rifle shot broke the deep silence, hurriedly the newcomers stopped and crouching behind the cars, looked around trying to locate the sniper, but there were no more shots and slowly they moved ahead again.

Since they did not seem antagonistic towards us, we tried to get closer to the highway, but as they noticed our movements, they made signs for us to go back, while two of them, leaving the group entered the dirt road and came forward. With the sunset shining behind them and blinding us, standing motionless with solemn faces we contemplated the newcomers, wondering what our fate would be now.

These were the two American soldiers that we had never seen, and we examined them from head to toe. As people they were not different from ourselves, as soldiers there was only the uniform to tell them apart from the Germans or the Italians. They wore a light green uniform made of a hardy twill material, a shirt stuffed into their trousers, with a wide khaki belt, calf length boots, that seemed to be made of very good leather, which I admired most of all, and a helmet resembling an Italian helmet, and holding in their hands a powerful automatic rifle. Although their intentions seemed friendly, they looked very nervous and uneasy, and once they got quite close to us, one of them asked in poor Italian, 'are there any German soldiers around?"

Everyone present understood perfectly what they wanted and, "Sandy, get Sandy", said papa, looking around, but since he was not present, mostly all the men stepped forward, they only asked for one, and appreciating the fact that I spoke a few words of English, they chose me to be their guide.

Following us like in a procession by the whole inhabitants of the small community, I accompanied them through the little canyon, and pointing toward a cliff opening, told them that there were two German soldiers concealed inside. Leaving me behind, and ordering everybody else to standstill, they warily approached the shelter, but before they had a chance to speak, the two frightened young German soldiers, who had scared the wits out of me earlier, stepped out from their hiding place with their hands clasped behind their heads. While one of the Americans kept the twp soldiers at gunpoint, the other walked to the tunnel entrance and picked up their guns threw them over his left shoulder and rejoined his friend who couldn't understand what one German meant, as he kept saying, "kaput, comrade, kaput," while pointing toward the old Roman house. I wasn't too sure, but I had a fairly good idea of what he was trying to say, and turning to the closest American, I said "there must be some dead soldiers up there."

We climbed the steep slope and crossed the dirt road, in the same trench that we saw them digging just before noon we found two soldiers sprawled against the old Roman house wall face down on the ground, dead forever, but still holding the guns tight in their stiff hands. We just looked at them and turned back. When we got down, still at gunpoint, the two prisoners were ordered to move and by the time we rejoined with the main group the tenseness in everybody's faces was gone, even the two German's seemed quite relaxed and resigned, as a matter of fact they seemed relieved that at last the war was over for them.

At one point, one of the prisoners was actually smiling, and then, of all the people, Mr. Fano stepped up closer to him and spat fully in his face, arousing anger among the crowd for his shameful behavior. Already he had forgotten the part he and his son had played in this rotten business, but we hadn't as we booed him and chased him away from us in disgust.

Once again, like a procession, we followed the Americans to the highway, where now a long line of armored tanks were moving lazily toward Rome, and could be seen on both sides of the road, extending far out into the distance in both directions, when a soldier from a tank, waving his helmet in the air called out loudly, "paisa, paisa". The ice was broken, and no words can describe the real live scene that took place, as our happiness, our joy, our gratitude was demonstrated. The hearty welcome we gave them, and the many strange things we did, as people jammed together at the entrance of the highway, slapping, patting, and hugging each other in mutual joy. Nonno Agostino, tears streaming down his face, while a tremulous smile played about his lips, fell to his knees and kissed the ground, then with arms upraised he prayed aloud unashamedly. Nonna Teresa kissing and hugging a soldier, Ruggiero and Ferrari's daughters were going from tank to tank, kissing the occupants and offering them flowers, others were shouting singing and waving their arms, or dancing with soldiers and laughing hilariously.

Nonno Edoardo, Ferrari, Piero, papa and many others, people that I never saw before, stood silently looking, then someone, I don't know from where, brought in a basket full of bottles of wine, and began passing them around to the ever thirsty soldiers, while the kids waved their little hands and shouted, "viva gli Americani, viva gli Americani."

That Sunday, the fourth of June will never be forgotten, it resembled a vast family reunion at Christmas time. Even though the many words that were passed back and forth were not understood, the meanings were unmistakable, and they rejoiced with us. Cigarettes, chocolates, candy and chewing gums were tossed to us by the handful, and while we scrambled frantically in the dust for these tokens of friendship, they laughed uproariously at our mad antics.

This is exactly how Rome was conquered, and this went on and on. Everybody was so excited, that it was impossible to understand such exuberance of joy, such explosion of exultation, yet it was the most natural reaction of the people, who after a long time of oppression and tyranny, for the first time was savoring the taste of freedom.

As for myself, I was busy running back and forth with Carmine catching small packages of Old Gold cigarettes, when suddenly like a stoke of lightning, a terrible thought entered my mind, if Ada and Rosa were there, where was Sandy? Usually they were always together, in fact we had started to call them the inseparable, and especially now, in this glorious moment, more than ever, they should have been celebrating together.

"Ada, Ada," I called out loudly to attract her attention. "Have you seen Sandy?" "No, and come to think of it, I haven't seen him for quite awhile. Where in the devil is he hiding?" More than ever preoccupied, I asked Carmine, papa, mamma, and everybody around, but among that indescribable confusion, no one had paid any attention. Was it possible that he had already joined the troops without saying a word to any of us? No, not Sandy, he would never do such a thing, after all we were his family, we loved him and he loved us just as much. Then, suddenly the great suspicion began to tighten my heart and like a madman I started running toward the house. When I got there my frightened doubts were immediately confirmed, there he was lying on our bedroom floor, all covered with plaster and dust, a long piece of glass with a point as sharp as a needle stuck in his temple, a dried up streak of blood running down alongside his cheek.

Suddenly I felt as though someone had dealt me a terrible blow, and the severe shock immobilized me. I couldn't touch, I couldn't talk or think. The reawakening was brutal and bitter, and my mouth was very dry. Why, why I asked myself? Why God had to allow such an unjust thing like this to happen? To die like Sandy did was cruel, unfair,, inhuman, especially now that there was so much at stake, deliverance was so near, with a whole future ahead, a whole new life with meaning, a new horizon. The freedom for whom he had suffered and fought for so strongly, so passionately, finally was here, had been regained, no one was going to take it away from us anymore. Why was he denied the right to enjoy it? Why did he have to die now? Damned, damned cruel and freaky destiny.

There is no way to describe and express the pain, sorrow and dismay caused by the news of Sandy's death among not only our family, but on the whole inhabitants of our small community that had learned how this great, good, simple, and soft spoken brother of ours was going to be missed.

Next morning, as the endless line of vehicles moved steadily forward in a continued stream, people kept hailing at the troops, but no one cared much for the lonely American soldier who laid on the side of the road, opposite Mr. Oliva's pub, dead with a bullet hole through his heart. The sniper's only shot that greeted the soldier's arrival, found a target after all, and he lay just a few feet from where ten months ago, another young man, an Italian lieutenant was killed by another German bullet. This American soldier was one of many that gave his life, the most precious possession he had, to earn us the freedom and peace, like himself, Sandy and all the others that died for this cause, will always have our eternal gratitude.

Thank you, thank you all!

Before I close this chapter, I would like to mention another freak and bizarre joke destiny had played, that was revealed to me, when that same afternoon, an open cheap hearse mule drawn, came to pick up the bodies of the two German soldiers which had been entirely robbed of their clothes, resting side by side next to the American soldier. While two men went inside to get Sandy, in order to make room for him, the third attendant had to push close to each other the corpses of the former enemies, that ironically alive couldn't get along peacefully, but in death had to share the same bed, breath the same air, and lay in the same cart.

Between a crying double line of friends, in whom you could see the real sorrow showing in their faces, the body of Sandy was brought out and laid in place. Before they moved away, papa gave the head attendant a piece of paper saying that Sandy was a soldier in the British army, stating his full name, serial number and regiment, but he was also of Jewish faith, and if it was possible to take him to the Jewish cemetery. "Mister, I am sorry to say that we don't know ourselves yet where we have to take them," answered the older of the three. "Besides, do you think it will make much difference where they are buried? Look at them, conqueror and conquered, Jews and Christians alike, what's the difference. Their lives are gone forever, and now up there, in the eyes of God they are all the same, they are all His sons."

THE END